SHW

BESTSELLING
BOOK SERIES

Healthcare Online For Dummies®

Cheat Sheet

D0474064

Top Health Tools

Drug information

drkoop.com's Drug Checker	www.drugchecker.com

Drug and pharmacy product prices

DestinationRX	www.destinationrx.com

General health information

healthfinder	www.healthfinder.gov
MEDLINE*plus*	www.medlineplus.gov
NOAH	www.noah-health.org

Medical journal articles

Internet Grateful Med	igm.nlm.nih.gov

Medical terms

MEDLINE*plus* ADAM Medical Encyclopedia	medlineplus.adam.com
MedTerms	www.medterms.com

Hospital background

Hospital Select	www.hospitalselect.com
QualityCheck	www.jcaho.org

Online pharmacies

Verified Internet Pharmacy Practice Sites	www.nabp.net/vipps/consumer/search.asp

Patient information and support

DIRLINE: Directory of Health Organizations	dirline.nlm.nih.gov

Physician background

AMA Physician Select	www.ama-assn.org/aps/amahg.htm

Research studies

ClinicalTrials.gov	www.clinicaltrials.gov
CenterWatch	www.centerwatch.com

For Dummies: Bestselling Book Series for Beginners

Healthcare Online For Dummies®

Medical Megasites

Web Site Name	URL
CBSHealthWatch	www.cbshealthwatch.com
drkoop.com	www.drkoop.com
HealthAnswers	www.healthanswers.com
HealthAtoZ.com	www.healthatoz.com
HealthCentral.com	www.healthcentral.com
InteliHealth	www.intelihealth.com
MayoClinic.com	www.mayoclinic.com
WebMD Health	my.webmd.com
WellnessWeb	www.wellnessweb.com
Yahoo! Health	health.yahoo.com

Handy Online Calculators

Activity Calorie Calculator: www.primusweb.com/fitnesspartner/jumpsite/calculat.htm

Body Fat Estimator: www.stevenscreek.com/goodies/pi.shtml

Body Surface Calculator: www.halls.md/bsa.htm

Breast Cancer Risk: www.halls.md/breast/risk.htm

Calorie Calculator: www.caloriescount.com/calculator.html

Children's Growth Calculator: www.healthatoz.com/atoz/growthdiary/growthcalculators.asp

Dessert Wizard: my.webmd.com/dessertwizard

Due Date Calculator: www.babycenter.com/calculators/duedate

Exercise Risk Calculator: www.drkoop.com/tools/calculator/exercise.asp

Pregnancy Calendar: www.babycenter.com/calendar/getinfo

Target Heart Rate Calculator: my.webmd.com/heartrate

For a comprehensive list of calculators on health and other subjects, go to author Judi Wolinsky's Measure 4 Measure at www.wolinskyweb.net/measure.htm.

Hungry Minds, the Hungry Minds logo, For Dummies, the For Dummies Bestselling Book Series logo and all related trade dress are registered trademarks or trademarks of Hungry Minds, Inc. All other trademarks are the property of their respective owners.

Copyright © 2001 Hungry Minds, Inc. All rights reserved.
Cheat Sheet $2.95 value. Item 0684-6.
For more information about Hungry Minds, call 1-800-762-2974.

For Dummies: Bestselling Book Series for Beginners

SHW

ALLEN COUNTY PUBLIC LIBRARY

JAN 0 8 2004

™

References for the Rest of Us! ®

BESTSELLING BOOK SERIES

Are you intimidated and confused by computers? Do you find that traditional manuals are overloaded with technical details you'll never use? Do your friends and family always call you to fix simple problems on their PCs? Then the For Dummies® computer book series from Hungry Minds, Inc. is for you.

For Dummies books are written for those frustrated computer users who know they aren't really dumb but find that PC hardware, software, and indeed the unique vocabulary of computing make them feel helpless. For Dummies books use a lighthearted approach, a down-to-earth style, and even cartoons and humorous icons to dispel computer novices' fears and build their confidence. Lighthearted but not lightweight, these books are a perfect survival guide for anyone forced to use a computer.

> *"I like my copy so much I told friends; now they bought copies."*
> — *Irene C., Orwell, Ohio*

> *"Quick, concise, nontechnical, and humorous."*
> — *Jay A., Elburn, Illinois*

> *"Thanks, I needed this book. Now I can sleep at night."*
> — *Robin F., British Columbia, Canada*

Already, millions of satisfied readers agree. They have made For Dummies books the #1 introductory level computer book series and have written asking for more. So, if you're looking for the most fun and easy way to learn about computers, look to For Dummies books to give you a helping hand.

Hungry Minds™

1/01

Healthcare Online FOR DUMMIES®

by Howard Wolinsky and Judi Wolinsky

Foreword Henry Heimlich, M.D., Sc.D.

Hungry Minds™

HUNGRY MINDS, INC.

Best-Selling Books • Digital Downloads • e-Books • Answer Networks • e-Newsletters • Branded Web Sites • e-Learning

New York, NY ◆ Cleveland, OH ◆ Indianapolis, IN

Healthcare Online For Dummies®

Published by
Hungry Minds, Inc.
909 Third Avenue
New York, NY 10022
www.hungryminds.com
www.dummies.com

Copyright © 2001 Hungry Minds, Inc. All rights reserved. No part of this book, including interior design, cover design, and icons, may be reproduced or transmitted in any form, by any means (electronic, photocopying, recording, or otherwise) without the prior written permission of the publisher.

Library of Congress Control Number: 99-69389

ISBN: 0-7645-0684-6

Printed in the United States of America

10 9 8 7 6 5 4 3 2 1

1B/SZ/QV/QR/IN

Distributed in the United States by Hungry Minds, Inc.

Distributed by CDG Books Canada Inc. for Canada; by Transworld Publishers Limited in the United Kingdom; by IDG Norge Books for Norway; by IDG Sweden Books for Sweden; by IDG Books Australia Publishing Corporation Pty. Ltd. for Australia and New Zealand; by TransQuest Publishers Pte Ltd. for Singapore, Malaysia, Thailand, Indonesia, and Hong Kong; by Gotop Information Inc. for Taiwan; by ICG Muse, Inc. for Japan; by Intersoft for South Africa; by Eyrolles for France; by International Thomson Publishing for Germany, Austria and Switzerland; by Distribuidora Cuspide for Argentina; by LR International for Brazil; by Galileo Libros for Chile; by Ediciones ZETA S.C.R. Ltda. for Peru; by WS Computer Publishing Corporation, Inc., for the Philippines; by Contemporanea de Ediciones for Venezuela; by Express Computer Distributors for the Caribbean and West Indies; by Micronesia Media Distributor, Inc. for Micronesia; by Chips Computadoras S.A. de C.V. for Mexico; by Editorial Norma de Panama S.A. for Panama; by American Bookshops for Finland.

For general information on Hungry Minds' products and services please contact our Customer Care Department within the U.S. at 800-762-2974, outside the U.S. at 317-572-3993 or fax 317-572-4002.

For sales inquiries and reseller information, including discounts, premium and bulk quantity sales, and foreign-language translations, please contact our Customer Care Department at 800-434-3422, fax 317-572-4002, or write to Hungry Minds, Inc., Attn: Customer Care Department, 10475 Crosspoint Boulevard, Indianapolis, IN 46256.

For information on licensing foreign or domestic rights, please contact our Sub-Rights Customer Care Department at 212-884-5000.

For information on using Hungry Minds' products and services in the classroom or for ordering examination copies, please contact our Educational Sales Department at 800-434-2086 or fax 317-572-4005.

Please contact our Public Relations Department at 212-884-5163 for press review copies or 212-884-5000 for author interviews and other publicity information or fax 212-884-5400.

For authorization to photocopy items for corporate, personal, or educational use, please contact Copyright Clearance Center, 222 Rosewood Drive, Danvers, MA 01923, or fax 978-750-4470.

LIMIT OF LIABILITY/DISCLAIMER OF WARRANTY: THE PUBLISHER AND AUTHOR HAVE USED THEIR BEST EFFORTS IN PREPARING THIS BOOK. THE PUBLISHER AND AUTHOR MAKE NO REPRESENTATIONS OR WARRANTIES WITH RESPECT TO THE ACCURACY OR COMPLETENESS OF THE CONTENTS OF THIS BOOK AND SPECIFICALLY DISCLAIM ANY IMPLIED WARRANTIES OF MERCHANTABILITY OR FITNESS FOR A PARTICULAR PURPOSE. THERE ARE NO WARRANTIES THAT EXTEND BEYOND THE DESCRIPTIONS CONTAINED IN THIS PARAGRAPH. NO WARRANTY MAY BE CREATED OR EXTENDED BY SALES REPRESENTATIVES OR WRITTEN SALES MATERIALS. THE ACCURACY AND COMPLETENESS OF THE INFORMATION PROVIDED HEREIN AND THE OPINIONS STATED HEREIN ARE NOT GUARANTEED OR WARRANTED TO PRODUCE ANY PARTICULAR RESULTS, AND THE ADVICE AND STRATEGIES CONTAINED HEREIN MAY NOT BE SUITABLE FOR EVERY INDIVIDUAL. NEITHER THE PUBLISHER NOR AUTHOR SHALL BE LIABLE FOR ANY LOSS OF PROFIT OR ANY OTHER COMMERCIAL DAMAGES, INCLUDING BUT NOT LIMITED TO SPECIAL, INCIDENTAL, CONSEQUENTIAL, OR OTHER DAMAGES. THE INFORMATION IN THIS BOOK IS NOT INTENDED TO SUBSTITUTE FOR EXPERT MEDICAL ADVISE OR TREATMENT; IT IS DESIGNED TO HELP YOU MAKE INFORMED CHOICES. BECAUSE EACH INDIVIDUAL IS UNIQUE, A PHYSICIAN OR OTHER QUALIFIED HEALTH CARE PRACTITIONER MUST DIAGNOSE HEALTH CARE CONDITIONS AND SUPERVISE TREATMENTS. IF AN INDIVIDUAL IS UNDER A DOCTOR OR OTHER QUALIFIED HEALTH CARE PRACTITIONER'S CARE AND RECEIVES ADVISE CONTRARY TO INFORMATION PROVIDED IN THIS REFERENCE BOOK, THE DOCTOR OR OTHER QUALIFIED HEALTH CARE PRACTITIONER'S ADVISE SHOULD BE FOLLOWED, AS IT IS BASED ON THE UNIQUE CHARACTERISTICS OF THAT INDIVIDUAL.

Trademarks: For Dummies, Dummies Man, A Reference for the Rest of Us!, The Dummies Way, Dummies Daily, and related trade dress are registered trademarks or trademarks of Hungry Minds, Inc. in the United States and other countries, and may not be used without written permission. All other trademarks are the property of their respective owners. Hungry Minds, Inc. is not associated with any product or vendor mentioned in this book.

Hungry Minds™ is a trademark of Hungry Minds, Inc.

About the Authors

Judi Wolinsky was in the right place at the right time. She was a graduate student in library science at the University of Illinois at Urbana-Champaign, when Mosaic, the first Internet graphic browser, was introduced there. The Internet changed everything for her — and for everyone else.

She's now head of reference services at the Homewood (Illinois) Public Library, where she and her able staff use the Net and old-fashioned print resources to find the answers to their patrons' questions.

Wolinsky manages the library's Web site. She also teaches a class in Internet searching for librarians at the Suburban Library System.

She has spoken at the Internet Librarian conference and written for the journal, *Public Libraries*.

Wolinsky has several popular Web sites, which you can visit at www.wolinskyweb.net, including Word Play and Measure 4 Measure.

Howard Wolinsky spent his first week as a medical writer on the Chicago Sun-Times in March 1981 covering the attempted assassination of President Reagan. He's been on the run there ever since, having written over 3,000 articles for the paper.

He spent 15 years writing health stories for the paper. The National Press Club, the Associated Press Managing Editors, and the Chicago Newspaper Guild have recognized Wolinsky's work. His health reporting has won a slew of other awards, including from the American Public Health Association, the American Bar Association, and Mental Health Association. *Gay Chicago* magazine named him *Hero to the Community* for his early coverage of the HIV/AIDS crisis.

Following exposés they wrote for the Sun-Times on the American Medical Association, Wolinsky and former Sun-Times reporter Tom Brune wrote the book, *The Serpent on the Staff: The Unhealthy Politics of the American Medical Association* (Putnam, 1995).

In 1994, the Internet bug, which wife Judi brought home from Urbana, bit Howard, and he switched to covering the Net and tech for the Sun-Times.

Wolinsky was a journalist-in-residence at the University of Michigan, where he studied medical ethics, medical economics, and other medical topics. He received M.S. and B.S. degrees in journalism from the University of Illinois at Urbana-Champaign.

The Wolinskys live in Flossmoor, Illinois, with their sons, Adam and David, and their pup, Rufus.

Dedication

Judi Wolinsky dedicates this book to her parents, Gladys and Leo Epstein, and to her sister, Beverly Feldt. Howard Wolinsky dedicates this book to his sibs, Steve, Gary, and Faith (in birth order).

Author's Acknowledgments

Many people helped make this book happen.

We'd like to thank Tom Heine, our acquisitions editor at Hungry Minds, Inc. We appreciate Tom choosing us to do this book and his (almost) weekly phone calls to check on our progress. During a cold, harsh Chicago winter, Tom sometimes was our only contact with the outside world — aside from e-mail, of course. Thanks to Shirley Jones, our project editor, who led us through the maze of the *For Dummies* process. Shirley kept us on track and on time. Thanks also to all the editors and production people at Hungry Minds, especially senior copy editor Kim Darosett (who made this book shine), senior editor Diana R. Conover, copy editor Rebecca Huehls, production coordinator Maridee Ennis, editorial assistant Jean Rogers, and technical editor Karen L. Kennedy, MD.

Thanks to our sons, Adam and David, and to the rest of our extended family, friends, and our colleagues from the Homewood (Illinois) Public Library and Chicago Sun-Times. We appreciate your support while we were lost in cyberspace for the months it took to complete this project.

Judi: I want to thank Cindy Rauch, administrative librarian of the Homewood Public Library, for her vision of librarianship and technology. Thanks for always encouraging me to spread my wings and supporting me in doing this book. Also, thanks to the Board of Trustees for granting me a leave of absence. I want to thank Carol Henry for encouraging me to go to grad school in library science, and Linda Rutz for sharing the ride and her friendship on the Road to Urbana and back. Thanks to Jenny Levine for her leadership in Internet library services in our area. I also want to thank Larry Gelfius, Janet Lewis, and George McFarland for showing me that librarians can make a difference.

Howard: I want to thank Dan Miller, my editor at the Chicago Sun-Times, for his view from 50,000 feet and his understanding that sometimes a person needs to get away and do something else. Thanks to our managing editor, Joyce Winnecke, and the other editors who agreed with Dan and granted me a leave of absence. Many people have helped, inspired, and motivated me along the way. Here are a few: Gene Arbetter, Alan Blum, Mark Bloom, John Bowman, Tom Brune, Len Cerullo, Joe Dragonette, Jan Glidewell, Thomas Guback, David Jacobson, Jack Kitson, Cathey Lowman, Bob Mendelsohn, Louise Morgan, Irwin Saltz, and Gordon White.

To anybody we forgot, and you know who you are, we're sorry. We'll catch you in the next edition.

Publisher's Acknowledgments

We're proud of this book; please send us your comments through our Hungry Minds Online Registration Form located at www.dummies.com.

Some of the people who helped bring this book to market include the following:

Acquisitions, Editorial, and
Media Development

Project Editor: Shirley A. Jones

Acquisitions Editor: Tom Heine

Senior Copy Editor: Kim Darosett

Senior Editor: Diana R. Conover

Copy Editor: Rebecca Huehls

Technical Editor: Karen L. Kennedy, M.D.

Permissions Editor: Carmen Krikorian

Editorial Manager: Leah Cameron

Editorial Assistant: Jean Rogers

Production

Project Coordinator: Maridee Ennis

Layout and Graphics: Amy Adrian, Joe Bucki, Jill Piscitelli, Jacque Schneider

Proofreaders: Laura Albert, John Greenough, Angel Perez, TECHBOOKS Production Services

Indexer: TECHBOOKS Production Sevices

Special Help: Christine Berman, Nicole Laux, Amy Pettinella, Rebecca Senninger

General and Administrative

Hungry Minds, Inc.: John Kilcullen, CEO; Bill Barry, President and COO; John Ball, Executive VP, Operations & Administration; John Harris, CFO

Hungry Minds Technology Publishing Group: Richard Swadley, Senior Vice President and Publisher; Mary Bednarek, Vice President and Publisher, Networking and Certification; Walter R. Bruce III, Vice President and Publisher, General User and Design Professional; Joseph Wikert, Vice President and Publisher, Programming; Mary C. Corder, Editorial Director, Branded Technology Editorial; Andy Cummings, Publishing Director, General User and Design Professional; Barry Pruett, Publishing Director, Visual

Hungry Minds Manufacturing: Ivor Parker, Vice President, Manufacturing

Hungry Minds Marketing: John Helmus, Assistant Vice President, Director of Marketing

Hungry Minds Production for Branded Press: Debbie Stailey, Production Director

Hungry Minds Sales: Roland Elgey, Senior Vice President, Sales and Marketing; Michael Violano, Vice President, International Sales and Sub Rights

◆

The publisher would like to give special thanks to Patrick J. McGovern, without whom this book would not have been possible.

◆

Contents at a Glance

Cartoons at a Glance

By Rich Tennant

"Oh, calm down. Sometimes it takes a long time to download an antidote on one of these things."

Ever since she got that thing, I'm afraid to fall asleep in my chair.

"...and whoever finds a cure for Mr. Pheeb's athletes foot gets extra credit."

"You know, anyone who wishes he had a remote control for his exercise equipment is missing the idea of exercise equipment."

"Gather around, kids! Your mother's found a home-tonsillectomy Web site."

"Hang on - I want to get a second opinion."

CYBERSIZERS
Thigh-Master Laptop
Nordic Server
Abdominizer Keyboard

TRAVIS AVOIDED DESCRIBING HIS SYMPTOMS IN AN E-MAIL BY FAXING HIS FACE TO THE DOCTOR

Cartoon Information:
Fax: 978-546-7747
E-Mail: richtennant@the5thwave.com
World Wide Web: www.the5thwave.com

Table of Contents

Foreword

I began using the Internet as a tool for communications, research, and social change about five years ago, before the Net started to hit the public consciousness. The Net has changed and will continue to change our world.

Thirty years ago, I created the Heimlich maneuver as a first-aid technique to help save the lives of people who are choking on food. The Heimlich maneuver is now used to save the lives of people who are drowning — it clears the water from their airways. The Maneuver also has been proven to save those gasping for breath from an asthma attack and, when used prophylactically, to prevent such attacks.

People are learning how to do the Heimlich maneuver online. Over 100,000 people have visited The Heimlich Institute Web site at www. heimlichinstitute.org in the past year. There, they can print off illustrated instructions on how to perform the Maneuver.

As a physician and medical researcher, I find the Net invaluable for keeping up on the latest news in medicine. Most importantly, anyone can learn to save the lives of loved ones online. Did you know, for example, that this year a study proved that mouth-to-mouth for heart attack victims increases their death rate, and that the American Heart Association no longer requires a rescuer to use mouth-to-mouth to save heart attack victims? Mouth-to-mouth is even worse for drowning victims who have water in their lungs. It's all online.

A friend told me his wife had multiple myeloma, a relatively rare disease. I sent him to the Net. In moments, he printed out comprehensive information about the disease. He was able to ask his wife's doctor intelligent questions and to help her make significant decisions when offered a choice of treatments.

E-mailing fellow researchers in China helps me coordinate an ongoing study funded by The Heimlich Institute on treating HIV with malariotherapy. We couldn't do the study without it. I also use the Net to promote "A Caring World." The Internet brings people together in the name of world peace and health.

This consumer-friendly book, *Healthcare Online For Dummies,* can help you get the information you need to be an informed patient. I have known one of the authors, Howard Wolinsky, for nearly 20 years. He is a veteran health and Internet reporter. Judi Wolinsky, his wife, is a pioneering Internet librarian. Combining their skills, they show you how to use the many resources on the Net to stay informed and healthy.

Use this book in good health.

Henry J. Heimlich

Henry J. Heimlich, M.D., Sc.D.

President, The Heimlich Institute

www.heimlichinstitute.org

Introduction

As a health consumer, we know that you're not a dummy. But the health-care system can leave you feeling as though you've landed a starring role in the movie *Dumb and Dumber*.

Even under the best of circumstances, seeing a doctor can be a nerve-racking experience. When you're sick, it's worse. You're vulnerable, and you hurt.

You'd like to make informed decisions about your health, but you don't have the answers. You often don't even have the questions. And the health professionals speak a language all their own, medicalese, and often are so time-crunched that they may not explain things as thoroughly as you'd like them to.

The Internet has made available — at the click of a mouse — storehouses of information of all kinds, including health and wellness information. You can use the Internet to find out just about anything you need to know about your health — maintaining it or restoring it, knowing what questions to ask your doctor, understanding the medicines you take, and so on. The Internet doesn't replace physicians, but it can help you build a strong partnership with your doctor.

This book's goal is to put you in touch with the trusted and reliable Internet resources you need in order to be able to make informed decisions about your health and wellness.

We're not doctors. We're a medical/technology reporter and a head of a reference department at a public library. We're trained in finding and evaluating information. It's our passion.

On our jobs, we're accustomed to finding comprehensive and reliable information on a deadline. The Internet has helped tremendously. It opened up access to new resources and people for us — both professionally and personally. It's all a heck of a lot of fun, too. Not a day goes by when we're not surprised and pleased to discover something new on the Web.

We're intrepid searchers. We love the hunt. There's nothing more satisfying than coming up with just the right resource to answer readers' questions and leading them to the information or the help that they need. The Internet has become our favorite hunting ground.

In this book, we're putting our Internet know-how to work for you in a couple of ways. We've shared with you our strategies for finding health Web sites that are reliable and are easy to use and understand. After reading this book, you'll have the tools you need to find your own way on the Net. We've also recommended health Web sites that we think are particularly worthwhile. We've looked for sites that are free or carry minimal charges.

Healthcare sites are among the most popular destinations online. But finding the *right* information can be difficult as you click through the vast number of health-related Web sites. A major criticism of health resources on the Internet *is* the vastness. So many Web sites, so little time. Another criticism is that much of the information is superficial or (worse) is inaccurate or was created by dot-con artists who are out to fleece you.

Keep in mind that medicine is marked by debate and disagreement on even the most fundamental points. Finding truth is a process. We aim to aid in that process by sharing information from authoritative sources. We trust that you, the reader — with support from your family, friends, and health professionals — will find your own truths.

About This Book

This book is a reference. You don't have to read the chapters in order. You can read it back to front, front to back, or start in the middle. If you wish, try reading it upside-down. We support you in whatever you do as far as reading this book goes.

But we want to remind you, however, that while you're using this book, you shouldn't make any decisions about your health based solely on what you read on the Internet. Consult on such matters with your personal doctor, who, after all, knows you and your health history best.

Both the world of medicine and the online world are constantly changing. Like medicine, the Internet is an ever-evolving work in progress. Web sites come, are tinkered with, get facelifts, and sometimes fade into oblivion.

We've made every attempt to pick sites that have reliable information and that will be there for you when you need them. But things change. The best that any book like this can do is to give you a snapshot of health resources on the Net at the time of writing. You know this, and so do we.

If you get to a Web site that's gone down, we feel your pain. But keep on trucking, er, searching. Hopefully, something better has come along. It probably has. That's the way of the Web.

Foolish Assumptions

We figure that you know how to use a computer. We assume that you know how to use a mouse to click and point and scroll up and down a page. We also assume that you have Internet access (or know someone who does) and that you have basic Internet skills, such as how to get to a Web page if given the address and how to navigate by using your browser.

To view some of the information at Web sites listed in this book, you must have Adobe Acrobat Reader installed on your computer. If you don't already have this program, you can download it for free from www.adobe.com/products/acrobat/readstep2.html.

How This Book Is Organized

We divided this book into seven main parts. Plus, we've included an Internet directory. You can read the pages at random or just look up what interests you. Here's an overview of what you can find in each part.

Part I: Getting Started

We give you a taste of what's to come in this part. We share pointers on how to evaluate health Web sites, how to avoid online quacks, hucksters, and rip-off artists, and how to protect yourself against having your online privacy invaded. You also find out how to stock your own black bag with Internet tools so you can find whatever you want at health Web sites. You find out, too, about exploring the medical megasites and locating clinical trials and support groups (as well as where you can scan the latest medical news and where you can find medical libraries).

Part II: Tapping into the Power of the Web

If you need help finding a doctor, hospital, or health insurance plan (including Medicare), this part is just what the, er, doctor ordered. We tell you about Internet tools that you can use to find out more about a doctor than his mother probably knows. You also can locate the best hospitals. And you can take a course in Health Insurance 101 to find out how to understand those mind-numbing details. We make it as easy as possible, so that you'll get an *A*. Guaranteed. You have an in with the teacher.

Part III: Researching Your Medical Concerns Online

This part shows you how to how to research a disease. We take you step-by-step through the process of finding information in medical dictionaries and encyclopedias and finding support groups, clinical trials, and relevant medical journal articles. We show you how to find a lot of information all at once at our favorite medical megasites. We also show you how to find out about your medications, including their benefits and potential side effects and interactions. In this part, we also show you some of the major Web sites for alternative healthcare.

Part IV: Using the Web to Research Major Illnesses

In this part, you find out about the Web resources that can provide you with information on the major diseases affecting Americans. These include heart disease, stroke, cancer, diabetes, arthritis, and infectious diseases, including HIV/AIDS and hepatitis. Here, you also find information about and links to self-help groups.

Part V: Staying Healthy in All the Seasons of Life

In this part, we take a life-stage approach to health and wellness on the Web. Here, you can find health Web sites with reliable information that addresses the issues and concerns for infants, children, teens, women, men, and seniors.

Part VI: Using the Web for Wellness

This is the part where you find Web sites with helpful information on eating right, staying fit, dealing with smoking and other addictions, and coping with stress, anxiety, and depression.

Part VII: The Part of Tens

This part contains only two brief chapters. In the first chapter, we've organized a virtual health fair where you can stop by the various booths to check out your stress level, how well balanced your diet is, and risks for major diseases, including heart disease, stroke, cancer, HIV, depression, anxiety, and osteoporosis. See you at the fair.

In the final chapter, we list our ten (count 'em, ten) must-see, must-use health Web sites. David Letterman eat your heart out. (Dave, there's a chapter here on heart disease. And, by the way, we'd love to do the show. Call our agent. We'll do sushi.)

Healthcare Online For Dummies Internet Directory

When you're flipping through the book, you can't help but notice the section of screaming yellow pages. You can't look up the local hardware store there. This is our *Healthcare Online For Dummies Internet Directory,* where you can quickly find Web sites organized by topic. The *Directory* lists additional Web sites on topics we've already covered plus lots of Web sites on topics we didn't have room to cover elsewhere. We also include some sites that were so cool that we just had to share them with you.

Conventions Used in This Book

This book has many step-by-step lists designed to make your life easier so you'll know what to do when you visit certain Web sites for the first time. Each step starts off with a boldface sentence telling you what you need to do. Directly after the bold step, you may see a sentence or two in regular type telling you what happens as a result of the bold action.

Whenever we list an online address, or URL, for a Web site, we put that address in a special typeface: www.wolinskyweb.net. Whenever we direct you to click a link on a page, we underline the link in the book: <u>Health Info</u>.

Icons Used in This Book

Throughout the book, you come across small round pictures in the margins. These are icons. They're designed to call your attention to paragraphs for a variety of reasons. Here are the icons used in this book and what they mean.

This icon won't help you win a bet at the track. But it is the fast track to some worthy tricks and hints that can save you time and trouble.

This icon is the closest thing we have in our icon arsenal to a flashing red light. It's designed to caution you about potential pitfalls or dangers.

This icon is used to flag information you should remember. Bet you won't forget this one.

This icon highlights the really nerdy stuff. Skip it if you wish.

Where to Go from Here

If you have a particular health or wellness concern, that's the place you should begin. Look in the Table of Contents or Index for the appropriate part or chapter number. Or if you want to start in the yellow pages or Chapter 1, that works for us, too.

At any rate, ladies and gents, fire up your computers and let the browsing begin.

Part I
Getting Started

In this part . . .

The chapters in this part help you get started in exploring the vast storehouse of health and wellness knowledge that's available online.

Chapter 1 tells you how to protect your personal information at Web sites and helps you evaluate health Web sites for accuracy and reliability. You also find out how to avoid dot-con artists and identify urban myths and Internet health hoaxes.

In Chapter 2, you assemble a bag of Internet tools. You find out how to locate support groups to help you cope with a disease or lose those extra pounds, and discover medical megasites that offer lots of information on a variety of health topics. This chapter also helps you develop a nose for news by introducing you to the best sites for tracking health news online.

Chapter 1

Getting Ready to Pan for Health Gold Online

In This Chapter

▶ Evaluating healthcare sites

▶ Protecting your privacy

▶ Avoiding Internet scams and hoaxes

*T*he Rush is on — the Internet Healthcare Information Gold Rush, that is. The fact that you're reading these words means that you want to get in on the action to find healthcare information online. You've got lots of company. In the year 2000, a whopping 100 million Americans ventured onto the Internet to find health information. That's up from 70 million in 1999, according to a Harris Interactive poll.

We know you're chomping at the bit to get started. Can't blame ya. But, there's a whole lot of fool's gold on the Net mixed in with the real stuff. This chapter gives you the picks and pans you need to cash in on the safest, most reliable, and most credible health and wellness Web sites.

The information in this chapter helps you avoid wading through the muck of sites that offer miracles but are more likely to deliver false promises. We show you how to steer clear of dot-con artists, hucksters, and marketeers who are trying to sell you a bill of goods and invade your privacy. So, gather your gear and get ready to go prospecting. There's healthcare gold in them thar Internet hills.

Warnings, Precautions, and All That Jazz

Your medication has warning labels, so does this book. This is it.

We're not doctors. We don't even play doctors on TV — let alone on the Internet. This book is not a medical manual; it's about medical and health-related Web sites. It's a book aimed at pointing you to Web sites that may help you.

When it comes to your heath, the partnership between you and your doctor is what counts. (Though we may refer at times to a *doctor* or *physician,* you can substitute other types of healthcare practitioners, such as a nurse practitioner or a physician assistant, depending on your personal situation.) If you encounter any new ideas for care while you're researching online, you should discuss them with a practitioner who knows you personally and is familiar with your health history.

Keep in mind that your physician may or may not want you to bring in a sheaf of printouts from the Net. A doctor's day is only so long, and even though most doctors themselves go online for research, they may not appreciate your cluttering up their desks with more papers. Ask your doctor what his or her feelings are about reviewing such information.

In any case, your doctor, regardless of how Net savvy he or she is, won't want you to use online material that is confusing, irresponsible, or downright dangerous. After all, your life and health are at stake here.

You shouldn't rely on the Internet in an emergency. Keep the phone number for your doctor, your hospital, and the nearest poison control center taped to your refrigerator and in your wallet so that it's quickly accessible. Also, have a printed first-aid manual at the ready so that you don't have to rely on your finicky Internet service provider and busy Internet sites when lives are at stake.

You can take a minute now to prepare for an emergency by reviewing these sites:

- ✔ **The American College of Emergency Physicians** (www.acep.org): The American College of Emergency Physicians (ACEP) offers excellent information about how to prepare for emergencies. To find out what you should do in a medical emergency, check out www.acep.org/library/index.cfm/id/402. To find out what you should have in your first-aid kit, go to www.acep.org/library/index.cfm/ID/1020.pdf.

- ✔ **American Association of Poison Control Centers** (www.aapcc.org): Click <u>Follow This Link</u> to go to a page where you can locate the nearest poison control center by entering your zip code.

- ✔ **The Heimlich Institute** (www.heimlichinstitute.org/howto.htm): This site offers printable instructions for performing the Heimlich maneuver to save yourself, an infant, and others who are choking (see Figure 1-1).

3 1833 04463 603 0

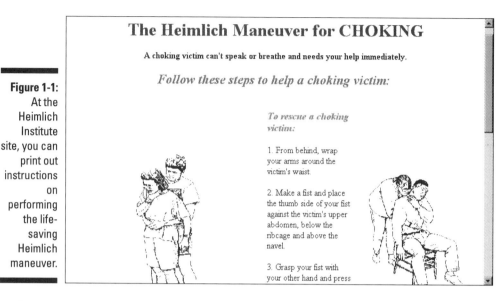

Figure 1-1:
At the
Heimlich
Institute
site, you can
print out
instructions
on
performing
the life-
saving
Heimlich
maneuver.

Whether in an emergency or a non-emergency situation, nothing, not even Internet technology can replace that old-fashioned, hands-on, in-person doctor-patient relationship. Nothing.

Judging Whether Web Sites Are Up to Code

Doctors and health organizations are worried about the quality of information at health-related Web sites, and you should be, too. The Web can serve up the best information from the most reputable sources, but it also is a free-wheeling, no-holds-barred environment where any kook with an ax to grind can grind away. Further, special interests, such as drug companies and insurance lobbies, also present their agendas at their sites without balance. Separating the good from the bad and the ugly may not be easy.

Honest Web site operators disclose to you their points-of-view, their sponsors, their privacy policies, and whether they are supported by ads. However, many sites may be less than honest. You need to have your suspicion radar on at all times on the Web, especially where your health is concerned.

Still, it's not mission impossible to find sites that are on the up and up. Some online groups have written prescriptions for health Web site quality that help you find the most authoritative, reliable, and credible sites. And, your common sense can take you a long way.

Guidelines for evaluating Web sites

The Internet Healthcare Coalition (`www.ihealthcoalition.org`) has developed this ten-point guide for evaluating sites:

1. Choosing an online health information resource is like choosing your doctor. You wouldn't go to just any doctor and you may get opinions from several doctors. Therefore you shouldn't rely on just any one Internet site for all your health needs. A good rule of thumb is to find a Web site that has a person, institution or organization in which you already have confidence. If possible, you should seek information from several sources and not rely on a single source of information.

2. Trust what you see or read on the Internet only if you can validate the source of the information. Authors and contributors should always be identified, along with their affiliations and financial interests, if any, in the content. Phone numbers, e-mail addresses or other contact information should also be provided.

3. Question Web sites that credit themselves as the sole source of information on a topic as well as sites that disrespect other sources of knowledge.

4. Don't be fooled by a comprehensive list of links. Any Web site can link to another and this in no way implies endorsement from either site.

5. Find out if the site is professionally managed and reviewed by an editorial board of experts to ensure that the material is both credible and reliable. Sources used to create the content should be clearly referenced and acknowledged.

6. Medical knowledge is continually evolving. Make sure that all clinical content includes the date of publication or modification.

7. Any and all sponsorship, advertising, underwriting, commercial funding arrangements, or potential conflicts should be clearly stated and separated from the editorial content. A good question to ask is: Does the author or authors have anything to gain from proposing one particular point of view over another?

8. Avoid any online physician who proposes to diagnose or treat you without a proper physical examination and consultation regarding your medical history.

9. Read the Web site's privacy statement and make certain that any personal medical or other information you supply will be kept absolutely confidential.

10. Most importantly, use your common sense! Shop around, always get more than one opinion, be suspicious of miracle cures, and always read the fine print.

© 2000 Internet Healthcare Coalition. All rights reserved. Reproduced with permission. For more information, refer to the Web site at `http://www.ihealthcoalition.org`.

The HONcode seal

Sometimes you may encounter a multi-colored HONcode seal at health sites. This seal comes from the Health On the Net Foundation (www.hon.ch), a non-profit health group whose goal is to help you separate good sites from potentially dangerous ones.

Sites that subscribe to the Health On the Net Foundation Code of Conduct (HONcode) for medical and health Web sites can put a HONcode seal on their sites. The HONcode system is strictly voluntary and self-policing. The HON Foundation reviews all sites applying for its seal and checks them out periodically. For more on how sites are judged, check out the "HONcode of Conduct Principles" sidebar.

The HON Foundation also has built a tool, shown in Figure 1-2, that enables you to evaluate a site for reliability and credibility. To locate this tool, click the HONcode of Conduct link on the site's main page and then click the Site-Checker link in the left-hand column.

Keep in mind that not all good sites have applied for the HONcode seal. The HONcode approach is not perfect, but it's a start toward improving the quality of health Web sites and protecting your health.

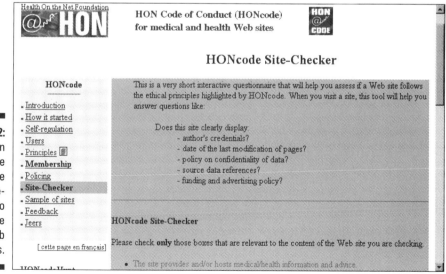

Figure 1-2:
You can use the HONcode Site-Checker to evaluate health Web sites.

HONcode of Conduct Principles

The HONcode suggests these standards for evaluating medical and health Web sites for reliability and credibility, which are listed at `www.hon.ch/HONcode/Conduct.html`:

✔ **Authority.** Any medical or health advice provided and hosted on this site will only be given by medically trained and qualified professionals unless a clear statement is made that a piece of advice offered is from a non-medically qualified individual or organization.

✔ **Complementarity.** The information provided on this site is designed to support, not replace, the relationship that exists between a patient/site visitor and his/her existing physician.

✔ **Confidentiality.** Confidentiality of data relating to individual patients and visitors to a medical/health Web site, including their identity, is respected by this Web site. The Web site owners undertake to honor or exceed the legal requirements of medical/health information privacy that apply in the country and state where the Web site and mirror sites are located.

✔ **Attribution.** Where appropriate, information contained on this site will be supported by clear references to source data and, where possible, have specific HTML links to that data. The date when a clinical page was last modified will be clearly displayed (e.g. at the bottom of the page).

✔ **Justifiability.** Any claims relating to the benefits/performance of a specific treatment, commercial product or service will be supported by appropriate, balanced evidence in the manner outlined in the fourth principle.

✔ **Transparency of authorship.** The designers of this Web site will seek to provide information in the clearest possible manner and provide contact addresses for visitors that seek further information or support. The Webmaster will display his/her e-mail address clearly throughout the Web site.

✔ **Transparency of sponsorship.** Support for this Web site will be clearly identified, including the identities of commercial and non-commercial organizations that have contributed funding, services or material for the site.

✔ **Honesty in advertising and editorial policy.** If advertising is a source of funding it will be clearly stated. A brief description of the advertising policy adopted by the Web site owners will be displayed on the site. Advertising and other promotional material will be presented to viewers in a manner and context that facilitates differentiation between it and the original material created by the institution operating the site.

Protecting Your Privacy Online

When you venture out on the World Wide Web, you can't be certain that the Web's not looking back at you. Marketeers may be watching your clicks as you move within or between sites. And some Web site operators develop and sell lists of e-mail addresses and other information of those who register at their Web sites.

That's the way of the Web. Sorry.

Still, you can harvest Internet riches while keeping the invasion of your privacy to a minimum. You can take steps to put at least partial blinders on those prying eyes. Here are some points to consider when you're going online for health information:

- ✔ **Protect your passwords.** Be creative when you make up passwords to access different sites. Avoid the obvious: Don't use a telephone number, a birth date, or a portion of your Social Security number. Rather combine numbers, letters, and symbols in a way that can't be guessed. And, of course, don't share your passwords with anyone.

- ✔ **Don't conduct research at the office.** Your boss may be monitoring what Web sites are frequented by staffers. If you're visiting health Web sites on the company's clock (which we don't recommend), you may inadvertently be sharing personal health information with your employer.

- ✔ **Think twice about giving out your real name and personal information in online health-related discussion groups.** If you disclose personal information in these virtual groups to people you don't really know, you expose yourself to the possibility of having your real life invaded.

- ✔ **Before disclosing personal information — including your name, health condition, and credit card number — be sure to read the site's privacy policy.** The policy should be prominently displayed at the site. If the site is selling your information to other parties, you may not want to visit it, let alone register there.

Also be aware that some sites use *cookies,* small computer files written on your computer, to collect information about you. Check out the "Cookies" sidebar for more information.

TECHNICAL STUFF

Cookies

C is for cookie — on Sesame Street as well as on Internet Street. Cookies are files that are deposited on your computer when you visit some Web sites and when you register at others. A cookie identifies you — or actually your computer.

Cookies are what make it possible for Amazon.com to welcome you by name and to recommend books you might enjoy — like that new one, you know, *Healthcare Online For Dummies.* But you may not like the fact that Web sites and advertisers can use cookies to track you and your interests. Some people say it's good marketing. Others see it as an invasion of privacy.

Check with your Web browser's Help manual to find out how your browser handles cookies. You may be able turn cookies off or be given a choice whether you want to accept them.

Us? We like milk with our cookies, the kind with chocolate, not computer, chips.

If you want to find out more about online privacy, here are a few sites you may want to check out:

- ✔ Privacy Rights Clearinghouse (www.privacyrights.org)

- ✔ Online Privacy Alliance (www.privacyalliance.com/consumers)

- ✔ The Federal Trade Commission's online pamphlet, "Site Seeing On The Internet" (www.ftc.gov/bcp/conline/pubs/online/sitesee/index.html), shown in Figure 1-3.

Protecting Yourself from Dot-con Men

Anybody ever try to sell you the Brooklyn Bridge? It happens on the Internet every day. Dot-con artists are plying their trade at Web sites, in chat rooms, and through e-mail, preying on those who want to be healthy, slim, sexy, and youthful.

You can protect yourself by exercising a healthy dose of skepticism and taking the proper precautions. You also can blow the whistle on the scumbaggery and humbuggery.

Figure 1-3: The Federal Trade Commission online pamphlet, "Site Seeing On The Internet," gives you tips on staying safe on the Web.

Avoid being taken by Internet rip-offs

Hucksters and rip-off artists thrive wherever they pick up the scent of hope, and nowhere is this more true than in healthcare. If you haven't received it yet, you'll probably be getting an e-mail today trying to sell you a miracle cure for cancer, arthritis, or impotence. Or maybe while you're researching a medical concern online, you'll be steered toward a site that is selling false hopes with false promises.

But you can take the proper precautions from being fleeced *online,* just as you can in the *offline* world. The old adage still holds true, no matter where you go: If it sounds too good to be true, it probably is.

Consumer watchdogs at the Federal Trade Commission point out the warning signs for consumer health fraud for you at `www.ftc.gov/bcp/conline/edcams/miracle/index.html`. They suggest that you be cautious about pitches for drugs, diets, and other products that use the following:

✔ Phrases such as *scientific breakthrough, miraculous cure, exclusive product, secret formula,* and *ancient ingredient.*

✔ *Medicalese* — impressive-sounding terminology to disguise a lack of good science.

✔ Case histories from *cured* consumers claiming amazing results. Their testimonials also imply that their experience is typical for consumers using the product or service. When you see a testimonial, ask for proof of its *typical* nature.

✔ A laundry list of symptoms the product cures or treats.

✔ The latest trendy ingredient touted in the headlines.

✔ A claim that the product is available from only one source, for a limited time.

✔ Testimonials from *famous* medical experts.

✔ A claim that the government, the medical profession or research scientists have conspired to suppress the product.

Avoid being fooled by Internet rumors

Did you get that e-mail alert about the Klingerman virus? You know, the one where they warn you about a number of people becoming ill and dying from a viral infection after opening an oversized blue package and handling the sponge sent as a gift from the Klingerman Foundation.

Filing an Internet fraud complaint

If you've been taken by Internet health fraud, you can fight back. You can file a complaint with the appropriate authorities to try to get your money back and to prevent the scammers from taking advantage of someone else.

Here are some places to take your complaints:

✔ **The Federal Trade Commission (www.ftc. gov):** The FTC is the federal agency that protect consumers against unfair, deceptive, or fraudulent practices. The Commission is especially concerned about advertising, marketing, and credit/lending fraud. You can file a complaint online at this site. Look for the link on the site's main page.

✔ **Internet Fraud Complaint Center (www. ifccfbi.gov/complaint/default.asp):** The Federal Bureau of Investigation and the National White Collar Crime Center run this center. The Complaint Center specifically addresses Internet fraud, with auction fraud and non-delivery of payment or goods being the most common complaints.

✔ **National Association of Attorneys General (www.naag.org/about/ag1.cfm):** This site has a clickable map listing Web pages for your state's attorney general, whose staff investigates violations of state consumer fraud laws.

✔ **Better Business Bureau (www.bbb.org/ bbbcomplaints/SelectComplaintLink.asp):** This site fields consumer gripes about individual companies.

Or did you get the e-mail cautioning you not to eat bananas from Costa Rica because they're infected with necrotizing fasciitis (flesh-eating) bacteria? The disease reportedly nearly wiped out the monkey population in the Costa Rican rain forest.

Pretty frightening stuff, huh? Turns out there's no Klingerman virus. There's not even a Klingerman Foundation. And you can go ahead and have bananas with your corn flakes. It's all a hoax.

E-mail has made our lives easier as we contact friends, family, and business associates at the speed of light. Likewise, hoaxers and rumormongers are having a field day by spreading near-truths, half-truths, non-truths, misinformation, disinformation, and outright lies faster than a cold virus spreads in a kindergarten class.

But never fear. The Centers for Disease Control and Prevention, best known as the CDC, acclaimed for fighting all sorts of health menaces, from AIDS to the Ebola virus, is here to help. If you receive a suspicious e-mail about a health hazard, meander over to the CDC's Current Health Related Hoaxes and Rumors page at www.cdc.gov/hoax_rumors.htm. There, the CDC explodes health rumors that are making the e-mail rounds.

Some other great places to check out Internet hoaxes and urban legends include

- ✔ Urban Legends Reference Pages at `www.snopes.com`
- ✔ The AFU and Urban Legends Archive at `www.urbanlegends.com` (has an extensive medical section)
- ✔ NetSquirrel.com's Urban Legend Combat Kit at `www.netsquirrel.com/combatkit`
- ✔ Quackwatch's Health- and Safety-Related Urban Legends, Rumors, and Hoaxes at `www.quackwatch.com/04ConsumerEducation/urbanlegends.html` (see Figure 1-4)

Quackwatch℠

Your Guide to Health Fraud, Quackery, and Intelligent Decisions

Operated by <u>Stephen Barrett, M.D.</u>
Questions related to consumer health answered by e-mail.
If you write, please mention how you found this Web site.

Figure 1-4:
Quackwatch
debunks
erroneous
health
rumors and
urban
legends.

<u>Search Quackwatch</u> ||| <u>Ask a Question</u> ||| <u>Make a Comment</u> ||| <u>Join Our Advisory Board</u>
<u>Deutsch</u> ||| <u>Espanol</u> ||| <u>Francais</u> ||| <u>Portugues</u>
<u>Chirobase</u> ||| <u>MLM Watch</u> ||| <u>NutriWatch</u> ||| <u>NCAHF</u>
<u>Most Recent Additions to Our Web Sites</u>
<u>Free Electronic Newsletter (Consumer Health Digest)</u> NEW FEATURE

Have you been victimized by an Internet-related health scam?
Would you like to help people by telling your story to a reporter?
If so, please send an e-mail message to <u>victims@quackwatch.com</u> describing what happened.

Chapter 2

Tools for Finding Health Information Online

- -

In This Chapter

▶ Taking a look at medical megasites

▶ Finding support online

▶ Checking out Internet health libraries

▶ Getting medical news on the Web

- -

*I*n the days when doctors routinely made house calls, they'd keep a black medical bag filled with the necessary tools of their trade. They'd stock it with some essential medications, tongue depressors, a stethoscope, a flashlight, and a reflex hammer. They were ready at a moment's notice to take their medical practices on the road.

In this chapter, we help you assemble and use your medical bag of Internet tools. With these tools, you'll be well prepared to go out onto the Information Superhighway and find the health and wellness information you need.

This chapter adds the following tools to your medical bag:

✔ The best medical megasites, which put at your fingertips information on medications, conditions, and wellness, as well as provide access to online health communities

✔ Online groups that provide support when you're coping with a disease or trying to stick with an exercise program, shed pounds, or quit smoking

✔ Medical libraries with helpful librarians and deep stacks of information

✔ Online medical news you can use

Medical Megasites

The best place to begin any search for information on health or a disease is at a medical megasite. These sites are one-stop shops that offer a wide variety of health information.

Here's a sampling of what valuable information you can find at medical megasites:

- ✔ Disease information and symptom checkers
- ✔ Medical encyclopedias
- ✔ Medical dictionaries
- ✔ Detailed information on various medications
- ✔ Tips on dieting, exercising, and reducing stress
- ✔ Advice from medical, health, and fitness experts
- ✔ Communities/message boards/chat rooms
- ✔ Cool interactive tools and quizzes
- ✔ Up-to-the-minute health news
- ✔ Doctor and hospital finders
- ✔ Links to other useful health sites

When you're evaluating the information you find at a megasite, keep the following points in mind:

- ✔ **Advertisers could influence the information or how it is displayed.** Most, but not all, megasites support themselves with ads for prescription drugs, vitamins, and medical sundries, as well as laptops, life insurance, and books — typical Internet commerce. Therefore, advertisers may influence the information you find on the site.

  But just because medical megasites are selling something doesn't mean that their information isn't useful. Just use your best judgment and run anything affecting your health past your personal doctor.

- ✔ **Look for the HONcode seal, which signifies that the site adheres to the HONcode principles.** You can find out more about the HONcode in Chapter 1.

Many medical megasites exist. In the following sections, we introduce a few of our favorites in no special order and highlight some of their best features.

drkoop.com

Named for its founder, famed former Surgeon General C. Everett Koop, drkoop.com (`www.drkoop.com`) presents you with a broad array of information, including a medical dictionary and news feeds. (See Figure 2-1.)

The Special Reports area of the site (`www.drkoop.com/news/special-reports`) deals with health issues and conditions. In some cases, this area includes upfront and personal descriptions on living with certain conditions, and provides links to related Web sites and, egads, books.

You can check out the medications you're taking at drkoop.com's Drug Checker. You can access the Drug Checker by clicking the link on the site's main page or by going to `www.drugchecker.com`. This tool provides profiles on different medications and their interactions with other drugs and certain foods. You can find out more about this tool in Chapter 7.

drkoop.com also offers a selection of educational Webcasts on allergies, hair loss, breast cancer, and hundreds of other subjects. You watch the Webcasts right on your computer monitor. To access these videos, click the <u>Health Videos</u> link on the main page or go directly to the videos at `healthology.drkoop.com`.

Need a sounding board? In the Community section, you can discuss anything that's bothering you on message boards or in chat rooms (see the "Chats and message boards" section, later in the chapter). You can go to this area by clicking the <u>Community</u> link on the site's main page. In order to participate, you need to register and log in.

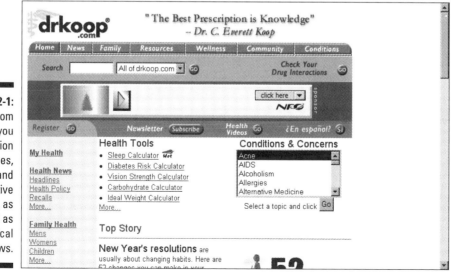

Figure 2-1: drkoop.com offers you information on diseases, drugs, and alternative medicine, as well as medical news.

TIP

Look it up, STAT!

The following sites are great resources for looking up medical terms on the Internet:

✔ **MedicineNet.com (www.medterms.com):** The fastest way to look up a medical term online is go to the Medical Terms dictionary at this site. You type the word into the Search the Dictionary box on the left side of the page or pick through an A-to-Z index. The site also has index information on symptoms, how the condition is diagnosed, procedures and tests, and medications.

✔ **HealthAtoZ.com (www.healthatoz.com):** This site offers a spelling checker of medical terms. On the site's home page, click the Spell Check link, which is located under the

search box. Then on the spell check page, enter the word you want to spell check.

✔ **MLANET (www.mlanet.org/resources/ medspeak/medspeaka_d.html):** Check out the Medical Library Association's "Deciphering Medspeak" for a list of medical terms from medical librarians.

✔ **Medspeak, the Language of ER (www. geocities.com/televisioncity/5196/noframes. html):** Trying to figure out what those doctors and nurses are saying on the TV show *ER*, where medicalese is as abundant as fake blood? Go to the Medspeak, the Language of ER Web site. In no time, you'll be able to tell a thoracotomy tray from a TV tray.

drkoop.com also has calculators to help you get the answers to such questions as what your risk for diabetes is and what your ideal weight is. You access these calculators at `www.drkoop.com/tools/calculator`.

WebMD Health

WebMD Health (`www.mywebmd.com`) covers all the bases you'd want covered at a medical megasite. From the site's home page, you can easily jump to information tailored to your interests. Scroll down the opening page to the Stay Healthy, Newly Diagnosed, and Living with Illness list boxes, and then select the topics that you're interested in.

You can also Ask An Expert, Talk With Others in weekly support chat groups, or Post a Message to a bulletin board or scan the latest health news. You must register to join a group and participate in Live Events.

In its Medical Library area, WebMD offers *The Yale University School of Medicine Patient's Guide to Medical Tests,* which explains major medical tests, and the *ADAM Medical Encyclopedia,* which contains thousands of entries on diseases, treatments, medical terms, and anatomy. You can also find Illustrated Guides that explain major diseases, such as asthma and osteoporosis.

healthfinder

Another site that's mega-cool is healthfinder (www.healthfinder.gov). This government site is a quick and easy way to access a treasure trove of reliable consumer health information.

The site provides a wealth of links to health publications, clearinghouses, databases, other Web sites, and support and self-help groups, as well as to government agencies and not-for-profits.

HealthCentral.com

HealthCentral.com (www.healthcentral.com), shown in Figure 2-2, is one of the largest health megasites. It features material from popular medical broadcaster Dr. Dean Edell, as well as the People's Pharmacy, where you can look up information about drugs and herbs. HealthCentral provides the typical medical online reference tools along with specialized encyclopedias on children's health as well as on sexual health.

MayoClinic.com

For years, people have traveled to Rochester, Minnesota, to see the experts at the famed Mayo Clinic. Now, you can tap into that Mayo expertise from your personal computer by going to MayoClinic.com (www.mayoclinic. com), as shown in Figure 2-3.

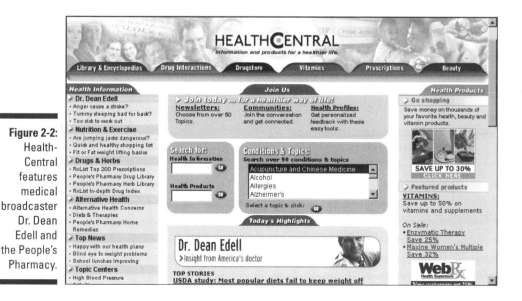

Figure 2-2: HealthCentral features medical broadcaster Dr. Dean Edell and the People's Pharmacy.

Visit the Condition Centers and Healthy Living Centers to get information and advice, without the usual advertising clutter you find at commercial megasites.

Got questions? Click the <u>Answers from Mayo Specialist</u> link to go to an area where you can find the Mayo staff's answers to questions e-mailed from readers. You can also find practical information in the First-Aid & Self-Care Guide, which covers a wide range of health concerns such as treating sunburns or avoiding back injuries.

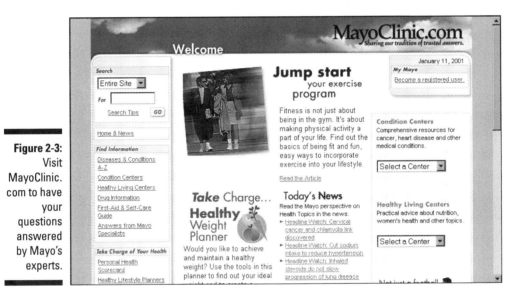

Figure 2-3: Visit MayoClinic. com to have your questions answered by Mayo's experts.

Check in at the Take Charge section to find personal planners on weight loss, exercise, smoking cessation, and stress reduction. These planners walk you through the steps of deciding to make a change to improve your health and then following through on that goal. You use online calculators to help set your goals, and you can find out how others are doing in meeting theirs. You have to register to join this health club, but you don't have to pay any monthly fees.

Some other megasites

Here are some other medical megasites that are worth a click:

- ✔ CBSHealthWatch at `www.cbshealthwatch.com`
- ✔ HealthAtoZ.com at `www.healthatoz.com`

✔ HealthAnswers.com at www.healthanswers.com

✔ InteliHealth at www.intelihealth.com

✔ WellnessWeb at www.wellnessweb.com

✔ Yahoo! Health at health.yahoo.com

The American Academy of Family Physicians' familydoctor.org Web site (www.familydoctor.org) offers some unique tools that are worth checking out (see Figure 2-4). For example, the Self-Care Flowcharts can help you decide whether you need to see a doctor, based on your symptoms.

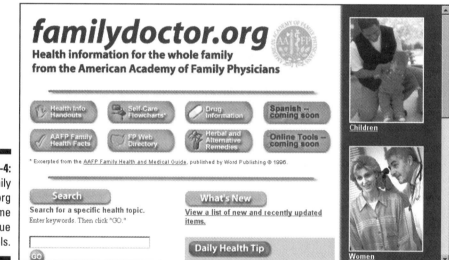

Figure 2-4:
Family
doctor.org
offers some
unique
tools.

Getting Support Online

Did you ever wish you had a circle of friends who would always be there for you with a sympathetic ear, and offer words of encouragement and just the right advice? The Internet can find you a group that will welcome you and answer your questions, even the ones you feel are too basic or silly to ask. And this group won't judge you by how you look or even how you spell.

Say you're struggling with a diet or a new exercise program. Or maybe you've just been diagnosed with a disease or have been coping with one for years. Whatever your health or wellness concern, many types of groups on the Internet are saving you a seat. Actually, you can just use your own seat in front of your computer.

Mailing lists

Everybody loves to get e-mail from friends. If you join a mailing list, you get lots of e-mail from people who have the same interests and concerns as you.

Mailing lists are dedicated to discussing one subject, such as a particular diet, a disease, parenting, menopause, or caregiving. Anyone who participates in the mailing list can ask questions, share an experience, commiserate, or just schmooze.

You join a mailing list by subscribing to it. Everyone who has signed on to the list receives a copy of every e-mail that's sent to the group. But be prepared; depending on how active the group is, you may be bombarded with e-mail.

You can respond to anything that interests you by sending a reply publicly to the group or privately to the sender. Some groups even keep archives of all the messages sent to the whole group.

How do you find a list? Try Liszt at www.liszt.com. *Franz*ly, er frankly, Liszt is a quick and easy way to locate a group. Here's how:

1. **Open your Web browser and go to** www.liszt.com.

2. **Click the <u>Health</u> link.**

3. **Scan through the list of subcategories and then click one that interests you.**

   If you can't find a subcategory that you're interested in, you can run a search by typing a keyword in the Find box near the top of the page.

   After you click a subcategory, a page appears, listing different mailing lists that match your topic.

4. **Click a mailing list that you're interested in subscribing to.**

   Usually, you can find a description of the group along with step-by-step instructions on how to subscribe *and* unsubscribe. These instructions vary, based on the specific mailing list, and you must follow them exactly.

After the e-mail starts coming in, you may want to just read the messages at first, rather than reply to them, to see if the mailing list is your cup of tea — this practice is called *lurking*. Reading through some of the messages helps you determine the personality of the group (quirky, warm, friendly, serious, well informed, and so on). And if the group isn't a good match, you can unsubscribe to the mailing list.

We suggest that you stick with mailing lists that are run by moderators. A moderator keeps the group on track, stops any bickering, and keeps out unwanted advertising. Sometimes health professionals or folks who are passionate about the topic run these mailing lists.

You can also find other e-mail groups at Topica at www.topica.com and Yahoo! Groups at groups.yahoo.com.

And as always, be skeptical of what other participants say and discuss any questions relating to your care with your doctor.

Newsgroups

If you don't want your e-mail box filled with missives from a mailing list, try the alternative: newsgroups. Newsgroups are electronic bulletin boards where you post and read messages.

Here are a few additional details about newsgroups:

- **Everything in newsgroups is archived and public.** The rant you write bleary-eyed at 3:00 a.m. to set the world straight may remain in the archives forever. So if you don't want others to read it, don't post it.

- **You need special newsreader software to participate in newsgroups.** Chances are your Internet Explorer or Netscape Communicator browser has a built-in newsreader. Look in your browser's Help section for details.

- **You can go to special sites to find newsgroups.** At Google (groups.google.com), for example, you can search for a newsgroup by entering a keyword in the Search Groups box. Then on the results page, you can peer into the archives to see what people have to say about that subject. Checking out some of these messages is a great way to determine if you want to join the newsgroup.

Chats and message boards

You can "talk" in real time to people who have similar health interests and concerns in chat rooms. Of course, "talking" in chat rooms means typing messages back and forth.

Probably the best way to link up with health-related chats is through the communities or forums run by medical megasites. At these sites, you can often chat with people like you or with experts. For example, you can find chats by clicking the <u>Community</u> link at HealthAtoZ.com (`www.healthatoz.com`) or by clicking the <u>Member Communities</u> link at WebMD Health (`www.mywebmd.com`). You have to register to join in on chats and events.

Many medical megasites also offer message boards, where you can post questions and share your thoughts on health subjects that interest you. Moderators run some of the message boards, and other boards are open forums. You have to register to join message boards. If you're interested in finding a message board, try clicking the <u>Community Resources</u> link at CBSHealthWatch (`www.cbshealthwatch.com`) or the <u>Community</u> link at drkoop.com (`www.drkoop.com`).

Keep those lines of communications open.

Visiting Virtual Health Libraries

The Internet has been described as a vast library of information. And online, you can find libraries with vast amounts of health information. Check out the virtual health libraries in the next few sections, where every library is your local branch and your books are never overdue.

MEDLINEplus

The National Library of Medicine is the mother ship of health libraries. It's consumer-friendly MEDLINE*plus* site (`www.medlineplus.gov`) is in a class of its own and worthy of medical megasite status (see Figure 2-5). You won't find any flashing banner ads for credit cards or vitamins here. This is an uncluttered, easy-to-navigate site, filled to the rafters with links to information.

Whether you're checking out a disease such as lupus or a wellness issue such as stress, start your search by clicking the <u>Health Topics</u> link. From there, you can click the first letter of the subject you're researching, or you can work your way through a subject list. Either way, you can choose from a dazzling array of well-organized links to related information about the disease or condition. You get links not only to the basics about diagnosing and treating the condition, but also to a whole host of additional goodies such as consumer brochures, glossaries, and doctor finders for the particular specialty.

With just a click, you can find relevant research studies that you can join, as well as do a MEDLINE search to find articles on a specific topic in doctors' journals.

MEDLINE*plus* has a direct link to the lushly illustrated *ADAM Medical Encyclopedia:* `medlineplus.adam.com`. You can search ADAM via an alphabetical list or by category (poison, symptom, surgery, test, injury, and so on).

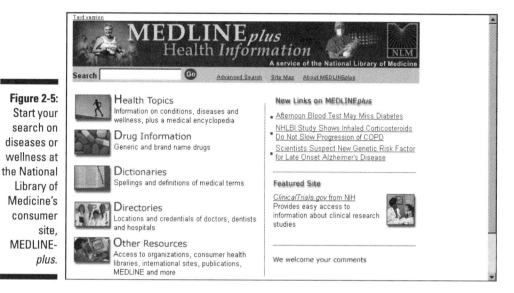

Figure 2-5:
Start your
search on
diseases or
wellness at
the National
Library of
Medicine's
consumer
site,
MEDLINE-
plus.

Other libraries

You can put the expertise of librarians to work for you on the Internet. The
following sites contain lists of high-quality Web sites, as chosen by librarians:

- ✔ The Medical Library Association's Top Ten Most Useful Websites for
  Health Consumers at `www.mlanet.org/resources/medspeak/`
  `topten.html`

- ✔ The Internet Public Library's Reference Center at `www.ipl.org/ref`
  (click the <u>Health & Medical Sciences Shelf</u> link)

- ✔ Emory MedWeb from the Emory Health Sciences Center Library at
  `www.medweb.emory.edu/MedWeb`

- ✔ Librarians' Index to the Internet (Health and Medicine section) at
  `www.lii.org/search/file/health`

You can also get help and health information from brick-and-mortar libraries
(consumer, hospital, and medical school libraries) that have a Web presence.
Here are some sites that provide links to those libraries:

- ✔ **The National Library of Medicine's MEDLINE*plus*** (`www.nlm.nih.gov/`
  `medlineplus/libraries.html`): Here, you find links to consumer and
  public libraries with excellent medical collections. Some of the library
  Web sites even have an Ask the Librarian e-mail service as well as lists of
  health Web sites that are recommended by librarians.

> ✔ **The Consumer and Patient Health Information Section of the Medical Library Association** (`caphis.njc.org/Directory/Find.HTML`): This site enables you to search for libraries that specialize in certain subjects, such as AIDS or alternative medicine. You get a description of what's in the library, as well as the library's phone number, address, and Web address. The description also notes whether librarians will answer questions via e-mail, by phone, or in person.
>
> ✔ **The National Network of Libraries of Medicine** (`www.nnlm.nlm.nih.gov/members`): This site helps you find medical libraries that provide medical reference services to the public.

Read All About It: Finding Health News Online

The Internet is the newest news medium. If health news is your dish, you can feast on a smorgasbord of online versions of newspapers, magazines, TV and radio stations, and medical journals. Some Web sites combine print and video media for a unique blend of news that's available only online. You can even go online to tap the original sources that the doctors read and the medical reporters rely on.

Checking out newspapers online

Victor Cohn, the late, great medical writer at *The Washington Post,* used to say there were two kinds of health stories: No Hope. And New Hope. Vic's point was that medical news sells papers — which explains all those front pages of newspapers and magazine covers with health news headlines.

The online versions of *The Washington Post* and *The New York Times* are as accessible as your local Daily Kazoo, and these papers have great health coverage you may not see in the Kazoo:

> ✔ **Washingtonpost.com**, shown in Figure 2-6, provides comprehensive health coverage with staff and wire reports at `washingtonpost.com/wp-dyn/health`. It also provides specialized health coverage on women, men, kids and seniors, alternative medicine, nutrition, fitness, chronic conditions, and more. The *Post* works with InteliHealth, the health megasite, to offer information on medications and diseases.
>
> ✔ **The New York Times on the Web** has a Health section with staff and wire reports (`www.nytimes.com/pages/health/index.html`). You get coverage on aging, children's health, fitness, genetics, men's health, nutrition, psychology, and women's health — *all the health news that's fit for your browser.*

Figure 2-6:
Washington-
post.com
offers you a
wide variety
of health
news and
features.

Read what your doctor reads

You probably don't subscribe to *The Journal of the American Medical Association* or *The New England Journal of Medicine.* But your doctor does.

You can peek over your doctor's shoulder by visiting medical journals online. Here are some of the more popular ones:

✔ The Journal of the American Medical Association at www.jama.com

✔ The New England Journal of Medicine at www.nejm.org

✔ The Lancet at www.thelancet.com

✔ Annals of Internal Medicine at www.annals.org

✔ Pediatrics at www.pediatrics.org

For a list of links to tons of other journals, check out the Southern Illinois University

Medical Library at www.siumed.edu/lib/webresources/webjournals.html.

The journals generally won't give you full text unless you're a subscriber. But they do share their tables of contents and detailed summaries of their articles, which are called *abstracts.* You'll probably need a medical dictionary to plow through them, so check out the dictionaries we list earlier in this chapter.

If the spirit moves you and you want to get the full text of the articles, you may be able to get them through your local public or medical library. Or, you can get them, for a fee, through the National Library of Medicine's Loansome Doc service. You can find instructions for ordering articles at www.nlm.nih.gov/loansomedoc/loansome_home.html.

Just what the doctor ordered.

Evaluating health information

You shouldn't read or view any health news — online or offline — without a critical eye.

Health Insight, a project directed by Assistant Professor Kimberly Thompson at the Harvard School of Public Health Center for Risk Analysis, has prepared a list of ten questions to help you evaluate health information and the risks involved in making healthcare decisions for yourself and your family. (You can find more information at www.health-insight.harvard.edu.)

Here are the questions the Harvard researchers urge you to ask:

✔ **What is the message?** Get past the presentation to the facts.

✔ **Is the source reliable?** Think about the quality of the information. Information comes from many sources, good and bad.

✔ **How strong is the evidence overall?** Understand how this information fits in with other evidence. Some sources are generally encouraged to provide unbiased coverage, while others may be intentionally biased. Consider how many sides of the story you hear and whether your source tells you about all of the possibilities.

✔ **Does this information matter?** Determine whether the information changes your thinking and leads you to respond.

✔ **What do the numbers mean?** Remember that understanding the importance of a risk requires that you understand the numbers.

✔ **How does this risk compare with others?** Put the risk into context.

✔ **What actions can be taken to reduce risk?** Identify the ways that you can improve your health.

✔ **What are the tradeoffs?** Make sure you can live with the tradeoffs associated with different actions.

✔ **What else do I need to know?** Focus on identifying the information that would help you make a better decision. Remember that scientific information is always somewhat uncertain even if it is not reported that way.

✔ **Where can I get more information?** Try your doctor, library, the original source, government agencies, consumer groups and the Internet.

Finding other news sources

1stHeadlines has a unique approach to health news. Its health section, 1stHealthNews (www.1sthealthnews.com), pulls together its front page on health from 98 newspaper, broadcast, and online sources. So in one place, you can link to and read health reports from ABC.com, *The Chicago Sun-Times,* Fox News, MSNBC, *The Philadelphia Inquirer*'s Philly.com, *USA Today,* and WebMD.

For a quick scan of the latest health headlines, go to Yahoo! Health (health.yahoo.com) and scroll down to the Today's Health News area. This area lists the most recent health news from the major news wire services: Reuters, the Associated Press, and HealthScout.

Or you can go directly to Reuters Health (www.reutershealth.com) for its Health eLine reports for consumers and separate reports aimed at health professionals. Reuters Health also profiles medications you may be taking and provides a quick way into MEDLINE searches of the medical literature.

These sites are also worth a click for finding health news:

- ✔ USA Today at www.usatoday.com
- ✔ MSNBC at www.msnbc.com
- ✔ CNN.com at www.cnn.com

You can find additional news sites in the *Healthcare Online For Dummies Internet Directory.*

You can also find news releases that are prepared by medical schools, hospitals, and others in hopes that reporters will bite and turn them into stories. Go to Newswise at www.newswise.com and click the MedNews link. Or go to EurekAlert! at www.eurekalert.org and click the This Week's Releases link.

Part II
Tapping into the Power of the Web

The 5th Wave   By Rich Tennant

"Oh, calm down. Sometimes it takes a long time to download an antidote on one of these things."

In this part . . .

Need help finding a doctor, a hospital, or an insurance company? Or maybe you want to see how they rate? The Internet has a whole host of tools that makes it easy to locate doctors, hospitals, and insurers that meet your needs. In this part, we tell you where you can find these tools on the Net, and we walk you through the process step-by-step, inch-by-inch.

Chapter 3 focuses on finding a doctor by location and specialty and deciding whether he or she is your Dr. Right. Chapter 4 helps you locate the best hospitals. And Chapter 5 puts the spotlight on finding your way through the insurance maze.

Chapter 3

Finding Dr. Right

. . . .

. . . .

*H*ere's our favorite doctor joke: A woman dies and goes to heaven. St. Peter is giving her a tour. When they reach the Heaven Cafeteria, a frantic figure with a flowing white mane rushes in. He's decked out in a white coat and has a stethoscope dangling from his neck. Without apology, he pushes to the head of the line, grabs his food, and hurries out. "Who was that?" the newbie asks. "That's God," says St. Peter, "He thinks He's a doctor."

Doctor bashing aside, love 'em or hate 'em, everyone still needs a doctor. Finding a physician you like and trust can be as tricky as finding a mate.

We can't promise you a match made in heaven, but we can help you try to find Dr. Right. This chapter can help you use the Internet to locate and evaluate your prospects.

Selecting Your Doctor

Perhaps you've just moved to town and don't know a soul or have found out that your doctor isn't on your insurance company's preferred provider list. Whatever your reason for looking for a new doctor, the best way to start your search is to figure out what you need.

You may need a family physician who can care for mom, pops, sis, and junior, or maybe you want an *internist* — a doctor specializing in adult care — for the adults and a pediatrician for the kids. If you're a woman, you may want a gynecologist. Mix and match as you wish. You can compile a list of candidates and check them out online.

When you're ready to go online and search for Dr. Right, we think the best place to begin is with the American Medical Association Physician Select — the most complete listing of medical doctors in the country. AMA Physician Select provides basic background on more than 690,000 doctors of medicine and doctors of osteopathic medicine, including where they went to medical school and trained, office addresses and phone numbers, and sometimes even their hours. Although the AMA doesn't recommend individual doctors, Physician Select helps you generate a list of qualified physicians in your area based on medical specialty.

Searching for a doctor by location and specialty

Here's how you can use Physician Select to find family doctors near your home:

1. **Open your Web browser and go to the AMA Physician Select Web site at** `www.ama-assn.org/aps/amahg.htm`.

2. **Scroll down the page and click the <u>We Invite You to Search for a Physician by Name or Medical Specialty</u> link.**

    A page of explanations and disclaimers appears.

3. **Click the <u>Accept</u> link at the bottom of the page.**

    You see a page inviting you to search by physician name or medical specialty.

4. **Click the <u>Medical Specialty</u> link.**

    An online form appears.

5. **Enter your state, city, and zip code in the corresponding text boxes and select the radio button next to the type of doctor that interests you.**

    To broaden your search, search for doctors in zip codes for neighboring communities.

    You can choose from a variety of specialties, including Family Practice, General Practice, Internal Medicine, Pediatrics, or Obstetrics & Gynecology.

6. **Scroll down the page and click the search button.**

    You see a list of doctors who practice near you. Click a doctor's name to find out about his or her education and training, office address, phone number, and possibly hours.

From the list that Physician Select generates, you can pick potential candidates based on your preferences. For example, if you're a woman, you may choose only female gynecologists from the list. You may want a younger or older physician. Maybe only graduates of Harvard or Yale interest you. Just remember the old joke: No matter what school a doctor graduated from or his or her class rank, a doctor's *first name* is still doctor.

Searching by a doctor's name

The Internet isn't the only network that can help you find a personal physician. You may want to use your *personal* network for leads. Time-honored sources are friends, family, and coworkers as well as your friendly neighborhood pharmacist or a nurse on staff at your local hospital.

On the other hand, if you belong to a Health Maintenance Organization (HMO), you may not have much of a choice, because your HMO gives you a list of its approved doctors. Still, you have to find the doctor who is right for you.

You may be saying to yourself, "I've got this list of names. Now where do I go for the 4-1-1?" You can get what you need 24/7/365 (366 on leap years) on the Net.

Go to AMA Physician Select, where you can find verified background information on your list of physicians, including their specialties, medical education, and training. Follow Steps 1 through 3 in the preceding section. Then click the <u>Physician Name</u> link and enter the physician's first and last name and state.

TIP

If you're not sure of the spelling, the AMA search engine can perform a sounds-like search. Just select the sounds-like check box below the Zip Code text box.

TIP

Your insurance company's Web site might also provide you with information about physicians online. Go to UltimateInsuranceLinks at `www.UltimateInsuranceLinks.com/lifelist.htm` to find a list of insurers. Click the name of your insurance plan. You may have to root around your insurance company's site to find a Doctor Finder feature.

Selecting a Medical Specialist

Every doctor's mom thinks he or she is special. But some are more special, make that *specialized,* than others. A dizzying array of specialists is out there, and we're sure that any day now, the right earlobe specialist will be hanging up her shingle. We hope she is across the street from the left-lobe guy.

Searching online for a specialist

You can use the American Medical Association Physician Select at `www.ama-assn.org/aps/amahg.htm` to find all manner of specialists. Follow the steps in the section, "Searching for a doctor by location and specialty," earlier in this chapter.

If you don't see the specialty you're looking for on the list, return to the Search by Physician Specialty page and click the <u>Search from an Expanded List of Medical Practice Specialties</u> link at the bottom of the page.

The American Medical Association isn't the only organization that can help you find a specialist. Some other doctor groups also offer online lists of their members' names. And some groups of non-physician health professionals, such as dentists and podiatrists, also have lists online. Table 3-1 lists other health professional groups' Web sites where you can find health professionals who are happy to care for you.

Table 3-1	Web Sites to Find Health Professionals	
Type of Specialist	*Professional Group*	*Web Site*
Allergist	The American Academy of Allergy, Asthma, and Immunology	`www.aaaai.org/scripts/ find-a-doc/main.asp`
Arthritis specialist	The American Academy of Rheumatology	`www.rheumatology.org/ directory/geo.html`
Cancer specialist	American Society of Clinical Oncology	`www.asco.org/people/ db/html/m_db.htm`
Chiropractor	The American Chiropractic Association	`www.amerchiro.org/ aspdb/memsearch.asp`
Dentist	The American Dental Association	`www.ada.org/public/ directory/index.html`
Ear, nose, and throat specialist	The American Academy of Otolaryngology – Head and Neck Surgery	`www.entnet.org/aao-cgi/fastweb?search form+aaoedupat`
Eye doctor	The American Optometric Association	`www.allaboutvision. com/asp/search.asp`

Type of Specialist	Professional Group	Web Site
Family doctor	The American Academy of Family Physicians	`www.familydoctor.org/cgi-bin/finddoc.pl`
Foot doctor	American Podiatric Medical Association	`www.vicinity.com/apma/startprx.hm`
Hearing specialist	American Academy of Audiology	`www.audiology.org/consumer/faa.php`
Neurologist	The American Academy of Neurology	`www.aan.com`
Obstetrician/Gynecologist	The American College of Obstetricians and Gynecologists	`www.acog.org/member-lookup`
Orthopedic surgeon	The American Academy of Orthopaedic Surgeons	`www3.aaos.org/memdir/public/memdir.cfm`
Plastic surgeon	The American Society of Plastic Surgeons	`www.plasticsurgery.org/findsurg/finding.htm`
Skin doctor	The American Academy of Dermatology	`www.aad.org/findaderm_intro.html`

Finding medical specialists at top hospitals

Your personal doctor or a nearby specialist can meet most of your healthcare needs. But if you have a condition that baffles Dr. Welby, you need to find a doctor's doctor.

The *U.S. News* Best Hospitals Finder at `www.usnews.com/usnews/nycu/health/hosptl/tophosp.htm` can come to the rescue. Editors here sift through surveys of top specialists, data on death rates, and other information on teaching hospitals around the country. The result is the Best Hospitals Finder.

You can use the Best Hospitals Finder to generate your own list of the best hospitals for particular conditions. In most cases, this list leads you to the home pages for the highly rated hospitals. After you have decided on a hospital, you can follow the link to the hospital's Web page and look for a Doctor Finder tool or online contact to reach the physicians who helped the hospital make it on the *U.S. News* list.

You can find more on how to use Best Hospitals Finder in Chapter 4.

Checking a Doctor's Credentials

Doctors like to show off their fancy diplomas and certificates to inspire confidence and trust. Now you can do more than read the writing on the wall. You can put on your Internet gumshoes and peek behind doctors' sheepskins.

Finding out about the status of a doctor's credentials used to be difficult. But with your mouse in hand, your computer powered up, and your electric bill current, you can be a regular Mulder or Scully. The truth is out there.

Though disclosure differs from state to state, your doctor's online X-File may reveal:

✔ Status of a doctor's license

✔ Whether a doctor has been disciplined

✔ Whether a doctor is board certified

Doctor's license and disciplinary actions

Some people say that a license to practice medicine is a license to mint money. These days, we're not so sure about that. The people who grant doctors their licenses have information that can help you in your quest to find out more about your doctor.

State medical boards have the job of protecting patients. They decide whether a doctor is entitled to a license. Doctors found unprofessional or incompetent may have their wings clipped or even lose their right to practice.

You often can find out online whether a doctor's license is in order and whether a doctor has ever been disciplined. Most state medical boards have Web sites where you can check this out, but tracking down the information while you're at the sites can be a bit tricky. The states vary on the amount of information they release and how they label it, so you may have to dig around.

Public Citizen's Health Research Group can help. This group is a long-time crusader against bad doctors. Its book, *20,125 Questionable Doctors,* lists doctors who have been disciplined and why, and outlines what you can do to be safe when choosing a doctor. The book's companion Web site at `www.questionabledoctors.org` doesn't name names. You have to read the book for that. But on the Web page, you can get the scoop on how to reach your state's medical board, which has the lowdown on questionable doctors in your state.

Investigating malpractice

Sometimes, a patient-physician relationship turns into a plaintiff-defendant relationship. No doubt, many lawsuits are frivolous. Likewise, cases where a patient should have sued a physician and didn't also occur.

Information about malpractice suits is just starting to become available online. The Massachusetts Board of Registration in Medicine at `www.docboard.org/ma/df/masearch.htm` pioneered public access to malpractice information as part of its Physician Profile.

These model profiles can tell you whether a doctor is accepting new patients; which insurance plans are accepted; and about the doctor's hospital affiliations, awards, education, training, and board certification. The profiles also let you know whether the state board or a hospital has disciplined the physician or whether the physician has had any criminal convictions. In addition, information on malpractice payments is available.

The Florida Department of Insurance at `www.doi.state.fl.us` also lists malpractice complaints.

More states should make this information available.

At the Web site (`www.citizen.org/HRG/QDSITE/map.htm`), you'll see a clickable United States map with a listing of the individual states below, shown in Figure 3-1. Click your state or your state's name, and you come to a page that shows you the number of doctors disciplined in your state and how your state ranks among the others.

Figure 3-1:
Public Citizen's Health Research Group at www.questionabledoctors.org can help you locate your state medical board.

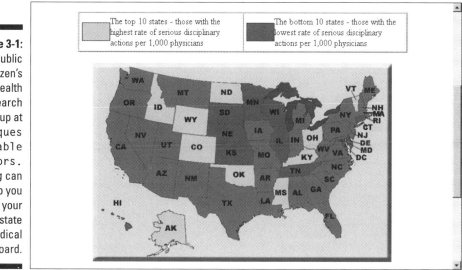

Scroll down, and you'll see charts on how well your state fares. If numbers fascinate you, enjoy. But if you're hot on the trail of your state medical board, keep scrollin' to the bottom of the page. There, you can find, in most cases, the link to the state medical board's Web site along with its mailing address and phone number and possibly e-mail address. Clicking the link takes you to the state board's Web site.

At your medical board's site, you may have to put on your detective cap and take out your magnifying glass. The clue you're looking for is a button that refers to licensure, credentials, or verification. The name of the button varies from state to state, and not all states disclose this information on their Web sites.

If your state does, plug in the doctor's name, properly spelled of course, and see what you will see. The amount of information is different from state to state. You can usually find out whether the doctor's license is active or inactive and whether any disciplinary actions have been taken against him or her. The listing may include the doctor's birthday and birthplace — which is great if you're astrologically inclined.

Some states tell all for free; others are stingy with information and may charge for it. A few require you to send an e-mail or an old-fangled letter by snail mail to get the information.

State medical boards, for reasons of confidentiality, cannot confirm whether an investigation of a doctor is pending.

The shortest distance to a state medical board Web site can be the Federation of State Medical Boards (`www.fsmb.org/members.htm`). This is a fast-loading, no-nonsense text list of contact names, addresses, phone numbers, and Web sites for state boards. However, we find that the Public Citizen's Health Group's list is more up-to-date.

Got a gripe?

State medical boards are not only places to find out about a doctor's record, but also places to file a complaint about such concerns as:

✔ Quality of care and treatment that a physician provides (such as negligence)

✔ Violation of drug laws or misprescribing medication

✔ Substance abuse by the physician

✔ Sexual misconduct by the physician

✔ Dishonesty (including filing fraudulent claims for insurance, Medicaid for indigents, or Medicare for the elderly)

✔ Practice of medicine by an unlicensed person

Many state medical board's Web sites tell you how to file a complaint and may even make online printable forms available.

The Public Citizen's Health Group has launched a new DocInfo service at `www.docinfo.org` that allows you to run a background check of disciplinary actions against physicians for a $9.95 fee. You can get immediate results online or have them e-mailed or mailed. The site has information on 115,000 disciplinary actions taken against 35,000 physicians since the early 1960s.

Checking for specialty certification

There are specialists and then there are specialists. Doctors can say they specialize in an area without necessarily having gone through board certification: a rigorous process involving advanced training for three to seven years and passing qualifying exams. The doctors whose names you find listed as specialists at many sites on the Web may or may not be board certified.

But fear not, you can quickly confirm whether a doctor successfully ran the gauntlet.

The American Board of Medical Specialties can verify whether a doctor is board certified. Just go to `www.abms.org/newsearch.asp` and plug in the doctor's first and last name.

TECHNICAL STUFF

What's board certification?

Doctors who have completed their internships and obtained their state licenses can hang out a shingle to practice any type of medicine they want. But the most qualified specialists and subspecialists earn their chops with extra training. Physicians who complete an accredited residency take exams to become board certified.

The American Board of Medical Specialties (`198.76.30.75/which.asp`) lists the following requirements for a doctor to be board certified:

✔ A doctor must complete of a course of study that leads to degrees in doctor of medicine or doctor of osteopathy from a recognized school of medicine.

✔ A doctor must receive three to seven years of full-time training in an accredited residency program designed to train specialists in the field.

✔ Some medical specialty boards require assessments of individual performance and competence.

✔ Most medical specialty boards require that the person seeking certification have an unrestricted license to practice medicine to take the certification exam.

✔ Some boards require the doctor have experience, typically two years, in full-time practice in the specialty before taking the exam.

✔ Each candidate for certification must pass a written examination that the specialty board gives. A similar process is followed for specialists who want to become subspecialists.

Certification may last only seven to ten years, requiring the doctor to be recertified.

Meeting Dr. Right

Having done all the research, you probably know more about the doctor than his or her own mother does. If you're satisfied with your choice, it's time you to make an appointment.

The Agency for Healthcare Research and Quality (AHRQ) has an excellent online pamphlet, "Choosing a Doctor," which is available at `www.ahcpr.gov/consumer/qntascii/qntdr.htm`. The pamphlet is full of tips on what to do before, during, and after the appointment. The (AHRQ) recommends that you find out if your health plan covers this doctor and whether this doctor is accepting new patients. If all systems are go, you can use the form in the "Contact the Doctors' Offices" section of the pamphlet. The form contains the following questions that you can ask the office manager, receptionist, or other staffer:

- ✔ Which hospitals does the doctor use?
- ✔ What are the office hours?
- ✔ How many other doctors cover for the doctor when he or she is not available? Who are they?
- ✔ How long does it usually take to get a routine appointment?
- ✔ How long might I need to wait in the office before seeing the doctor?
- ✔ What happens if I need to cancel the appointment? Will I have to pay for it anyway?
- ✔ Does the office send reminders about prevention tests, for example, pap smears?
- ✔ What do I do if I need urgent care or have an emergency?
- ✔ Does the doctor or a nurse or a physician assistant give advice over the phone for common medical problems?
- ✔ Can someone in the office speak the language that I'm most comfortable using? (This question is useful if you or your family is more comfortable communicating in another language.)

Here's hoping you're on the way to building a long, healthy relationship with your new doctor.

Need help finding the doctor's office? Go to MapQuest at `www.mapquest.com` to get door-to-door driving instructions and maps.

Chapter 4

Locating the Best Hospital

· ·

In This Chapter

▶ Searching online for the best hospital

▶ Getting hospital ratings

▶ Finding the best hospitals

· ·

Some 60 million Americans go to the hospital each year. They don't go there for the food. Modern medical centers provide care for everything from minor mishaps to life-and-death illnesses.

Behind every bed in these hallowed halls of medicine is a story. And these stories translate into measures of how well the doctors, nurses, and staff treat their patients and how successful those treatments are.

Even under the best circumstances, when you or members of your family are admitted to the hospital, it's a stressful, scary affair. The food's not great. You're surrounded by sick people. The healthcare professionals tell you to sleep, but they keep waking you up so they can take your temperature. And the folks in charge of your fate speak a language all their own.

It's hard to believe, but the Internet *can't* solve all these problems. But it *can* help you find the best possible hospital for you. That's what this chapter is all about.

Finding a Hospital with Hospital Select

If you have a common health problem, chances are that the community hospital near you has everything that you need to get better. But if your problem is more complicated, you may need to go to a hospital that offers more services.

Not too many years ago, ferreting out information about hospitals, such as the death rate from surgeries, was difficult. The consumer revolution has helped break this information loose, and now the Internet revolution is making increasing amounts of this data on hospitals and other health facilities available to you online.

Even if you're a member of a Health Maintenance Organization (HMO) and have a limited choice of hospitals, you can use this online information to choose among hospitals in your plan. You may even want to choose an HMO based on what you discover online about its affiliated hospitals.

Whether you have an insurance plan or not, this chapter shows you where to go online to find what you need to know to make an informed choice when selecting a hospital.

Searching by name

Imagine that your HMO has given you the names of a few hospitals near your home or office, or imagine that you're new in town and you've found some hospital names in the Yellow Pages. In any case, you've got some hospital names to work with.

Now what? We recommend that you go to the Hospital Select Web site at www.hospitalselect.com (shown in Figure 4-1) and follow these steps:

1. **In the Hospital Name text box, type in the name or a keyword from the name of the hospital you're interested in checking out, use the drop-down list box to select the state where the hospital is located, and click the Search button.**

   If you want to narrow the search, type the name of the city where the hospital is located.

   The name of the hospital appears on the Search Results page.

2. **Click the <u>Hospital Name</u> link to see a detailed profile of the hospital.**

   At the top of the profile page is basic contact information for the hospital, including the hospital's address and phone number.

3. **Scroll down the page to view a bunch of numbers that tell how big the hospital is and how busy it is.**

   If a term on this page is unfamiliar to you, you can click it for an explanation.

4. **Scroll still further down the page to find a list of medical services available at the hospital.**

   If you need a kidney transplant or open heart surgery, this is where you find out if you can get those services at this hospital.

5. **Scroll down further to find a list of groups (such as the American College of Surgeons and the federal government's Medicare program) whose standards the hospital has met.**

   Here, you also can find out whether the hospital is affiliated with a medical school.

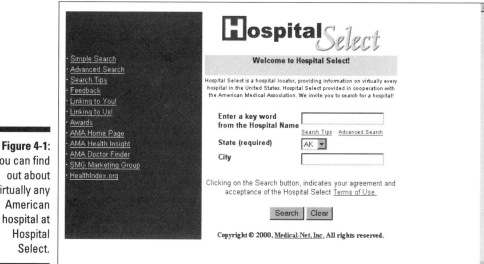

Copyright © 2000, Medical-Net, Inc. All rights reserved.

Figure 4-1:
You can find out about virtually any American hospital at Hospital Select.

You can get a feel for a hospital and find out about its services by visiting its Web site. HospitalWeb, at `neuro-www.mgh.harvard.edu/hospitalweb.html`, has links to hospital Web sites around the United States. Click the name of a state to see a list of Web sites for hospitals in that state.

Hospital sites may feature a directory of staff doctors with their backgrounds, a listing of health and fitness classes, a schedule of free screenings, and so on, as shown in Figure 4-2.

Figure 4-2:
Hospital Web sites often have information about staff doctors, screenings, and classes.

Reading your rights as a hospital patient

As any loyal fan of TV's *Law & Order* will tell you, the perps must have their Miranda rights read to them. It's the law.

It oughta be a law that patients are afforded their rights and dignity. In fact, it is a law in a number of states. And hospital groups encourage their member hospitals to adopt a Patients' Bill of Rights.

Here are some points adapted from New York State's Patients' Bill of Rights. If you want more details, go to the New York State Department of Health's Web site at `www.health.state.ny.us/nysdoh/hospital/english2.htm#patients`.

As a patient in a hospital, you have the right to

- Receive care without discrimination as to race, color, religion, sex, national origin, disability, sexual orientation, or source of payment.

- Receive considerate and respectful care in a clean and safe environment free of unnecessary restraints.

- Receive emergency care if you need it.

- Be informed of the name and position of the doctor who is in charge of your care.

- Know the names, positions, and functions of any hospital staff involved in your care and refuse their treatment, examination, or observation.

- A non-smoking room.

- Receive complete information about your diagnosis, treatment, and prognosis.

- Receive all the information that you need to give informed consent for any proposed procedure or treatment, including possible risks and benefits of the procedure or treatment.

- Receive all the information you need to give informed consent for an order not to resuscitate. You also have the right to designate an individual to give this consent for you if you are too ill to do so.

- Refuse treatment and be told what effect this may have on your health.

- Refuse to take part in research.

- Privacy while in the hospital and confidentiality of all information and records regarding your care.

- Participate in all decisions about your treatment and discharge from the hospital.

- Review your medical record without charge. Obtain a copy of your medical record for which the hospital can charge a reasonable fee.

- Receive an itemized bill and explanation of all charges.

Searching by location

What if you're not sure about which hospitals are nearby and what they offer, or maybe you're scouting out a hospital for your mother-in-law in Little Rock?

The Hospital Select Web site can help you compile a list of the hospitals in your area or in your mother-in-law's area. To compile this list, you need to use Hospital Select's Advanced Search feature. Here's how:

1. **Open your browser and go to the Hospital Select Web site at** `www.hospitalselect.com`.

   The Welcome to Hospital Select page appears (refer to Figure 4-1).

2. **On the left-hand side of the page, click the <u>Advanced Search</u> link.**

   A second page, with expanded search options, appears.

3. **Select the state of your choice from the State drop-down list box. Choose the type of medical service you're interested in from the Service Line drop-down list box. Finally, type in the names of as many as four cities.**

   In our example, we wanted to find information about hospitals in Little Rock, Arkansas, that offer open heart surgery. We chose AR from the State drop-down list box, we chose Open Heart Surgery from the Service Line drop-down list box, and we typed in *Little Rock, Pine Bluff,* and *Hot Springs* as our choice of cities, as shown in Figure 4-3.

4. **Scroll down and click the Search button.**

   Our search, shown in Figure 4-4, came up with 11 qualified hospitals.

5. **Click the name of a hospital to see a profile of that hospital.**

   You see a profile of the hospital you selected. The profile lists basic contact information for the hospital, including the address and phone number, statistics on how big and busy the hospital is, the medical services offered, the groups whose standards the hospital has met, and whether the hospital is affiliated with a medical school.

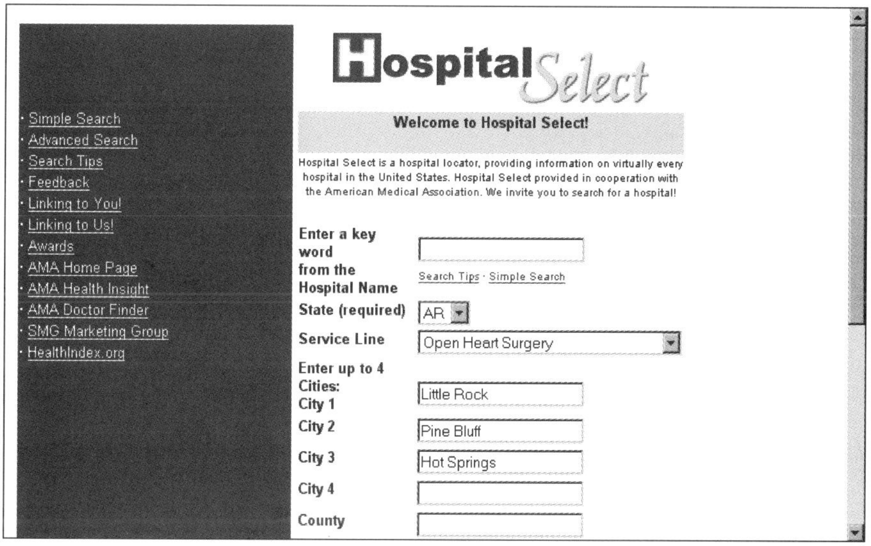

Figure 4-3: The Hospital Select Advanced Search form enables you to look at up to four cities in the same state at one time.

Search Results

You found 11 hospitals according to your search criteria of:

- Simple Search
- Advanced Search
- Search Tips
- Feedback
- Linking to You!
- Linking to Us!
- Awards
- AMA Home Page
- AMA Health Insight
- AMA Doctor Finder
- SMG Marketing Group
- HealthIndex.org

Hospital Name:		City 2: Pine Bluff		Page: 1 of 2
	State: AR	City 3: Hot Springs		County:
	City 1: Little Rock	City 4:		Zipcode:

Data provided by SMG Marketing Group, Inc. Copyright © 2000

Hospital Name	City	State	County	Zipcode
Arkansas Childrens Hospital	Little Rock	AR	PULASKI	72202
Arkansas Heart Hospital	Little Rock	AR	PULASKI	72211
Baptist Medical Center	Little Rock	AR	PULASKI	72205
Baptist Memorial Medical Center	North Little Rock	AR	PULASKI	72114
Central AR	Little			

Figure 4-4: Results show 11 qualified hospitals in the Little Rock, Arkansas area.

If you want even more data about a hospital, go to the American Hospital Directory at www.ahd.com and click the <u>Free Services</u> link. By filling in a community name or an individual hospital's name, you can generate hospital profiles. Tapping into statistics from the American Hospital Association, this site provides the average length of stay and cost for common procedures. You can also take a look at the hospital's bottom line, if you're so inclined, and see whether the hospital is healthy or not. In any case, this site gets you the numbers STAT.

Checklist for choosing a hospital

In its "Choosing a Hospital Worksheet" (www.ahcpr.gov/consumer/qntascii/ qnthosp.htm), the Agency for Healthcare Research and Quality urges you to consider these questions when choosing a hospital:

✔ Does the hospital meet national quality standards?

✔ How does the hospital compare with others in your area?

✔ Does your doctor have the right to admit patients to the hospital?

✔ Does your health plan cover care at the hospital?

✔ Does the hospital have experience with your condition?

✔ Has the hospital had success with your condition?

✔ How often is the procedure you need done there?

✔ How often does your doctor perform the procedure? (Practice makes perfect.)

✔ How well do the patients do? What's the success rate?

How Does Your Hospital Rate?

Okay, you've got a list of hospitals in mind. How do you know which ones are *St. Elsewhere* and which are *Chicago Hope*? You can go to places online that can give you the information you need to help you decide.

Making the grade

At HealthGrades (www.healthgrades.com), you can get a hospital report card that makes it easy to tell which hospitals are at the head of their class. The hospitals get graded on how patients who underwent a variety of common procedures (including coronary bypass, open heart surgery, back surgery, and hip replacement surgery) fared. We like the simple star grading system — the hospitals get five stars for best results, three stars for average results, and one star for poor results.

Here's how to get a hospital report card:

1. **Go to www.healthgrades.com by using your browser's address feature.**

   You see the HealthGrades opening screen.

2. **Under Healthcare Report Cards, click the <u>Hospitals</u> link.**

   You see the Hospital Report Cards page, as shown in Figure 4-5.

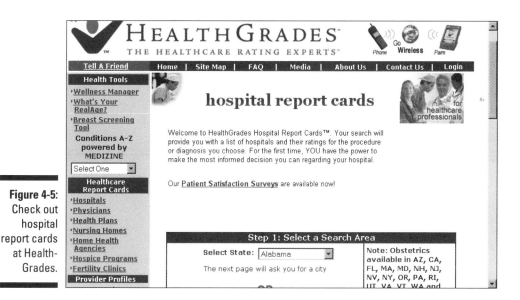

Figure 4-5: Check out hospital report cards at Health-Grades.

3. **Under Step 1: Select a Search Area, select your state from the drop-down list box or enter your zip code. Under Step 2: Select a Procedure/Diagnosis, select the radio button next to the procedure you're interested in checking out. Scroll down to the bottom of the page and click Go.**

   For our example, we selected Arkansas and Heart Attack-Hospitals That Do Open Heart Surgery, as shown in Figure 4-6.

   You now see Step 3 with a choice of Select by Area or Select by Hospital Name.

4. **Choose by area or by hospital name and then click the word Go that appears immediately under the choice you selected.**

   For our example, we selected by area and chose the Little Rock Area from the drop-down list box.

5. **You now come to the HealthGrades User Agreement screen. Read the agreement, and if you agree, select the I Agree radio button. Then click the See Search Results button.**

   Note: Depending on what browser you're using, you may not see a See Search Results button. In that case, just click I Agree.

   You see another Hospital Report Cards page. Scroll down to see the grades the hospitals received based on class rank, from best to worst, as shown in Figure 4-7.

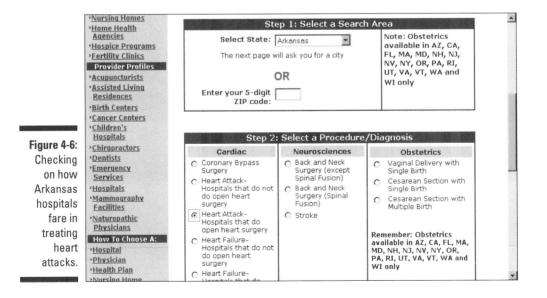

Figure 4-6: Checking on how Arkansas hospitals fare in treating heart attacks.

		2001 Analysis (3 years ending 1999) Heart Attack-Hospitals that do open heart surgery				
	Hospital	City State	# of Medicare Cases	Inhospital Deaths/Mortality	Inhospital +1 Month Deaths/Mortality	Inhospital +6 Months Deaths/Mortality
▸Nursing Homes ▸Home Health Agencies ▸Hospice Programs ▸Fertility Clinics						
Provider Profiles	ARKANSAS HEART HOSPITAL Complete a Survey See Survey Results	LITTLE ROCK AR Map	428	★ ★ ★ ★ ★	★ ★ ★ ★ ★	★ ★ ★
▸Acupuncturists ▸Assisted Living Residences						
▸Birth Centers ▸Cancer Centers ▸Children's Hospitals	ST JOSEPHS REGIONAL HEALTH CENTER Complete a Survey See Survey Results	HOT SPRINGS AR Map	514	★ ★ ★	★ ★ ★	★ ★ ★
▸Chiropractors ▸Dentists ▸Emergency Services	BAPTIST MEDICAL CENTER Complete a Survey See Survey Results	LITTLE ROCK AR Map	1138	★ ★ ★	★ ★ ★	★ ★ ★
▸Hospitals ▸Mammography Facilities ▸Naturopathic Physicians	NATIONAL PARK MEDICAL CENTER INC Complete a Survey See Survey Results	HOT SPRINGS AR Map	200	★ ★ ★	★ ★ ★	★ ★ ★
How To Choose A: ▸Hospital ▸Physician ▸Health Plan	JEFFERSON REGIONAL MEDICAL CENTER Complete a Survey See Survey Results	PINE BLUFF AR Map	496	★ ★ ★	★ ★ ★	★ ★ ★

Figure 4-7:
This Health-
Grades
hospital
report card
shows class
rankings.

By clicking a hospital name on a HealthGrades hospital report card, you get a brief profile of the hospital. Other links in the report card give you printable maps with driving directions to the hospital.

HealthGrades offers information on a variety of other medical facilities, including hospices, assisted living residences, birth centers, cancer centers, mammography centers, nursing homes, emergency services, and walk-in clinics. However, aside from hospitals, grades are only available for nursing homes and home health agencies.

Digging deeper

When you buy a house, you get a professional home inspector to check out your prospective digs. The inspector looks in the nooks and crannies to make sure that the wiring and plumbing are sound, the roof isn't leaking, and the foundation is solid.

When you're being admitted to the hospital, you can't hire your own inspector to check out the joint, but you can have *The Joint* check out the place for you.

The Joint is short for the Joint Commission on Accreditation of Healthcare Organizations (JCAHO). The Joint Commission evaluates whether hospitals, outpatient surgery centers, mental hospitals, nursing homes, and other medical facilities meet standards for such things as medical and nursing care, safety, infection-control procedures, and patients' rights. Hospitals may need Joint Commission approval to get their state licenses and Medicare payments.

Here's how you can investigate the results of the Joint Commission's hospital surveys online at its QualityCheck service to find out whether your hospital is up to snuff:

1. **Open your Web browser and go to the QualityCheck Web site at** www.jcaho.org/qualitycheck/directry/directry.asp.

   You see the QualityCheck Organization Search Criteria page, as shown in Figure 4-8.

2. **Select Hospitals from the Type of Organization drop-down list box. If you want to find the standing of all the hospitals in your state, select a state from the Geographic Location drop-down text box. Then click the Search button.**

   You can narrow your search by typing in a city, zip code, and/or county in the appropriate boxes. If you want to search for a specific hospital, type in the hospital's name in the Organization Name box.

   In our example, we selected Arkansas because we wanted to find out how the hospitals in the state fared. So our results page, shown in Figure 4-9, is a list (in alphabetical order by city) of the hospitals in Arkansas that chose to go through the Joint Commission survey process.

From your results list, you can click a hospital name to go to the QualityCheck Organization Details page to find its accreditation standing as well as its street address, phone number, and possibly a link to its Web site and e-mail address. Underlined accreditation terms on the page are linked to a glossary.

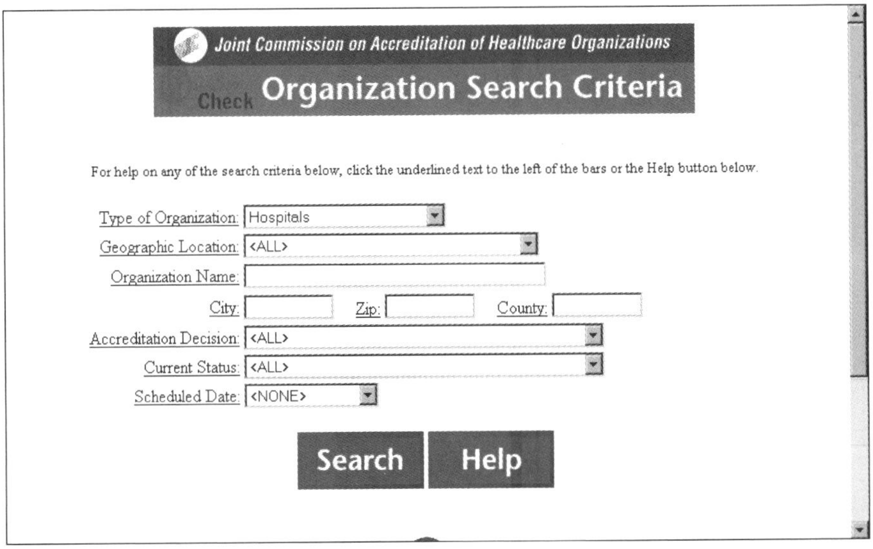

Joint Commission on Accreditation of Healthcare Organizations

Check **Organization Search Criteria**

For help on any of the search criteria below, click the underlined text to the left of the bars or the Help button below.

Type of Organization:	Hospitals
Geographic Location:	<ALL>
Organization Name:	
City:	Zip:	County:
Accreditation Decision:	<ALL>
Current Status:	<ALL>
Scheduled Date:	<NONE>

Search   **Help**

Figure 4-8: By filling in this form at Quality-Check, you begin the search for a hospital's accreditation credentials.

Figure 4-9:
Results of
a Quality-
Check
search for
Arkansas
hospitals at
the Joint
Commission
on Accredi-
tation of
Healthcare
Organiza-
tions' Web
site.

Joint Commission on Accreditation of Healthcare Organizations		
Check **Organization Search Results**		

Type of Organization: Hospitals **Geographic Location:** AR

Organization Name	City	Scheduled Survey
Baptist Medical Center Arkadelphia	Arkadelphia	
White River Health System	Batesville	
CCS/Rivendell Behavioral Health Services	Benton	
Saline County Medical Center	Benton	
Carroll Regional Medical Center	Berryville	
Baptist Memorial Hospital - Blytheville	Blytheville	Nov 09, 2000
Ouachita County Medical Center	Camden	
Conway Regional Medical Center	Conway	
Medical Center of South Arkansas	El Dorado	
HealthSouth Rehabilitation Hospital	Fayetteville	
VA Medical Center	Fayetteville	
Vista Health	Fayetteville	
Washington Regional Medical Center	Fayetteville	
Baptist Memorial Hospital - Forrest City, Inc.	Forrest City	Oct 31, 2000

Unless a survey of the hospital is in progress, you can read online the complete performance report on which the accreditation status was based. Look
for the link at the bottom of the Organization Details page.

The QualityCheck feature at the Joint Commission Web site also can be used
to check out long-term care centers, ambulatory surgical centers, mental hospitals, addiction treatment facilities, imaging centers, home care services,
clinical laboratories, and a host of other types of medical services. If you find
a less-than-favorable report, bring any concerns you have to the attention of
your doctor, insurance plan representative, or the hospital administrator.

If you have a concern about conditions in a hospital or other accredited
healthcare organization, the Joint Commission encourages you to first bring
your complaint to the attention of the organization's leaders. If this does not
lead to resolution, you can lodge an online complaint with the Joint
Commission.

You can find directions for reporting a complaint at www.jcaho.org/compl_
frm.html. You have a couple of choices on how to proceed. You can send an
e-mail message to complaints@jcaho.org, or you can print out a complaint
form (shown in Figure 4-10) from www.jcaho.org/compform.html and mail
or fax it in.

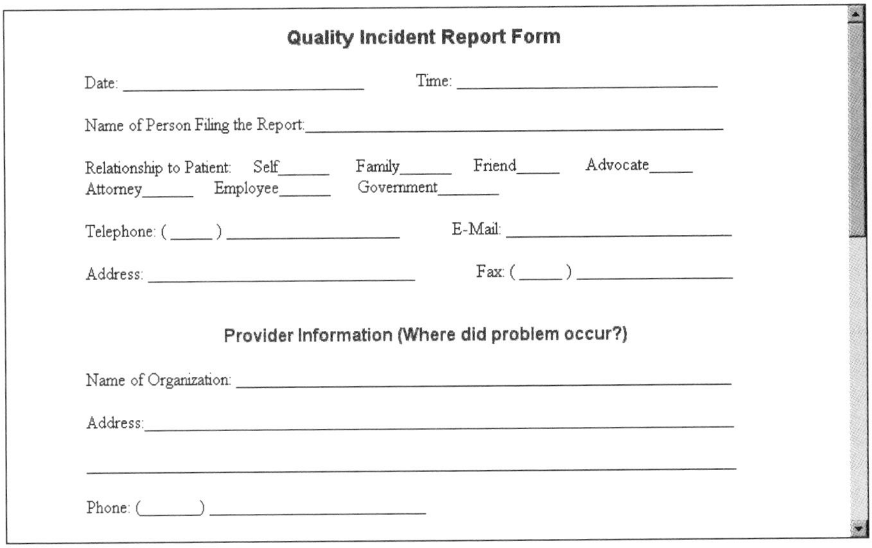

Figure 4-10:
You can
print out this
form at the
Joint
Commis-
sion's Web
site to file a
complaint
against a
hospital.

> ### Quality Incident Report Form
>
> Date: _____   Time: _____
>
> Name of Person Filing the Report: _____
>
> Relationship to Patient: Self_____   Family_____   Friend_____   Advocate_____
> Attorney_____   Employee_____   Government_____
>
> Telephone: (_____) _____   E-Mail: _____
>
> Address: _____   Fax: (_____) _____
>
> ### Provider Information (Where did problem occur?)
>
> Name of Organization: _____
>
> Address: _____
>
> _____
>
> Phone: (_____) _____

Best of the Best: Finding the Top Hospitals

For dog lovers, the big event each year is the Westminster Kennel Club's competition for Best of Breed. In the hospital world, it's the annual America's Best Hospitals issue of *U.S. News.* The hospitals that make this prestigious list get bragging rights for being the best of their breed. There's not a dog in the lot.

U.S. News is the first to admit that you don't need this list unless you have a critical illness that is compromising your quality of life or your survival. This list of 173 hospitals — out of 6,247 nationally — would come in handy in those rare instances in which you have a condition beyond the abilities of the docs at your community hospital.

The Best Hospitals Finder at `www.usnews.com/usnews/nycu/health/hosptl/tophosp.htm` (shown in Figure 4-11) can help you find the most highly rated programs for 17 different specialties, from cancer through urology.

If you're interested in national rankings of the best hospitals to treat a particular medical condition, select the condition from the For Nationwide Rankings drop-down list box and click Go.

Figure 4-11:
The Best
Hospitals
Finder helps
you find the
top-ranked
teaching
hospitals in
the country.

To find the hospitals, in a certain region or state, with the best reputation for treating the condition, make sure that the medical condition is selected (as noted in the preceding paragraph), select the region or state from the To Narrow Your Search drop-down list box, and click Go.

You can also find the list of the overall best hospitals in a city or region. Just select the city or region from the Find a List of Top Hospitals Near You drop-down list box and click Go.

Best Hospitals Honor Roll

U.S. News lists at its Web site at www.usnews.com/usnews/nycu/health/hosptl/honroll.htm the most highly rated hospitals, which it calls its Best Hospitals Honor Roll. Each July, *U.S. News* publishes a new list. Here is the list from the July 17, 2000, issue — drum roll, please:

1. Johns Hopkins Hospital, Baltimore, MD (www.hopkinsmedicine.org/hopkinshospital)

2. Mayo Clinic, Rochester, MN (www.mayo.edu/mcr)

3. Massachusetts General Hospital, Boston, MA (www.mgh.harvard.edu)

4. Cleveland Clinic, Cleveland, OH (www.clevelandclinic.org)

5. UCLA Medical Center, Los Angeles, CA (www.medctr.ucla.edu)

(continued)

(continued)

6. Duke University Medical Center, Durham, NC (www.mc.duke.edu)

7. Barnes-Jewish Hospital, St. Louis, MO (www.bjc.org/bjh_main.html)

   Stanford University Hospital, Stanford, CA (www.med.stanford.edu/sumc/stan.html)

8. Brigham and Women's Hospital, Boston, MA (www.partners.org/bwh)

9. Hospital of the University of Pennsylvania, Philadelphia, PA (www.pennhealth.com)

10. University of California, San Francisco Medical Center, San Francisco, CA (www.ucsfhealth.org)

11. University of Michigan Medical Center, Ann Arbor, MI (www.med.umich.edu)

12. University of Washington Medical Center, Seattle, WA (www.washington.edu/medical/uwmc/index.html)

13. University of Chicago Hospitals, Chicago, IL (www.uchospitals.edu/index_js.html)

14. University of Pittsburgh Medical Center, Pittsburgh, PA (www.upmc.edu)

Chapter 5

Navigating the Health Insurance Maze

*W*oody Allen said there are worse things in life than death. He went on to ask, "Have you ever spent an evening with an insurance salesman?" We understand just what he means. The health insurance maze can be frustrating, confusing, and exhausting. Your eyes can glaze over with all the gobbledygook.

Are you in the market to choose a plan? Or are you wondering how your plan stacks up against others? Understanding and choosing insurance isn't easy.

We can show you the way through this mess. This chapter helps you use the Internet to cut through the jargon, see how the various health plans measure up, and find out where you can go online to get help or gripe. You will be rewarded at the end of the maze with a chunk of cheese — low-fat cheese, of course.

Health Insurance 101

Are you confused about the differences among HMOs, PPOs, or POSs? Despite rumors to the contrary, HMO isn't short for "Hey, Moe," as in Dr. Moe

Howard of *The Three Stooges* fame. In medical circles, Moe Howard is still honored for making the breakthrough discovery that a poke in both eyes helped patients forget their other pains.

The Agency for Healthcare Research and Quality (AHRQ), a federal bureau that researches the cost and quality of healthcare, offers a crib sheet for Health Insurance 101 that would win Dr. Moe Howard's Seal of Approval. N'Yuk. N'Yuk. N'Yuk.

At the agency's site at `www.ahcpr.gov/consumer`, look under the section on Health Plans for two online booklets entitled "Checkup on Health Insurance Choices" and "Choosing and Using a Health Plan." (See Figure 5-1.)

These two electronic booklets can answer your questions about health insurance, sorting out the differences between fee-for-service plans and HMOs, group insurance versus individual insurance, and so on. The booklets also feature checklists of questions you should ask insurers.

The AHRQ also has links to Insure Kids Now (`www.insurekidsnow.gov`), a program aimed at providing no-cost or low-cost insurance to children. One of the great scandals of American life is that more than 40 million people have no health insurance, and many of them are kids.

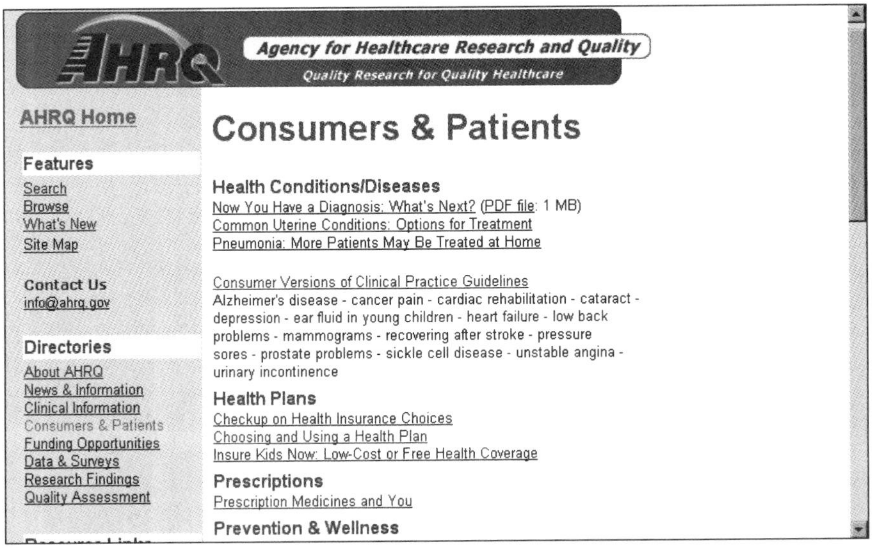

Figure 5-1:
The AHRQ
Web site is
chock-full of
consumer-
friendly
health
information.

Checklist on your insurance needs

The Agency for Healthcare Research and Quality recommends at its Web site that you give your need for insurance a checkup before choosing a plan. You have to decide what is most important to you. All plans have tradeoffs. Ask yourself these questions:

✔ How comprehensive do you want coverage of health care services to be?

✔ How do you feel about limits on your choice of doctors or hospitals?

✔ How do you feel about a primary care doctor referring you to specialists for additional care?

✔ How convenient does your care need to be?

✔ How important is the cost of services?

✔ How much are you willing to spend on premiums and other health care costs?

✔ How do you feel about keeping receipts and filing claims?

You can find other checklists to help you sort out your health insurance choices at the Agency's Web site at www.ahcpr.gov/consumer.

Can't *indemnify* some insurance language? Doctors speak medicalese. Insurers apparently speak insurancese. You can get help from the glossary provided by the BlueCross BlueShield Association at www.bcbs.com/Glossary/glossary.html.

How Your Health Plan Rates

People used to get the mushroom treatment about health plans. You know: kept in the dark and sprinkled with, er, fertilizer.

There's a new day now, folks, thanks to the Internet. The information you need to evaluate and choose a health plan is only a click or two away.

The National Committee for Quality Assurance — *NCQA* as it's known to its many fans — is an independent, nonprofit group that evaluates the quality of the nation's managed care organizations. These managed care organizations, which include HMOs, provide healthcare in return for preset monthly payments and coordinate care through a network of primary care physicians and hospitals.

NCQA makes available Health Plan Report Cards for hundreds of HMOs and Point of Service (POS) plans at hprc.ncqa.org, where you can find out which health plans are getting straight *As* and which health plans are repeating their senior years.

In preparing the report cards, NCQA checks on whether each doctor in a particular HMO or POS is licensed and trained to practice medicine. NCQA determines whether patients in that HMO or POS are receiving appropriate tests and care, and it measures how happy the patients are with their physicians.

Most Fortune 500 corporations and federal and state agencies use the NCQA's information to choose health plans for their employees. Now you can, too. Here's how:

1. **Open your browser and go to the NCQA Web site at** hprc.ncqa.org.

   The NCQA's Health Plan Report Card page greets you with a welcome message.

2. **At the bottom of that page, click the <u>Create Report Card</u> link.**

   You see the Terms of Use for NCQA.org.

3. **Select I Agree by clicking the words under the Terms of Use box.**

   You see a page inviting you to search by Plan Name, type of insurance, state, or zip code, as shown in Figure 5-2.

4. **Fill in as much information as possible.**

   For example, if you live in New York select that state from the Enter Your State drop-down list box, or simply type your zip code in the Enter Your Zip Code text box.

5. **Click the Submit button.**

   The results of your search now appear in the form of a chart, as shown in Figure 5-3. NCQA rates the plans — zero to five stars — for easy comparison. Better your plan should be a hero than a zero.

You may be able to compare NCQA's findings with those at HealthGrades at www.healthgrades.com. The HealthGrades site offers advice on choosing different types of health plans, including various managed care plans and traditional health insurance. Health Pages (www.thehealthpages.com) also offers ratings, including doctor's opinions of various health plans in more than 20 metropolitan areas. Some traditional fee-for-service health plans are rated here as well.

Buying health insurance online

Employers typically provide health insurance plans. But if you have no coverage at work, are running a small business, or are a senior looking for supplemental Medicare insurance, you can go online to get insurance quotes and even apply for coverage. Some places you may want to check out are eHealthInsurance.com at www.ehealthinsurance.com, InsWeb at www.insweb.com, and Quotesmith.com at www.quotesmith.com.

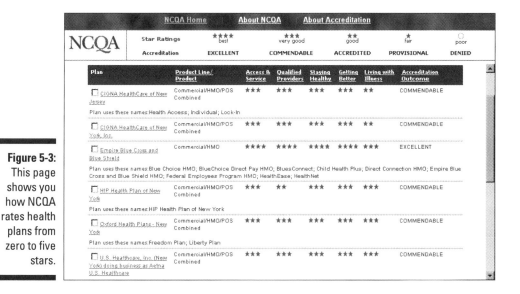

Figure 5-2:
Filling in the NCQA form gives you a report card on your health plan.

Figure 5-3:
This page shows you how NCQA rates health plans from zero to five stars.

Contacting Your Health Insurer

The Web offers lots of additional information on individual insurers. By going to the insurers' sites, you often can find out about benefits, which medications are covered by your plan, and the backgrounds of affiliated physicians. You also may be able to download a copy of an insurance claim form and check your account online.

Imagine, by using the Web instead the phone, that you'll get the information you need without complicated "press-3-now" routing menus, and you won't have to listen to endless Muzak renditions of Beatles' songs. You'll change your tune from "Help! I need somebody" to "I get by with a little help from my mouse!"

The Health Insurance Association of America provides a list of health insurers' Web sites at `www.hiaa.org/member/memb-hiaa/cat1.htm`. Not all health plans belong to the association. If you don't find your plan there, check UltimateInsuranceLinks at `www.ultimateinsurancelinks.com/LIFELIST.HTM`.

Calling the Insurance Commish

If you do have problems that your health plan does not resolve to your satisfaction, you can always call the Commish — that is, your insurance commissioner. Or, even better, send him or her an e-mail message or a Web complaint form, as shown in Figure 5-4.

Each state has an insurance commissioner whose job it is to explain your rights as a healthcare consumer and to help you understand your insurance coverage. The commissioner is supposed to help you with any complaints or problems. The Commish can also tell you which insurance plans get the most complaints. In addition, you can find out whether an insurance agent is licensed.

The National Association of Insurance Commissioners Regulators page at `www.naic.org/1regulator/usamap.htm` has a clickable map that can take you directly to your state insurance commissioner's Web site.

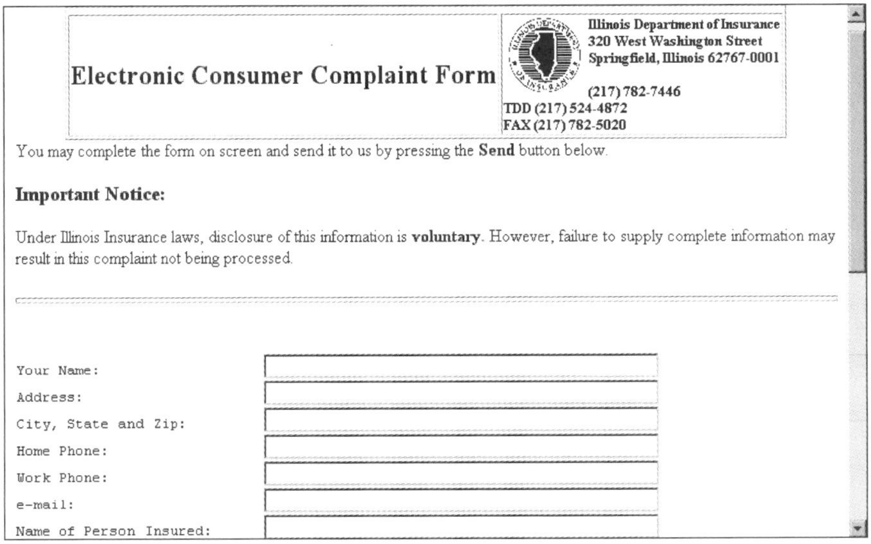

Figure 5-4:
You complain about your insurance plan online using electronic complaint forms like this one to the Illinois Department of Insurance.

Electronic Consumer Complaint Form

Illinois Department of Insurance
320 West Washington Street
Springfield, Illinois 62767-0001

(217) 782-7446
TDD (217) 524-4872
FAX (217) 782-5020

You may complete the form on screen and send it to us by pressing the **Send** button below.

Important Notice:

Under Illinois Insurance laws, disclosure of this information is **voluntary**. However, failure to supply complete information may result in this complaint not being processed.

Your Name:
Address:
City, State and Zip:
Home Phone:
Work Phone:
e-mail:
Name of Person Insured:

Unlocking the secrets in your insurance file

Just as people worry about whether the information in their credit record is accurate, they harbor similar concerns about their health insurance file. Wrong information in your health insurance file could cause you to unfairly lose your coverage.

Now you can put MIB to work for you. *MIB* doesn't stand for *Men in Black.* Rather, that's the Medical Information Bureau. This association of insurance companies allows you to find out whether you've been red-flagged for something that potentially could affect your health, life, disability, or long-term care insurance rate. And MIB gives you the opportunity to set that record straight. You can get a copy of your record for $8.50. You apply online at www.mib.com/html/us_residents.html. (Black-rimmed shades not included.)

Getting to Know Medicare

Thanks to advances in public health and medicine, more and more of us are living into ripe old age. These days, you're not really considered old until your children are on Medicare.

Medicare is the federal government's health insurance program for people 65 years of age or older and people with certain disabilities.

Finding out Medicare basics

You can get the skinny on Medicare at the Medicare Web site at www.medicare.gov. Click the <u>Medicare Basics</u> link on the left-hand side of your screen, and you can find out about your coverage, eligibility, and enrollment, plus info on prescription drug assistance programs and info on getting help with healthcare costs.

From the Medicare main page, you can also follow a link to a list of the 20 most frequently asked questions. Fortunately, the Medicare folks also give the answers.

Medicare combines the worst of three worlds: medicine, insurance, and government. That makes for some tough sledding when it comes to figuring out what they're talking about. But you can decode Medicare terms by using its glossary at www.medicare.gov/Glossary/Search.asp. Click the first letter of the word you want to define and then scroll down to find your word — no secret decoder ring necessary.

Comparing Medicare plans

The Medicare Web site has a cool online tool, Medicare Compare, that can help you comparison-shop for Medicare health plans by looking at costs, benefits, and quality. To use Medicare Compare, follow these steps:

1. **Open your browser and go to the Medicare Health Plan Compare Web site at** `www.medicare.gov/MPHcompare/Home.asp`**.**

   The Medicare Health Plan Compare page appears on-screen, as shown in Figure 5-5.

2. **Scroll down to Select a Geographic Area, shown in Figure 5-6, and fill in your zip code or select a state/territory from the drop-down text box. Then scroll down and click the Next Step button.**

   You see the Health Plans Search page. Scroll down to see the various types of Medicare plans available in your area.

3. **Select the types of plans you want to compare by clicking the boxes to the left of the plan names. After you've selected all the plans you want, scroll down the page and click the Continue button.**

   You now see the Select a Topic page that enables you to compare basic or more-detailed information about the plans you've selected. Many, many choices are available here; but for our purposes, we chose to compare basic information, which includes cost, doctor and hospital choice, prescription drugs, and extra benefits.

Figure 5-5: Starting at the Medicare Health Plan Compare site, you can comparison -shop for a Medicare plan.

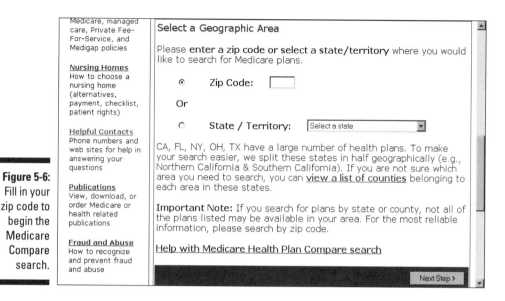

Figure 5-6:
Fill in your
zip code to
begin the
Medicare
Compare
search.

4. **Under the Cost and Benefits heading, select the Basic Information radio button. Then click the Go to Costs and Benefits button.**

   You now see the results of such a search, as shown in Figure 5-7. Information about each plan is presented in a table with side-by-side comparisons.

Figure 5-7:
Scrolling
down this
page
reveals the
costs and
benefits for
the selected
Medicare
plans.

What's Most Important To You	Aetna U.S. Healthcare, Inc. Aetna U.S. Healthcare Golden Medicare 10 (H0359 - 002) 1-800-810-5522	Intergroup of Arizona, Inc. SeniorCare (H0351 - 014) 1-800-438-7766
General Plan Information		
Plan Service Area	Phoenix	Maricopa County & Apache Junction
Plan Type	HMO (M+C)	HMO (M+C)
Federal Approval Status	Approved by Medicare	Approved by Medicare
Tax Status	For Profit	For Profit
Plan Contact	Medicare Customer Service	SeniorCare Inquiry Research

If you want more than basic information about the plans, choose from these additional options:

- **Detailed Information:** Select this option button to get a smorgasbord of two dozen categories, such as which preventive services are covered.

- **Go to Quality:** Click this button if you're interested in how happy or unhappy people are with the plans. From there, you can find out how members felt about how long they had to wait for care, how well they felt that the doctors communicated with them, and whether they got the care they needed.

- **Go to People Leaving Managed Care Plans:** Click this button to find out how many people with Medicare chose to leave specific, named managed care plans in the last two years. (How people vote with their feet may be the most important measure of how a plan is doing.) See Figure 5-8 for an example.

The Medicare Web site features a list of physicians who participate in the Medicare program. The site, in whole or in part, is available in Spanish and in Chinese and has a screen-reader-friendly version for the visually impaired.

Many Medicare beneficiaries attempt to fill in the gaps in coverage by buying supplemental Medigap policies. Medicare offers comparisons based on where you live for these policies and coverages at www.medicare.gov/MGCompare/Home.asp.

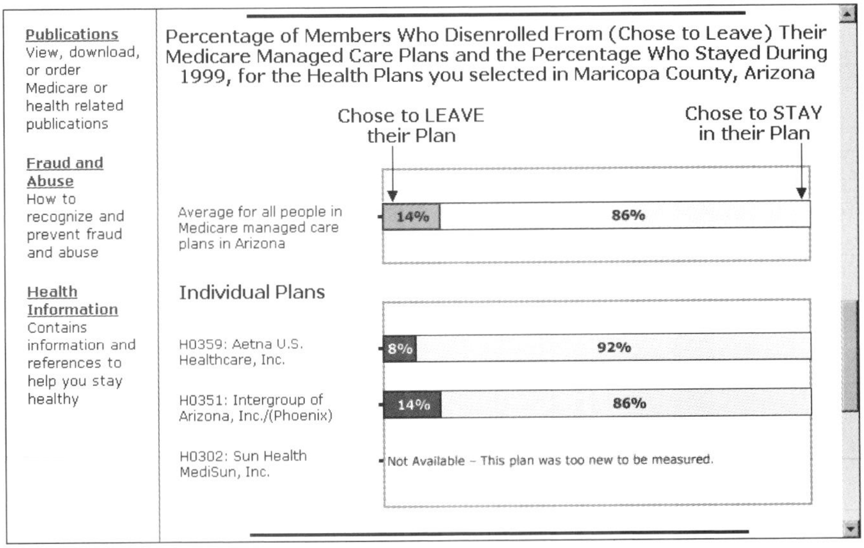

Figure 5-8:
Scroll to the bottom of this page to see how many people recently left the Medicare managed care plans you selected.

Publications
View, download, or order Medicare or health related publications

Fraud and Abuse
How to recognize and prevent fraud and abuse

Health Information
Contains information and references to help you stay healthy

Percentage of Members Who Disenrolled From (Chose to Leave) Their Medicare Managed Care Plans and the Percentage Who Stayed During 1999, for the Health Plans you selected in Maricopa County, Arizona

Chose to LEAVE their Plan | Chose to STAY in their Plan

Average for all people in Medicare managed care plans in Arizona — 14% | 86%

Individual Plans

H0359: Aetna U.S. Healthcare, Inc. — 8% | 92%

H0351: Intergroup of Arizona, Inc./(Phoenix) — 14% | 86%

H0302: Sun Health MediSun, Inc. — Not Available – This plan was too new to be measured.

Blowing the whistle on Medicare fraud

The elderly sometimes are easy marks for Medicare fraud. Medicare recommends being suspicious when a healthcare provider says one of the following:

- The test is free; I only need your Medicare number for my records.
- Medicare wants you to have the item or service.
- I know how to get Medicare to pay for it.
- The more tests I provide, the cheaper they are.
- The equipment or service is free; it won't cost you anything.

Be suspicious of providers that

- Routinely waive co-payments without checking on your ability to pay
- Advertise "free" consultations to Medicare beneficiaries
- Claim they represent Medicare
- Use pressure or scare tactics to sell you high-priced medical services or diagnostic tests
- Bill Medicare for services you do not recall receiving
- Use telemarketing and door-to-door selling as marketing tools

For information on how to report suspected Medicare fraud and abuse, go to www.hcfa.gov/medicare/fraud/REPORT2.HTM.

Part III
Researching Your Medical Concerns Online

The 5th Wave   By Rich Tennant

"Gather around, kids! Your mother's found a home-tonsillectomy Web site."

In this part . . .

You want to find out about a medical condition, a medication, or an alternative medical therapy. You've heard that the Internet is the place to go. And it is . . . if you know where to look.

The chapters in this part show you where to go to find what you're looking for quickly, from reliable sources, with as much or as little information as it takes to meet your needs

In Chapter 6, you find out how to research a medical condition, translate medicalese, and find support online. In Chapter 7, you discover how to research and shop for medications online. Finally, in Chapter 8, you can find out about alternative and complementary medicine.

Chapter 6

Researching a Disease Step-by-Step

*W*e've heard it said that if you give a man a fish, you'll feed him for a day, but if you teach him to fish, you'll feed him for the rest of his life. Our goal in this chapter is to show you how to use the Internet to fish for information on diseases and conditions.

We know that some of you will only need to fish from the shore. Maybe you heard about some condition that a distant cousin has been diagnosed with, and you want to skim the surface and find out a little about it. We help you find the resources you need, and we promise that you'll only have to dip your toes in the water.

Some of you may want to know more for your own reasons. Maybe you or a loved one have been diagnosed with a condition that is life-threatening or that is chronic and life-altering. For these situations, we introduce you to the tools you'll need to fish in deep waters.

So many people are casting their nets onto the Internet these days that the old expression about teaching a man to fish has been updated. Now it goes like this: Give a man a fish, and you'll feed him for a day, but if you show a man how to use the Internet, he won't bother you for weeks.

So hang your *Gone Fishin'* sign on the door 'cause here we go.

Look It Up, Quick

A good place to start any search or to quickly get the basics on a disease is with online encyclopedias and dictionaries. Both are easy to search and contain linked words that can lead you to more information.

Encyclopedias

We learned how to spell e-n-c-y-c-l-o-pedia from Jiminy Cricket on the old *Mickey Mouse Club* TV show. We've loved e-n-c-y-c-l-o-pedias ever since.

And the online versions can really be slick. You can readily get the general information, which may be all that you need, on a disease.

ADAM Medical Encyclopedia at MEDLINEplus

The online medical encyclopedia we like the best is the *ADAM Medical Encyclopedia* at the National Library of Medicine's MEDLINE*plus* Web site. It's easy to use, has thousands of articles, and features beautiful illustrations.

You can search the encyclopedia for information on diseases, tests, symptoms, injuries, and surgeries. Here's how:

1. **Open your Web browser and go to the *ADAM Medical Encyclopedia* at MEDLINE*plus* at** medlineplus.adam.com.

   The Disease Reference page, with an A-to-Z index toward the top of the page, appears.

2. **Click the first letter of the name of the disease that you're interested in checking out.**

   We clicked *M* because we are using migraine headache as our example.

   You see an alphabetical list of diseases that begin with the letter you chose. (In our example, we see the list of diseases that begin with the letter *M*.)

3. **Find the disease you're researching. Scroll down the page if necessary. Then click the disease.**

   In our example, scrolling halfway down the page, you see three choices for migraine: Migraine; migraine headache, classical; and migraine headache, common. We selected the first choice. (The three subjects are linked together in the encyclopedia. Selecting any of these choices provides you with a way to find the others.)

   You will then see the first page of the article, the Overview, on the disease.

Each Overview gives you a definition of the disease, its causes, its incidence, and its risk factors. Each article has, at the top of the Web page, links to the following additional sections:

- ✔ Symptoms, which includes a listing of symptoms, signs, and tests
- ✔ Treatment, which includes treatment, prognosis, complications, and a guide on when to call the doctor
- ✔ Prevention, which includes lowering risk factors or taking appropriate screening tests

Each article features underlined words that serve as links to other information. When you click the underlined words (links), you get more information about the words. Thumbnail (miniature) versions of related illustrations appear at the top of each page. Click a thumbnail (or click the words beneath a thumbnail) to see an enlarged version of the image.

Britannica.com

Encyclopaedia Britannica isn't a medical encyclopedia, but it packs a lot of medical information into its online version, Britannica.com (www.britannica.com). A search at this site not only gives you the basic information about a disease, but also links to Web sites and full-text articles in consumer magazines. The folks at EB don't spell *encyclopedia* the way old Jiminy Cricket did, but Britannica rules.

Dictionaries

If you need a medical dictionary, the one we like the best is MedicineNet.com's *MedTerms Medical Dictionary* at www.medterms.com. Just type your term in the Search the Dictionary box on the left side of the page and click the Go button. You can also use the site's A-to-Z index to find your word. We searched for *migraine,* and you can see the results in Figure 6-1.

The editors at MedicineNet.com describe their work as an *e-encyclopedic dictionary* because it not only provides short definitions but also provides more-detailed information.

Medical dictionaries are also available at InteliHealth (www.intelihealth.com) and CBSHealthWatch (www.cbshealthwatch.com). In addition, you may want to check out the *On-Line Medical Dictionary* at www.graylab.ac.uk/omd/index.html.

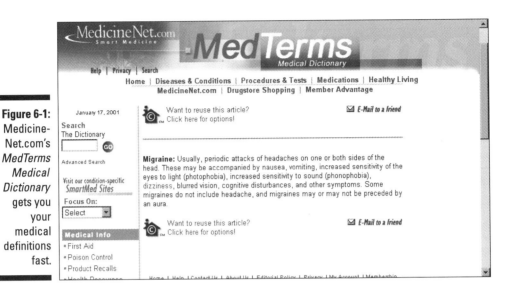

Figure 6-1: Medicine-Net.com's *MedTerms Medical Dictionary* gets you your medical definitions fast.

What are online health searchers after?

One of the major reasons Americans use the Internet is to look for health information. And the number-one type of health information they're seeking is disease information.

Harris Interactive has been tracking people like you to find out how they used the Internet to research health concerns. Here are the percentages of people who told the pollsters what they sometimes or often wanted:

- ✔ **61%** Information about specific illnesses
- ✔ **44%** To research symptoms they are experiencing
- ✔ **44%** Information about specific drugs

- ✔ **40%** Information about over-the-counter medications
- ✔ **19%** Support from people with the same medical condition
- ✔ **17%** Ratings of physicians
- ✔ **13%** To find a physician
- ✔ **8%** Advice via e-mail from a physician other than their own
- ✔ **4%** To obtain a prescription
- ✔ **3%** To fill a prescription
- ✔ **2%** To consult with a physician in "real time"

The Full Treatment: Finding Out How a Disease Is Diagnosed and Treated

A big part of researching a disease is finding out how the disease is diagnosed and treated. In this section, you find out how to get quick access to information on tests, surgery, and medications. We also show you how to get alternative medicine's view of the disease that you're researching.

Tests

In the course of researching a disease, you're likely to run across mentions of tests and procedures used to diagnose a condition. The fast track on test information is at the MEDLINE*plus* Test Reference section at `medlineplus. adam.com/ency/index/testidxa.htm`. This portion of the MEDLINE*plus* Web site features an A-to-Z index. You look for the test under the first letter of the test name.

In our example, migraine headache, head MRI scans sometimes are ordered. To find out more about this test, we went to the Test Reference section, clicked *H,* and found a <u>Head MRI Scan</u> link. This link led us to the Cranial MRI page, which explains the test and how to prepare for it. The Cranial MRI page also has links to more information on test risks and results and also to illustrations.

Medications

You can find out a lot about the medications for treating the disease you're researching, whether the medicines are prescribed by your doctor or purchased over the counter.

At CBSHealthWatch (`www.cbshealthwatch.com`), you can use a tool that enables you not only to get a profile on an individual medication but also to search by disease for the medications that are used to treat the condition you're interested in. To tap into this information at CBSHealthWatch, follow these steps:

1. **Open your Web browser and go to** `www.cbshealthwatch.com`.

   The CBSHealthWatch opening page appears.

2. **Under Resources on the left hand-side of the page, click the <u>Drug Directory</u> link.**

   The Drug Directory screen appears.

3. **In the text box below Enter Your Search Term, type either the name of a drug or a condition. Select the appropriate radio button — either Drug or Disease — and then click the nearby Search button.**

   In our example, we typed *migraine,* selected the Disease radio button, and then clicked Search.

   If you're not sure how to spell the name of a drug or disease, you can type in the first few letters. CBSHealthWatch automatically suggests possible matches.

   You see the results of your search.

4. **The results may consist of several likely choices. Click the best match.**

   For our example, we clicked the <u>Migraine</u> link.

   Next, you see the Drugs by Name page that lists the drugs used to treat that disease.

5. **After you have the list of drugs, you can click the links for individual ones you want to know more about.**

   In our example, we wanted to know more about sumatriptan succinate, the generic name for a drug sold under the brand name Imitrex. We were interested in the oral medication. After clicking the appropriate link, we were presented with the drug's profile.

If you have a particular medication in mind, you can search for it under either the generic or brand name under Search by Drug on the Drug Directory Search page in Step 3 of the preceding steps.

However you get there, drug profiles include the following information:

 ✔ Brand name or names

 ✔ Uses

 ✔ How to take this medication

 ✔ Side effects

 ✔ Precautions

 ✔ Drug interactions

 ✔ What to do if you miss a dose

 ✔ How to store this medication

In case you need to look up an unfamiliar word, CBSHealthWatch has, at the bottom of each drug profile page, a convenient <u>Medical Dictionary</u> link to the *Merriam-Webster Medical Dictionary.*

Another place for quick look-ups on medications is MEDLINE*plus* at `www.nlm.nih.gov/medlineplus/druginformation.html`.

Surgery

If an operation is suggested to treat the condition you're researching, you can get quick and complete information with surgical precision at the MEDLINE*plus* Surgery Reference section at `medlineplus.adam.com/ency/index/surgidxa.htm`. This section has an A-to-Z index. Click the first letter of the name of the surgical procedure for a list of operations. Then click the one you're looking for.

You'll find a rundown on the procedure, including alternative names, indications for the operation, how the operation is performed, its risks, and information about postoperative care and recovery.

Alternative medicine

If you want to include alternative medicine in your research of a disease, here are a couple of sites we like.

OneBody.com

At OneBody.com (`www.onebody.com`), you can find out what a variety of alternative therapies offers for the disease you're researching. OneBody has Care Centers with detailed overviews, including description of the conditions, causes, signs and symptoms, how it's diagnosed, prognosis, conventional treatments, alternative treatments, and self-care. You select the disease you're interested in from the drop-down text box under Care Centers.

The Natural Pharmacist

The Natural Pharmacist (`www.tnp.com`) has science-based natural health information. The Conditions A–Z section of *The Natural Health Encyclopedia* enables you to search for diseases and find out what research shows about the benefits of herbs, supplements, and other treatments.

Here's how to find the disease you're researching in the Conditions A–Z section of *The Natural Health Encyclopedia*:

1. **Open your browser and go to `www.tnp.com`.**

   The Natural Pharmacist home page appears on-screen.

2. **In the TNP Encyclopedia box near the top of the page, click the <u>Conditions A–Z</u> link.**

   The Conditions A–Z page, with an alphabetic index and a Search For text box at the top of the page, appears.

3. **Type in the disease you're researching in the Search For text box and click the Search button. (You could, instead, select the disease by clicking the first letter of the disease you're researching, in which case you would — on the page that appears — need to click the name of the disease.)**

In our example, we typed *migraine* into the Search For text box and clicked Search. This brought us to a search results page with several choices. We clicked the <u>Migraine Headaches</u> link, which took us to an article.

A Helping Hand: Getting Support

Whatever condition you or a loved one have been diagnosed with, know that you are not alone. Loads of other people out there are feeling the same pain and can lend you a helping hand with advice on coping, tips on the best places to obtain supplies, and leads on finding doctors or hospitals.

Support can take many forms, including self-help groups that may meet in a church basement or YMCA in your neighborhood to discuss mutual problems. In the Internet age, new forms of support — from virtual groups that turn the country or the world into your neighborhood by using e-mail, online chats, and other new technologies — are available.

Whether you think that traditional support groups or online support groups work better for you, the Internet can help you find what you're looking for.

Patient associations

We think that one of the best ways to find the support you're looking for is through a patient association. *Patient associations* are groups that were started by patients with a condition (such as migraine, cancer, or multiple sclerosis) and their family members — and sometimes doctors and other healthcare professionals. Such associations share information and provide support.

The Internet has created a new way for these groups to reach patients: Web sites, which typically have online brochures about the condition, links to the Web sites of related organizations, and often e-mail support groups, bulletin board discussion groups, and online chats. The associations frequently list contacts for traditional in-the-flesh support group meetings, too.

Patient association Web sites may also link to the sites of *professional associations,* groups made up of doctors specializing in the condition. The professional association sites may have online brochures on the condition and databases that can help you find doctors who are experts in the condition.

You can find patient associations online in several ways, but we think that the easiest way is through healthfinder at `www.healthfinder.gov`. (The U.S. Department of Health and Human Services runs healthfinder.) For a patient association or any other Web site to be included in healthfinder, it must measure up to healthfinder standards. These standards include providing reliable information and being able to respond to consumers via e-mail or traditional mail or phone.

Here's how to use healthfinder to track down patient associations:

1. **Open your Web browser and go to the healthfinder Web site at** `www.healthfinder.gov`**.**

   You see the healthfinder home page, as shown in Figure 6-2.

2. **Type in the condition you're researching in the Search For box and then click the Go button.**

   In our example, we typed *migraine* and clicked Go. The search results page appeared with results of our migraine search. The results page is divided into two sections — Web Resources and Organizations — as shown in Figure 6-3.

3. **To find out more about an individual organization, you can read its healthfinder review by clicking the <u>Details</u> link shown to the right of each organization's name.**

   In our example, we chose American Council for Headache Education (ACHE) and clicked the <u>Details</u> link to the right of its name. After we did that, the organization resource details page for ACHE appeared.

   The healthfinder's organization resource details pages include the following information on patient associations:

   - Web and e-mail addresses

   - Other contact information, such as addresses and phone numbers

   - Descriptions of their missions

   - Print resources they offer, such as brochures

4. **To go directly to the patient association's Web site, click the association's Web address (also called a URL).**

   In our example, we clicked the Web address for ACHE, as shown in Figure 6-4. By clicking in the list on the left-hand side of the site's main page, we could reach the following pages:

   - **Discussion Forums:** ACHE offers migraine patients two online bulletin board forums, Ask the Expert and Headache Talk.

     You can read or browse the messages without logging in, but to participate, you need to register. To do this, click the <u>Create a New User Account</u> link and enter a log-in name, a password, your e-mail address, and a screen name that you will use as your on-screen identity.

   - **Support Groups:** ACHE provides contact information for both online and offline support groups.

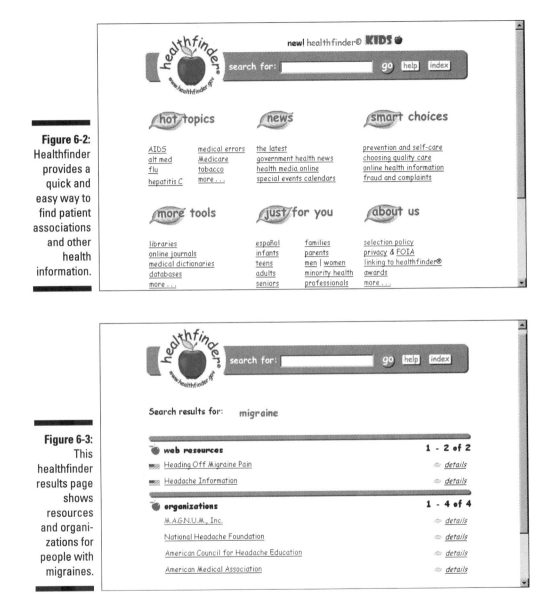

Figure 6-2:
Healthfinder
provides a
quick and
easy way to
find patient
associations
and other
health
information.

Figure 6-3:
This
healthfinder
results page
shows
resources
and organi-
zations for
people with
migraines.

Web sites from patient associations offer a variety of other services. These often include a library of basic patient care information, an online glossary of terms related to the condition, links to Web pages from other patient groups or professional associations, and news on the condition. Patient association Web sites also may have some unique features, such as the gallery of art by people with migraines at the ACHE site.

Figure 6-4:
The ACHE
Web site
lists online
forums and
support
groups for
people with
migraine
headaches.

The National Library of Medicine's DIRLINE: Directory of Health
Organizations at `dirline.nlm.nih.gov` provides another quick way to
locate patient and professional organizations. You can find more on patient
associations in the *Healthcare Online For Dummies Internet Directory*.

Online support groups

At a variety of places online, you can find groups that can provide you with
support, advice, and information on specific conditions. This information
comes from people who have walked a mile or more in your moccasins. Some
of these groups are run by passionate laypersons, and others are run by compassionate health professionals.

These online groups come in various forms, including mailing lists, newsgroups, electronic bulletin boards, and online chats. The term *mailing lists,* in
this case, refers to virtual support groups that exchange e-mail messages.
Newsgroups are places on the Internet where you, by using special software,
can post and read messages. *Electronic bulletin boards* are virtual places,
sometimes within Web sites, where you can post and respond to messages.
And *online chats* are real-time typed conversations. You can read more about
these online groups in Chapter 2.

Some places to look for online support for the disease you're researching
include the following:

✔ **Medical megasites:** These are those large, all-encompassing, often commercial health sites, such as WebMD Health (`my.webmd.com`), drkoop.com (`www.drkoop.com`), HealthCentral.com (`www.healthcentral.com`), and CBSHealthWatch (`www.cbshealthwatch.com`). Such megasites typically offer bulletin boards, chat events with health experts, and support chats with others who are dealing with the same condition.

✔ **Usenet groups:** Support-Group.com (`www.support-group.com`) provides links to online health-oriented bulletin boards, chats, and newsgroups, which also are known as Usenet groups. Google Groups (`groups.google.com`) enables you to search and read recent newsgroup postings.

✔ **Mailing lists:** Yahoo! Groups (`groups.yahoo.com`), Topica (`www.topica.com`), and Liszt (`www.liszt.com`) are a few places to go to sign up for mailing lists.

Tapping into Medical Research

Maybe the kind of research you need to do on a disease is beyond the basics. Maybe you're interested in finding a research study to participate in or in finding the results from one of those studies.

Clinical trials

In researching a disease thoroughly, you might want to know what studies are currently in the pipeline. You can go to the National Library of Medicine's ClinicalTrials.gov at `www.clinicaltrials.gov` to search for studies, primarily those funded by the federal government. In Chapter 7, we provide a step-by-step explanation on how to find a trial at this government site.

Using our example of researching *migraine,* we found two studies recruiting subjects at ClinicalTrials.gov, as shown in Figure 6-5.

Even if you don't want to join a study, you can note the names of the researchers conducting the trials to develop a list of experts you may want to contact about the disease.

You can also find trials, primarily those funded by the drug industry, at CenterWatch at `www.centerwatch.com`.

Medical literature

Today's research may be tomorrow's treatment. If you want to know what the researchers are saying about a disease, you can read all about it in the researchers' own words in the medical journals.

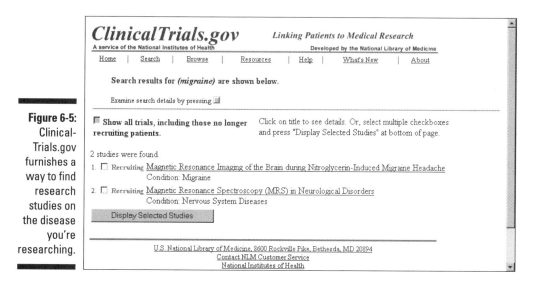

Figure 6-5:
Clinical-
Trials.gov
furnishes a
way to find
research
studies on
the disease
you're
researching.

The best way to locate the articles you want is through MEDLINE, a huge database of medical journal articles, from the National Library of Medicine. Its Internet Grateful Med (IGM) site at igm.nlm.nih.gov provides, by far, the easiest way to search MEDLINE.

These searches can be quite complicated, but we're going to start out with a simple search, using our example of researching migraine headaches.

The MEDLINE database has summaries of medical articles dating back to the time when Lyndon Johnson was president. If you simply type in the name of the disease you're researching, you could get thousands of hits. The results can be as overwhelming as the results of performing a search on AltaVista or Google.

So when we searched for articles on migraine headache in our example, we were very specific. We limited the search to those articles that discuss using acupuncture therapy for migraines. We also searched for only those articles that appeared in the journals in a one-year period. To perform such a search on Internet Grateful Med, follow these steps:

1. **Open your Web browser and go to the Internet Grateful Med Web site at** igm.nlm.nih.gov.

   You see the Internet Grateful Med opening page.

2. **Under Select Database to Search, click MEDLINE.**

   The National Library of Medicine: Internet Grateful Med Search Screen appears.

3. **Type in the disease in the first Search For text box. Then click the Perform Search button either at the top or at the bottom of the page.**

You may want to type in another term, such as *drugs* or *surgery,* in an And Search For box to get more-specific results. You also may want to use one or more of the drop-down text boxes in the Apply Limits area to limit your search to a particular language, to a type of study, or to a type of publication.

In our example, we typed *migraine* in the Search For box and typed *acupuncture* in the first AND Search For box. Next, in the Apply Limits area, we typed the year 2000 in both the Year Range Begin Year box and in the End Year box, as shown in Figure 6-6. Then we clicked the Perform Search button.

Next you see the National Library of Medicine: IGM Results Screen with the articles that match the words in your search. (In our example, we matched seven articles, as shown in Figure 6-7.)

You can click the Full Citation box to the left of each listing to see a short summary of each article.

If you want to get a copy of the complete article you found in your search at Internet Grateful Med, you can order it through the National Library of Medicine's Loansome Doc service for a fee. To do this, click the Order Documents button at the top of the IGM page. You must establish a Loansome Doc account to use this service.

You may also be able to obtain the article through a local library or through a library specializing in medical resources. You can get help in locating one of these special libraries in Chapter 2.

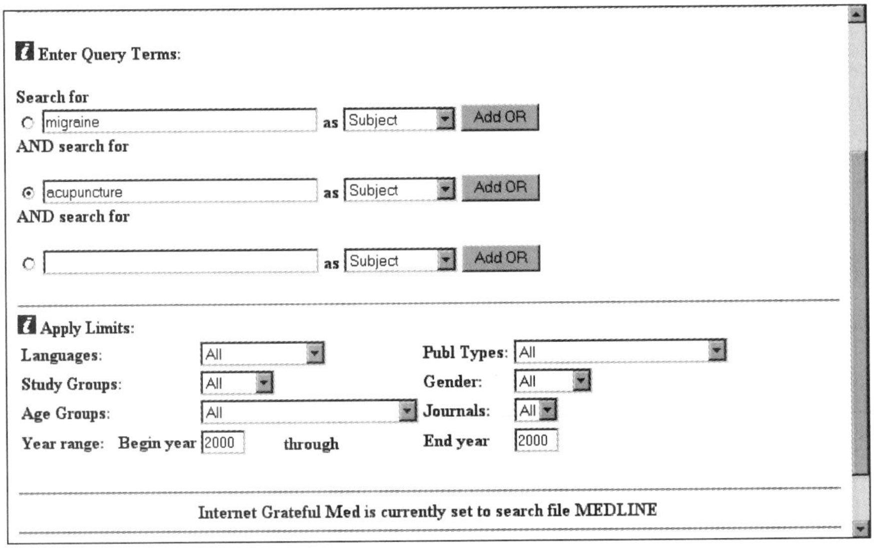

Figure 6-6:
IGM lets you
perform a
simple
search of
the medical
literature.

Enter Query Terms:

Search for
○ migraine   **as** Subject   Add OR
AND search for

◉ acupuncture   **as** Subject   Add OR
AND search for

○   **as** Subject   Add OR

Apply Limits:
Languages:	All	Publ Types:	All
Study Groups:	All	Gender:	All
Age Groups:	All	Journals:	All
Year range: Begin year 2000	through	End year	2000

Internet Grateful Med is currently set to search file MEDLINE

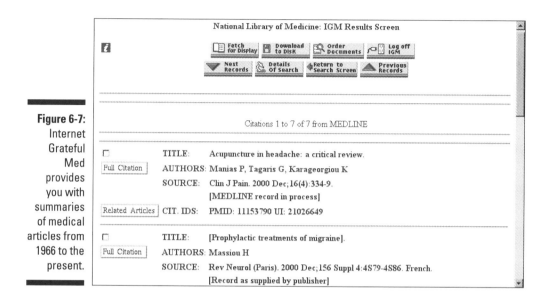

Figure 6-7:
Internet
Grateful
Med
provides
you with
summaries
of medical
articles from
1966 to the
present.

Why not Google?

So you're researching a disease. What's wrong with using your favorite general search engine, such as Google or Hotbot or AltaVista? Nothing. We use 'em. We like 'em.

Google is our current favorite. In fact, we've added a Google button to our browsers so we can have Google search for something for us from wherever we are on the Web. See `www.google.com/options/buttons.html` to find out how to do this yourself.

There are lots of reasons to use a search engine when you're researching a disease. Search engines are easy to use, fast, and as comfortable as an old pair of slippers. They can retrieve sites that will be exactly what you're looking for with lots of good information. But, on the other hand, search engines can have some downsides. They can virtually drown you in hits. And some of the hits will be way off target. Some of the sites they retrieve will mention the disease only in passing.

You may find yourself linked to someone's personal account of dealing with a disease, which may or may not be helpful to you. You may find yourself linked to dot-con artists, quacks and scammers, or people with axes to grind. You may be linked to oodles of sites that are completely irrelevant.

Some simple ways to make your searches more effective are possible, such as enclosing phrases in quotation marks and using specific (rather than general) search terms or keywords. If you really want to make your searches more efficient, read the Help pages at your favorite search engine. You can also pick up tips at Search Engine Watch (`www.searchenginewatch.com`) and at Search Engine Showdown (`www.searchengineshowdown.com`).

Another way to increase your success rate is to use the subject directories that most of the popular search engines now offer. These directories categorize sites by subjects, such as Health or Medicine. Look in the *Healthcare Online For Dummies Internet Directory* for the addresses of some search engines and subject directories that we recommend.

Go forth and search!

Finding All the Pieces to the Puzzle at One Site

Earlier in this chapter, we assume that you're looking for a piece or two of the disease-research puzzle. But what if you'd prefer to have all the pieces of the puzzle assembled neatly before you? Some places on the Web do this: the medical megasites.

We discuss megasites in Chapter 2, and any of the megasites in that chapter are worth checking out. But our own preferences, when researching a disease or other medical topic, are MEDLINE*plus* and MayoClinic.com.

MEDLINEplus

Elsewhere in this chapter, we recommend pieces of the MEDLINE*plus* Web site at `www.nlm.nih.gov/medlineplus`. It's a great place for looking at a medical encyclopedia and the like. But MEDLINE*plus,* a gift to the nation from the National Library of Medicine, can put all the information together in a tidy package.

Here's how to look for disease information at MEDLINE*plus:*

1. **Open your Web browser and go to** `www.nlm.nih.gov/medlineplus`.

   The MEDLINE*plus* home page appears.

2. **Click Health Topics.**

   The Health Topics page, with an A-to-Z index across the top of the page, appears.

3. **Click the first letter of the disease you're researching.**

   A listing of the MEDLINE*plus* topics that begin with the letter you clicked appears.

4. **Scroll down the page and click the topic you're interested in.**

   In our example, we clicked *M* and scrolled down the page to find *Migraine,* which refers to the <u>Headache and Migraine</u> link.

   You see the MEDLINE*plus* list of resources for the condition. (In our example, we came to the Headache and Migraine page, as shown in Figure 6-8.)

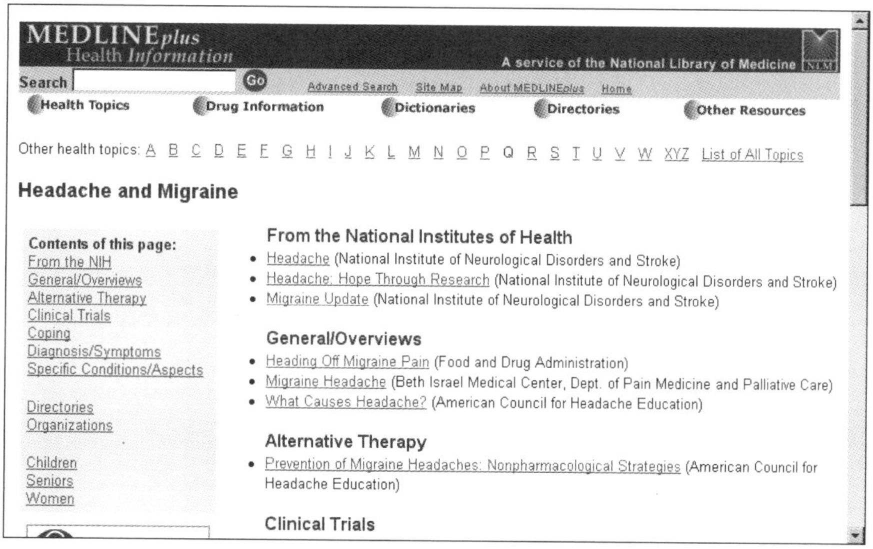

Figure 6-8:
MEDLINE-
plus gives
you a wide
array of
information
on
conditions.

A MEDLINE*plus* search on a disease gives you links to reliable information from government, major medical centers, professional associations, and patient groups. The search may give you links to support groups, glossaries of terms relating to the condition, guides on nutrition, and alternative medical therapy. The search also features links to online pamphlets, research, materials in Spanish and other languages, and information relating to special populations, such as children and seniors.

Something really cool here is that MEDLINE*plus* can generate a search for recent articles on the disease in MEDLINE, the National Library of Medicine's database of the medical literature. To get summaries of the latest articles on the condition, look for the links to the searches under Search MEDLINE in a box on the left-hand side of the page.

MEDLINE*plus* can also help you locate studies on the condition using the search engines at ClinicalTrials.gov and CenterWatch. Look for the links to the searches under the Clinical Trials heading on the right-hand side of the page.

MayoClinic.com

MayoClinic.com is an easy-to-use site to get the full picture of a disease. It's clean, uncluttered, and has the Mayo Clinic standing behind it.

Here's how to find what Mayo has to say about the disease you're researching:

1. **Open your browser and go to** `www.mayoclinic.com`.

   You see the MayoClinic.com home page.

2. **On the left-hand side of the page, under the Find Information heading, click the** <u>Diseases & Conditions, A–Z</u> **link.**

   The Diseases & Conditions page, with the A–Z index in the Select a Disease or Condition area of the page, appears.

3. **Click the first letter of the disease you're researching.**

   A list of diseases and conditions appears.

4. **Click the name of the disease you're researching.**

   In our example, we clicked *Migraine*.

   You see the MayoClinic.com page for the disease you're researching. (In our example, we came to the Migraine page, as shown in Figure 6-9.)

The MayoClinic.com articles on diseases have easy-to-navigate indexes that help you quickly get to information on symptoms, causes, risk factors, when to seek medical advice, diagnosis, treatment, prevention, self-care, coping strategies, and alternative medicine. You can also find information on medications by clicking the <u>Drug Information</u> link under Find Information on the left-hand side of the home page.

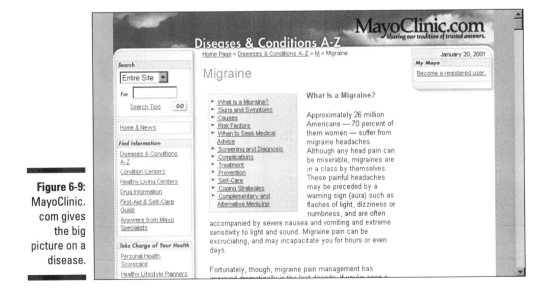

Figure 6-9: MayoClinic. com gives the big picture on a disease.

Chapter 7

Researching and Buying Medicines

*H*ave you heard the one about the doctor who jotted down some notes in preparation for an acceptance speech as Doctor of the Year from the local medical society? When the big day came, he got up to receive his award and couldn't make out his own scrawl. He broke up his colleagues when he asked, "Is there a pharmacist in the house?"

Just as pharmacists decipher physicians' poor penmanship, the Internet can help you figure out the puzzling world of pills and potions. You can find out online how your *meds* — as the health pros like to call them — work, their side effects, what foods and other drugs they interact badly with, and what to do if you miss a dose. You also can go online to check out the latest research on medications and to find out how to participate in a clinical trial of new or experimental drugs.

In this chapter, you find out about sites that can tell you everything you ever needed to know about the medications you take as well as how to purchase them online and what to look for in an online pharmacy.

Getting to Know Your Meds

Medications, whether prescription or over the counter, are supposed to help you feel better. And usually they do.

Knowing more about your medicines can make them easier to swallow. By going online, you can find a drug storehouse of knowledge about what your medicines are supposed to do. You can also find precautions about using them and get heads-up alerts if there are potential problems about mixing them with other medications and foods.

Your doctor and pharmacist are the best people to ask any questions you have about medicines. They know you, and they know the medications you are taking. The Internet offers you plenty of backup information if you need a reminder or want to know more.

Putting drkoop.com to work for you

drkoop.com — named for the famed former Surgeon General of the United States, Dr. C. Everett Koop — has a Drug Checker feature at `www.drugchecker.com` that can provide you with basic information about your medicines.

Here's how to use Drug Checker:

1. **Open your Web browser and go to the Drug Checker site at** `www.drugchecker.com`.

   You see the Welcome to the drkoop.com Drug Checker page, shown in Figure 7-1.

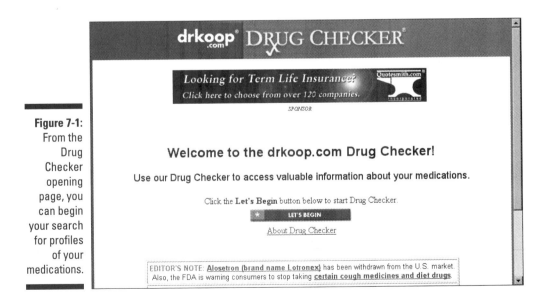

Figure 7-1: From the Drug Checker opening page, you can begin your search for profiles of your medications.

2. **Click the Let's Begin button.**

   The Drug Search screen appears.

3. **Begin your search by typing the name of the drug you're interested in checking out in the Search For text box; then click the Search button.**

   In our example, we checked out the cholesterol-lowering drug Lipitor, so we typed *Lipitor* in the box and clicked the Search button.

   Next, the Drug Search Results screen appears, listing drugs that Drug Checker thinks that you have in mind.

   Drug names, especially the generic ones, don't naturally roll off the tongue (or the fingertips, for that matter). If you're not sure how to spell a drug's name, type in your best guess and then select whichever of the radio buttons under the Search For box applies. You can take a stab at the name by using a part of the name (by using the Contains radio button); the beginning of the name (by using the Begins With radio button), or the sound of the name (by using the Sounds Like radio button).

4. **Select one of the drugs listed in the Search Results box by clicking the name of the drug; then click the Add Drug(s) To List button.**

   For our example, we selected *Lipitor* and then clicked the Add Drug(s) To List button.

   You then see the Drug List page with the drug (in our case Lipitor) in the Selected Drugs box on the right, shown in Figure 7-2.

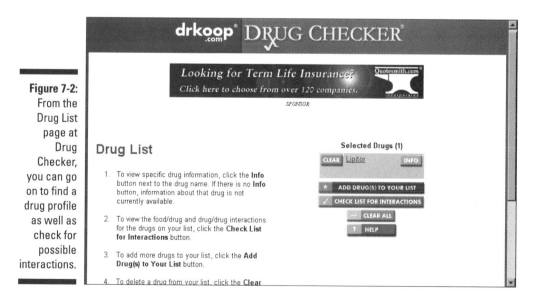

Figure 7-2: From the Drug List page at Drug Checker, you can go on to find a drug profile as well as check for possible interactions.

5. Click the Info button.

You then see the permissions page. Before viewing drug information, you must agree with the Disclaimer of Warranties statement.

6. Click the I Agree box beneath the disclaimer.

At long last, you come to the information you wanted. You see Drug Checker's basic drug leaflet, shown in Figure 7-3.

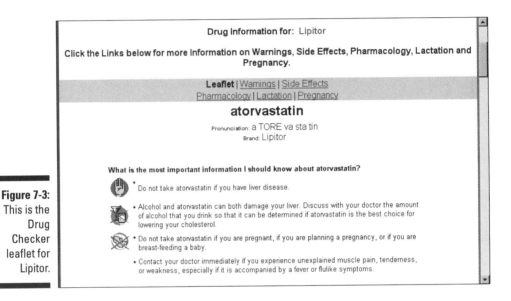

Figure 7-3:
This is the Drug Checker leaflet for Lipitor.

If you want even more information, don't miss the links at the top of the leaflet page for Warnings, Side Effects, Pharmacology, Lactation, and Pregnancy. To view the food/drug and drug/drug interactions for your medicine, click the Check List for Interactions button on the Drug List (refer to Figure 7-2) in Step 4 in the preceding steps. To see an example of the results, see Figure 7-4.

drkoop.com rates the seriousness of drug interactions and describes in medicalese what causes the problem. If you want to decode the language, you can use an online medical dictionary. (You can find more on online medical dictionaries in Chapter 6.)

Also, if you want to delve into the details, drkoop.com provides references to relevant articles in medical journals. Look in the References section on the Your Drug Interactions page for these references, some of which have More Info links to article summaries.

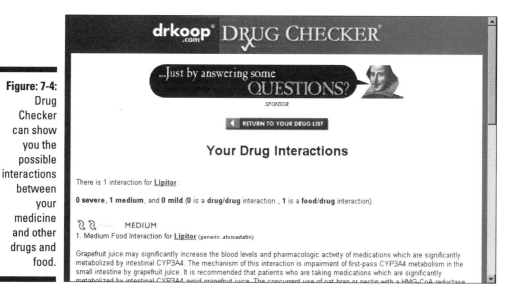

Figure: 7-4:
Drug
Checker
can show
you the
possible
interactions
between
your
medicine
and other
drugs and
food.

Cracking the drug code

Your doctor probably tells you that he's pre-scribing a medicine that you'll be taking, say, twice each day. He'll tell the pharmacist that you'll need it *bid.* That's short for *bis in die,* which is Latin for *twice a day.*

It's a time-honored tradition for docs to write with poor handwriting in Latin. Ever see *Rx*? That's an abbreviation for the Latin word for *recipe* or *prescription.* The use of all this Latin combined with poor penmanship has been, an, er, Rx for disaster, in some cases putting lives in danger and compromising patient care.

Some experts want computers to take the place of handwriting and plain English to replace the Latin abbreviations; that seems like a good idea. But until it happens, you may want to know what those abbreviations stand for. All this Latin was Greek to us until we found this list on the Food and Drug Administration's Web site at www.fda.gov/fdac/features/695_prescrip.html:

Latin	Abbreviation	Meaning
ante cibum	ac	before meals
bis in die	bid	twice a day
gutta	gt	drop
hora somni	hs	at bedtime
oculus dexter	od	right eye
oculus sinister	os	left eye
per os	po	by mouth
post cibum	pc	after meals
pro re nata	prn	as needed
quaque 3 hora	q 3 h	every 3 hours
quaque die	qd	every day
quater in die	qid	4 times a day
ter in die	tid	3 times a day

What to look for when researching a drug

Look for the answers to the following questions on any site that dispenses drug information:

✔ What does the drug do?

✔ Who shouldn't take it?

✔ How should you take it?

✔ What should you do if you miss a dose?

✔ What should you do if you take an overdose?

✔ What should you avoid while taking the drug?

✔ What are the possible side effects?

✔ What other drugs will interact with it?

✔ How should you store the drug?

Drug Checker can help you find out about some over-the-counter medications and herbal preparations, too. Another place to check on these is WebMD's Medical Library. It has profiles on over-the-counter drugs at `my.webmd.com/medcast_toc/pdr_drug_and_herb` from the *PDR Family Guide to Over-the-Counter Drugs.* WebMD also has an herbal directory at `my.webmd.com/medcast_toc/pdr_herbs_and_vitamins`. (See Chapter 8 for more information on herbal medicine.)

Getting second opinions on your meds

Plenty of credible Web sites can help answer your questions about medicines. But to be sure that you have the latest info, getting a second opinion by checking more than one Web site is a good idea. If you find any troublesome discrepancies, talk them over with your pharmacist or physician.

PDR.net

The trusty old print standby for drug information for consumers and physicians alike is the *Physicians' Desk Reference,* known popularly as *the PDR.* Not surprisingly, the PDR has a presence on the Web with features especially customized for consumers like you. Head on over to `consumer.pdr.net/consumer/index.htm`, shown in Figure 7-5.

Figure 7-5:
Known for
its book on
drugs, PDR
offers online
consumers
a variety
of drug
information.

You have to register to use this site. After you've registered and logged into the site, click the Drug Information link, which is the first link under Resources on the left. The Patient Education: PDR Family Guides Search page appears. On this page, PDR offers you three free sources of medical information. You can select one, two, or all three of the following: *PDR Family Guide to Prescription Drugs, PDR Family Guide to Women's Health,* and *PDR Family Guide Encyclopedia of Medical Care.* You must pay a subscription fee to gain access to the actual *PDR.*

If you research a medication here, you'll get a profile describing how it works, who should take it, its adverse effects, and so on. The site even has pictures to help you identify medications. The site also features related articles from trade publications from *PDR*'s publisher, Medical Economics.

The PDR site can be your source for the latest medical news from Reuters Health Information news wire. It also provides information, through its Getting Well Network, on seven common diseases: arthritis, allergy, breast cancer, depression, ear infection, hypertension, and osteoporosis. The Getting Well Network describes risk factors, detection, and treatment, offers advice on how to cope, and tests your knowledge about the condition.

Using the health megasites for drug information

Any health megasite worth its Epsom salts has a drug directory. Here are a few health megasites that we like:

- **CBSHealthWatch at** `www.cbshealthwatch.com`**:** Under Resources, click the Drug Directory link. There, you enter the first few letters of a drug's name and get a list of suggested medications. Drug Directory automatically runs a sound-alike feature to help the spelling impaired.

- **InteliHealth at** `www.intelihealth.com`**:** Clicking the Drug Search link from the menu on the left side on this screen brings you to the Drug Resource Center. There, you can use the Drug Index section of the page to get profiles on medicines. In addition, the Drug Resource Center has the latest news and features on medications, including drug updates from the Food and Drug Administration. Toward the bottom of the page, you see the Ask the Pharmacist feature, where you can submit questions about medications and read an archive of earlier responses to questions on particular drugs.

- **The National Library of Medicine's MEDLINE***plus* **at** `www.nlm.nih.gov/medlineplus/druginformation.html`**:** This page, shown in Figure 7-6, is a great one-stop shop. Here, you can get profiles on drugs, links to the latest news on drugs, consumer information from the Federal Drug Administration, and a link to MEDLINE, which allows you to scour the medical journals.

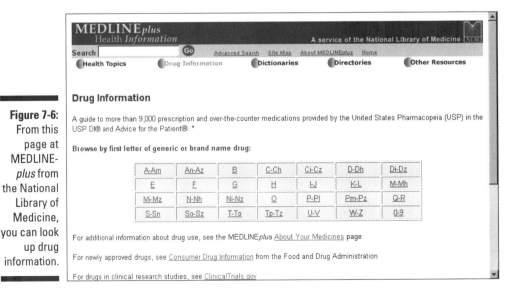

Figure 7-6: From this page at MEDLINE-*plus* from the National Library of Medicine, you can look up drug information.

MEDLINE

If you want to do a comprehensive search on a medicine, you should read what researchers have to say in the medical journals. And you don't have to subscribe to *The New England Journal of Medicine* or *Lancet* to do so. To find out what the doctors read, you can use MED-LINE, a free service offered by the National Library of Medicine. You can go directly to MED-LINE by clicking the <u>MEDLINE</u> link at Internet Grateful Med at igm.nlm.nih.gov.

MEDLINE combs the journals to find *abstracts,* or summaries, of relevant medical articles. You search based on keywords, the author's name, or the title of the article. You'll probably have to consult one of those handy online medical dictionaries to understand what's going on in an abstract.

If you want to know more than what's in the summary, you can head down to your nearest medical school library with abstract in hand to get a full-text version. Even better, save the gas and time and order a copy for a fee from a medical library through the Loansome Doc service at the National Library of Medicine. You can find details on this service at www.nlm.nih.gov/pubs/factsheets/loansome_doc.html.

Drug Trials without Tribulations

If you're not responding to standard drugs, you may need to go out on the cutting edge and try an experimental medicine in a clinical trial. A *clinical trial* is a research study designed to determine whether new drugs or treatments are both safe and effective. These studies are set up to reveal whether the drugs or other therapies work better than traditional treatment, no treatment, or treatment with inactive medications, known as *sugar pills* or *placebos*.

If you join a study, you could be among the first to get a crack at promising new therapies. But you should also be aware that if you get into a study, you might be among those who get placebos.

Ferreting out clinical trials used to be tedious and hard. But the Internet has made it as easy as pointing and clicking your mouse.

ClinicalTrials.gov

The U.S. National Institutes of Health, through its National Library of Medicine, has developed ClinicalTrials.gov (www.clinicaltrials.gov), which provides current information about clinical studies.

If you scroll down the site's main page (shown in Figure 7-7), you find the Resource Information section. There, if you click the <u>Understanding Clinical Trials</u> link, you can get a primer on how clinical trials work.

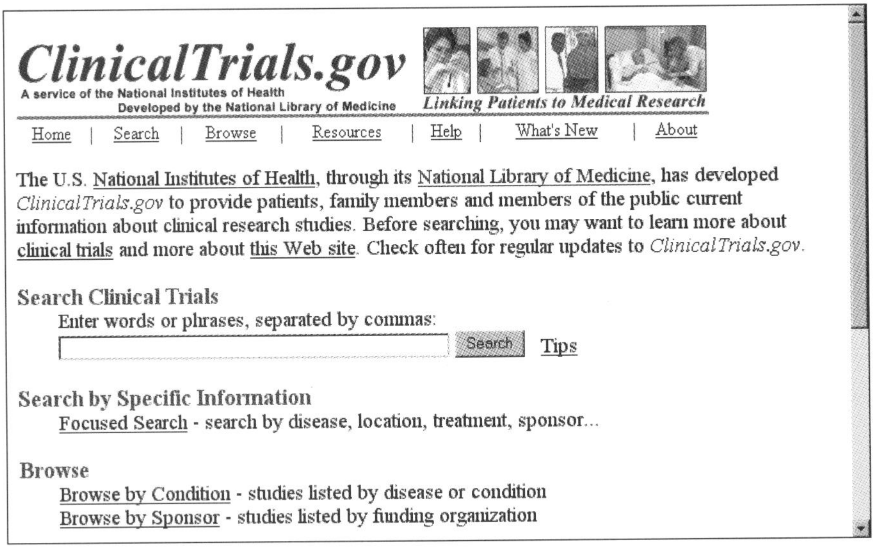

Figure 7-7: ClinicalTrials. gov makes getting the scoop on government-sponsored studies on new drugs easy.

ClinicalTrials.gov
A service of the National Institutes of Health
Developed by the National Library of Medicine
Linking Patients to Medical Research

<u>Home</u> | <u>Search</u> | <u>Browse</u> | <u>Resources</u> | <u>Help</u> | <u>What's New</u> | <u>About</u>

The U.S. <u>National Institutes of Health</u>, through its <u>National Library of Medicine</u>, has developed *ClinicalTrials.gov* to provide patients, family members and members of the public current information about clinical research studies. Before searching, you may want to learn more about <u>clinical trials</u> and more about <u>this Web site</u>. Check often for regular updates to *ClinicalTrials.gov*.

Search Clinical Trials
Enter words or phrases, separated by commas:

[Search] <u>Tips</u>

Search by Specific Information
<u>Focused Search</u> - search by disease, location, treatment, sponsor...

Browse
<u>Browse by Condition</u> - studies listed by disease or condition
<u>Browse by Sponsor</u> - studies listed by funding organization

ClinicalTrials.gov offers several ways to search for studies. It emphasizes studies sponsored by the federal government. You can browse by condition or by sponsor, such as the National Institutes of Health, other federal agencies, pharmaceutical companies, and universities. You'll probably find that the most useful way to check out clinical trials is under the Search by Specific Information heading. Here's how you do that type of search:

1. **Open your Web browser and go to the ClinicalTrials.gov site at** `www.clinicaltrials.gov`.

   You see the ClinicalTrials.gov opening page (refer to Figure 7-7).

2. **Click the <u>Focused Search</u> link in the Go to Search by Specific Information section.**

   You see the Focused Search form.

3. **Fill in only the boxes necessary for your search. Enter words or phrases separated by commas in any of the search boxes.**

   If you want to know more about what to put in a box, click the label to the left of the box for further explanation.

In our example, we searched for studies on _lupus,_ an immune system disorder, for people of all ages in Los Angeles.

4. **Click the Search button.**

In our example, the results page listed three studies, shown in Figure 7-8.

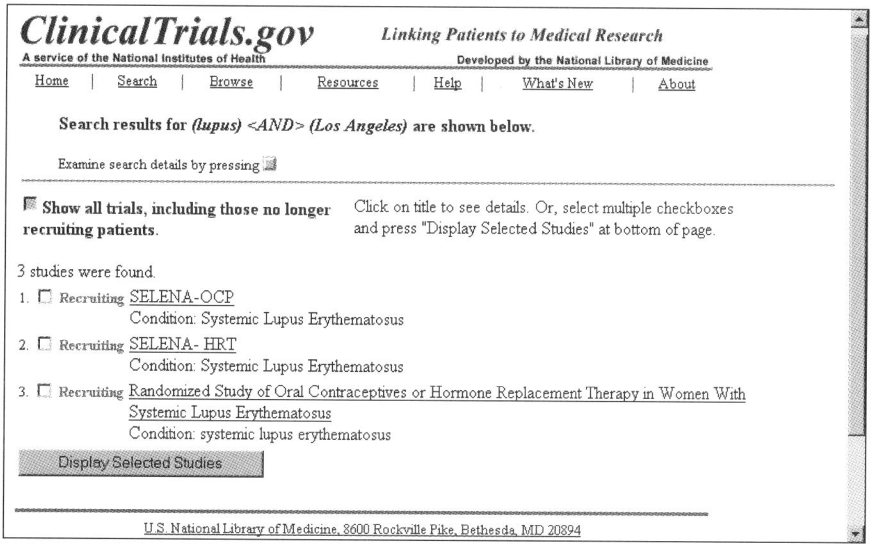

Figure 7-8: This page shows the results of a ClinicalTrials. gov search.

> **_ClinicalTrials.gov_**   _Linking Patients to Medical Research_
> A service of the National Institutes of Health   Developed by the National Library of Medicine
>
> Home | Search | Browse | Resources | Help | What's New | About
>
> Search results for _(lupus)_ _<AND>_ _(Los Angeles)_ are shown below.
>
> Examine search details by pressing
>
> ☑ **Show all trials, including those no longer recruiting patients.**   Click on title to see details. Or, select multiple checkboxes and press "Display Selected Studies" at bottom of page.
>
> 3 studies were found.
> 1. ☐ Recruiting SELENA-OCP
>   Condition: Systemic Lupus Erythematosus
> 2. ☐ Recruiting SELENA- HRT
>   Condition: Systemic Lupus Erythematosus
> 3. ☐ Recruiting Randomized Study of Oral Contraceptives or Hormone Replacement Therapy in Women With Systemic Lupus Erythematosus
>   Condition: systemic lupus erythematosus
>
> Display Selected Studies
>
> U.S. National Library of Medicine, 8600 Rockville Pike, Bethesda, MD 20894

5. **Click a study title to see its description.**

You see a detailed description of the study, including what is being studied, who is eligible, and contact information for the researcher (including address, phone number, and possibly an e-mail address).

Because the information on researchers is included with the results of a search, searching for a trial for a condition you're interested in is a good way to find many of the leading experts in the field.

You can print out the information and discuss it with your personal doctor or contact the study leader directly yourself.

Clinical trials, phase II

ClinicalTrials.gov is a rich source on research studies, but it isn't the only one. You can find trials by using other Web sites, such as the following:

✔ The National Cancer Institute's PDQ, at `cancernet.nci.nih.gov/ trialsrch.shtml`, has a huge listing on cancer studies.

✔ The federal government's AIDS Clinical Trials Information Service, at `www.actis.org/index.html`, helps locate studies to help people with HIV/AIDS.

✔ CenterWatch.com (`www.centerwatch.com`), shown in Figure 7-9, is the best way to get in touch with studies sponsored by the drug industry, which outspends the government nearly eightfold on research. This site lists studies by medical areas under Trial Listings.

You also can sign up at `www.centerwatch.com/patient/patemail. html` to be notified by e-mail when new studies are listed for a condition that you want to follow. You also can run a search at `www.centerwatch. com/patient/cwpipeline/default.asp` for the most promising experimental drugs that are moving close to approval.

Figure 7-9: You can search for drug-industry-sponsored research at Center-Watch.com.

Calling In the Feds

When a crime has been committed, you call the cops — maybe even the Federal B.I. When it comes to dangerous drugs, who you gonna call? The U.S. Food and Drug Administration (FDA). The FDA is available around the clock online at `www.fda.gov` and is ready, willing, and able to serve up a wealth of information.

Go to the FDA's site, shown in Figure 7-10, to find out about the latest drugs that the FDA has approved and which ones the FDA has recalled. The FDA giveth, and the FDA taketh away.

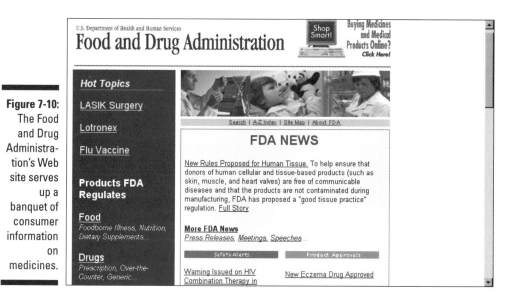

Figure 7-10:
The Food and Drug Administration's Web site serves up a banquet of consumer information on medicines.

The FDA site has loads of information on the products that it regulates, including prescription and nonprescription medications, dietary supplements, foods, medical devices, and cosmetics. It also has information on mammography, breast implants, cancer medications, and AIDS/HIV medications.

You can contact the FDA online for a variety of other reasons, too:

- ✔ **To report a bad reaction to a drug:** File a report at MedWatch at `www.accessdata.fda.gov/scripts/medwatch`.

- ✔ **To report suspected illegal sale of medicines at Web sites:** Fill in the online form at `www.fda.gov/oc/buyonline/buyonlineform.htm`.

- ✔ **To report e-mail messages promoting medical products that you think might be illegal:** Forward the e-mail messages to `webcomplaints@ora.fda.gov`.

If you're having an emergency that requires immediate action, such as a case of food-borne illness or a drug product that has been tampered with, call the FDA's main emergency number: 301-443-1240. It's staffed 24 hours a day.

Buying Medicine Online

Maybe you've heard of those innocent bygone days when Doc would call your prescription in to Pops, the pharmacist. When it was filled, Pops would send little Billy over on his shiny Schwinn with your medicine. If you had any questions, you'd call up Pops.

Well, those days are back again thanks to Internet pharmacies. Doc still can ring up PopsDrugs.com (not a real site) to call in your prescription (or perhaps fax it in). Lil' Billy is all grown up now. He'll deliver your prescription in his UPS or FedEx truck. And what if you have some questions for Pops about your medicine? Just give one of his pharmacists a jingle at a toll-free phone number.

Online pharmacies offer you the convenience of shopping at home at all hours in your jammies. Not only do they dispense your medicine, but their virtual shelves are brimming with a wide variety of stuff.

The jury is still out on whether you can save money by buying medicine online. However, with dozens of pharmacies only a click away, you can easily compare prices — just be sure that you're not comparing apples and oranges (or 60 milligrams of this with 30 milligrams of that).

A good online drugstore is open 24 hours a day and has a pharmacist available at all times to answer your questions about medications by phone. And typically, you can expect next-day delivery of prescriptions. Some pharmacies even promise same-day service. You can almost hear the bicycle bell ringing.

What you can find at an Internet pharmacy

Clicking your way through an Internet pharmacy is much like roaming up and down the aisles of your neighborhood megadrugstore. Head over to the likes of, DrugEmporium.com, or Rx.com, and you'll find tens of thousands of items for sale. In addition to prescription medications, you can select such items as the following:

- Nonprescription drugs for colds, headaches, and sinus problems
- Vitamins
- Herbal preparations, such as St. John's wort, valerian, and Echinacea

- Medical supplies, such as lancets and syringes for people with diabetes as well as bandages and first-aid kits
- Contact lenses and eye care products
- Home medical test kits for pregnancy and colon cancer
- Disposable diapers and baby oil
- Beauty products, such as blushes, hair colorings, and makeup mirrors
- Appliances, such as vaporizers
- Sports energy bars, diet products, and dietetic cookies
- Pet care products

You can search for an Internet pharmacy that meets your needs based on geography and specific services or products, such as same-day delivery, vitamins, and cosmetics. Fill in your specifics at www.nabp.net/vipps/consumer/search.asp.

Brick-and-mortar drugstores have displays of health pamphlets on diabetes, heart disease, and the like near the drug counter. Online pharmacies not only have electronic pamphlets on common diseases, but also provide articles on health issues and lots of links to useful health-related sites.

Online drugstores (such as DrugEmporium.com, shown in Figure 7-11) may have links to medical dictionaries, quizzes to test your knowledge of medical conditions, calculators to figure out your best weight or your target heart rate for exercise, and information on handling medical emergencies. You may even be able to sign up for e-mail reminders to refill your prescriptions.

You can comparison-shop for medications or sundries from online pharmacies at DestinationRx at destinationrx.com. The *Healthcare Online For Dummies Internet Directory* has information on obtaining medications at reduced prices or even for free, depending on need.

Avoiding risks at online pharmacies

The only prescriptions you should have filled online are those from a physician who has examined you in person initially or who truly knows your medical history. Some people have encountered otherwise-avoidable complications caused by medicines prescribed by online doctors who never saw them face to face, asked only a few questions in a chat room or in an e-mail message, and then wrote a prescription for a drug. Virtual prescribing doesn't cut it, nor does ordering medicine from a Web site from another country — a Web site that could be sending you a drug that doesn't meet U.S. safety standards.

Figure 7-11:
You can get pre-scriptions filled, buy medical supplies, and get drug information at online drugstores, such as Drug-Emporium.com.

With the right precautions, Internet pharmacies can help you get the pre-scriptions you need to get, or stay, well. A good way to check everything at an Internet pharmacy is to look for and click the VIPPS seal from the National Association of Boards of Pharmacy. *VIPPS* is short for Verified Internet Pharmacy Practice Sites. To protect the public, the association developed a system to certify online pharmacies that meet certain standards, such as complying with the licensing and inspection requirements in each state in which they dispense medicine.

VIPPS-approved Internet pharmacies also meet standards on protecting patient privacy, providing safe online transactions, having quality-assurance policies, and providing meaningful consultation between patients and pharmacists.

To see a list of pharmacies with VIPPS certification, go to www.nabp.net/vipps/consumer/listall.asp (see Figure 7-12). Click the Detail icon next to the pharmacy's name to see a profile with contact information, including the Web site for the pharmacy. And if you click the Click for Details icon on a pharmacy's profile page, you'll see the state where the pharmacy is licensed and a full list of services that the pharmacy provides.

You may see the TRUSTe seal at some Internet pharmacies. This seal means that the pharmacy agrees to tell you what personal information is being gath-ered about you and what it will do with that information. You can read more about this program at www.truste.com.

Figure 7-12:
At the
National
Association
of Boards of
Pharmacy
Web site,
you can
view a list
of Internet
pharmacies
that meet
consumer-
protection
standards.

If you are suspicious about an Internet pharmacy, you can bring your suspicions to the attention of the National Association of Boards of Pharmacy at its online complaint site at www.nabp.net/vipps/consumer/report.asp. The board will notify the appropriate state board of pharmacy or medicine, or a federal agency.

Chapter 8

Researching Alternative Medicine

* *

In This Chapter

▶ Discovering alternative medicine

▶ Finding alternative practitioners

▶ Finding studies on alternatives

* *

C all it *alternative* medicine. Call it *complementary* medicine. Call it *integrative* medicine. Call it *holistic* medicine.

Whatever you call it, and there are some differences in their meanings, chances are that you've had some first-hand experience with this increasingly popular brand of healthcare. Perhaps you've tried or are interested in acupuncture, chiropractic, herbs, homeopathy, massage, or naturopathic medicine.

This chapter explores the Web's resources on alternative health, including where to find out about the practices, how to find practitioners, and how to protect yourself from unsafe treatments.

Consider the Alternatives

Maybe you feel that conventional medicine isn't helping you. Or you feel that you'd like a more hands-on approach to your care, where the practitioner spends more time with you. Or you are tired of the pill-for-every-ill approach and worried about side effects from medications. Or you're curious about a treatment you heard about from a friend or on TV.

Whatever your reason, you can find out a lot about alternative care online. Just for the record, we're using the term *alternative medicine* broadly to include therapies intended to be *alternatives* to mainstream medicine as well as those intended to *complement* or to *integrate* with mainstream medicine.

The rise of alternative medicine

Although alternative medical practices often have found themselves as underdogs and disrespected in the medical world, they have been steadily gaining in popularity. Many people are tired of modern medicine's sometimes toxic and expensive drugs and rushed care. They've been turning in droves to alternative medicine.

Consider these findings from some surveys on alternative medicine:

✔ One-third to one-half of Americans use alternative medicine, though typically they don't share that information with their personal physicians.

✔ Nearly two-thirds of mainstream American medical schools offer classes on complementary medicine.

✔ The most common conditions for which alternative care is used are back pain, allergies, arthritis, insomnia, sprains or strains, headache, high blood pressure, digestive problems, anxiety, and depression.

✔ The most popular forms of alternative practices are chiropractic, massage, use of herbal medicines or megavitamins, meditation, homeopathy, naturopathy, and acupuncture.

If you want to read more, go to the Milbank Memorial Fund to read its report, "Enhancing the Accountability of Alternative Medicine," at `www.milbank.org/mraltmed.html`.

We're not advocating using any particular approach, and so many of them are available that we can't cover them all here. Look in the *Healthcare Online For Dummies Internet Directory* for links to additional alternative medicine sites.

Yahoo! Health

The best place to start your journey of alternative healing is Yahoo! Health (`health.yahoo.com`), as shown in Figure 8-1. On the site's main page, you can click the <u>Alternative Medicine</u> link (under Health Resources) for straight-shooting, commonsensical articles on alternative practices from acupuncture to yoga.

Yahoo! Health answers the following questions — all but the last of which should be asked of mainstream care as well — for alternative therapies:

✔ What conditions it is used for?

✔ How does the treatment work?

✔ What does the treatment hope to accomplish?

✔ Who should avoid this therapy?

✔ What side effects may occur?

✔ When should you stop the therapy?

✔ When should you see a conventional doctor?

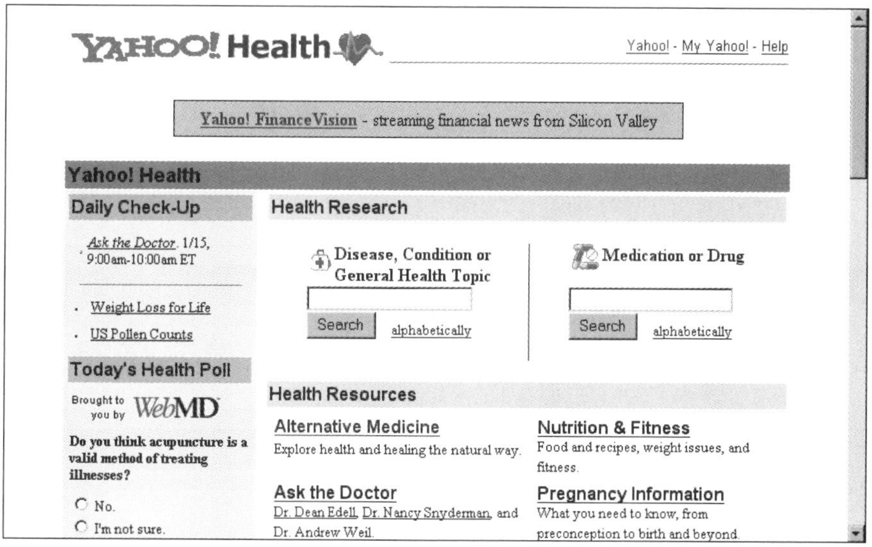

Figure 8-1:
Yahoo!
Health is
your portal
to informa-
tion on
alternative
health.

Yahoo! Health also lists links and contacts to organizations and books and magazines on the topic. Way to go, Yahoo!!

Other alternatives

HealingPeople.com (www.healingpeople.com), shown in Figure 8-2, focuses on Chinese medicine, homeopathy, aromatherapy, bodywork, Ayurveda, and western herbalism. It has the comprehensive *Natural Health Encyclopedia* (www.healingpeople.com/hp_html/primapub/encyclopedia.htm), which consists of the following parts:

✔ **Herbs and Supplements:** The latest scientific research on natural remedies and their uses

✔ **Conditions:** Information on natural remedies for conditions from acne to yeast infections, including references to scientific studies

✔ **Drug Interactions:** Listings of the interactions between medications and natural substances

Figure 8-2:
Healing People.com is a source on alternative practices, including Chinese medicine, homeopathy, and bodywork.

You can also go to the source for these tools at The Natural Pharmacist Web site at www.tnp.com.

The Alternative Medicine Homepage (www.pitt.edu/~cbw/altm.html), shown in Figure 8-3, is a thorough, well-organized list of links to Web sites on unconventional therapies. This site also links to directories of practitioners of Chinese medicine, homeopathy, chiropractic, and massage therapy.

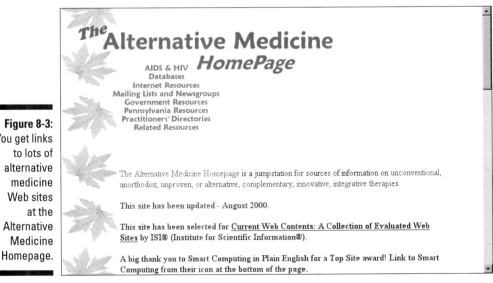

Figure 8-3:
You get links to lots of alternative medicine Web sites at the Alternative Medicine Homepage.

Some other good places with lists of Web sites on alternative medicine are the following:

- ✔ Alternative Health News Online at www.altmedicine.com
- ✔ Internet Public Library at www.ipl.org/ref/RR/static/hea04.00.00.html
- ✔ Librarians' Index to the Internet at www.lii.org/search/file/health
- ✔ NOAH (New York Online Access to Health) at www.noah-health.org/english/alternative/alternative.html

Unortho-Docs Online

Here's the short history of medicine found all over the Internet:

- ✔ 2000 B.C. — Here, eat this root.
- ✔ A.D. 1000 — That root is heathen, say this prayer.
- ✔ A.D. 1850 — That prayer is superstition, drink this potion.
- ✔ A.D. 1940 — That potion is snake oil, swallow this pill.
- ✔ A.D. 1965 — That pill is ineffective, take this antibiotic.
- ✔ A.D. 2001 — That antibiotic is artificial. Here, eat this root.

(If you want to see a rockin' version with animations, go to NonHealth.com at www.nonhealth.com/history.)

Whether your thing is roots and herbs or hands-on treatments, you can find out more about them on the Web.

Chiropractic

Chiropractic is the most popular type of alternative medicine and one of the fastest growing. This technique uses spinal manipulation, known as *an adjustment,* to restore normal function. Chiropractic sometimes is combined with nutritional and other nondrug approaches to treat backaches, headaches, and other problems.

You can find out about chiropractic and get information on where to find a chiropractor at the Web sites for the American Chiropractic Association at www.amerchiro.org and for the International Chiropractic Association at www.chiropractic.org.

Chiropractors are licensed by the states. You can verify the licenses of chiropractic physicians through state licensing boards. A listing of the boards and contact information, including Web sites and e-mail addresses, appears at the Federation of Chiropractic Licensing Board's Web site at `www.fclb.org/directory/index.htm`. Click the <u>United States</u> link in the left-hand column to see a listing of links for the individual state boards.

Searchpoint*e* (`www.searchpointe.com`) enables you to check a chiropractor's credentials for free. To do so, click the Chiropractor Search button on the site's main page. This brings you to the Chiropractor Search welcome page, where you click the Find a Chiropractor button. On the next page, enter the provider's information and then click the Search Now button to see the results of your search.

For a $9.95 fee, Searchpoint*e* will prepare a report on disciplinary actions against a chiropractor, such as for insurance fraud and other criminal charges. A similar service is available for medical doctors (MDs), but not for other practitioners.

Acupuncture

Western mainstream medicine has called acupuncture an experimental treatment. But this increasingly popular therapy, along with other Chinese techniques, has been around for thousands of years.

Many medical doctors, chiropractors, dentists, and even veterinarians are now using acupuncture. They insert hair-thin needles into certain spots in an effort to balance energy flows in the body. Acupuncture is used to treat a variety of ailments, including back pain, headaches, allergies, and chronic pain.

You can find out about acupuncture and also find a practitioner at Acupuncture.com (`www.acupuncture.com`), as shown in Figure 8-4. You can find medical doctors trained in acupuncture through the American Academy of Medical Acupuncture at `www.medicalacupuncture.org`. You can also check with the American Association of Oriental Medicine at `www.aaom.org`.

 About three dozen states regulate acupuncturists through state medical boards, boards of Oriental medicine, or other agencies. To check on the laws in your state, go to Acupuncture.com's United States Acupuncture Laws by State at `www.acupuncture.com/StateLaws/StateLaws.htm`.

Figure 8-4:
Acupuncture.com has information on how acupuncture is used and how you can find practitioners.

Naturopathy

As the name suggests, naturopathic doctors (NDs) take a natural approach to healing, employing diet and vitamins, herbal remedies, exercise, homeopathy, massage, spinal and soft tissue manipulation, hydrotherapy, light therapy, acupuncture, and other techniques. To find out more about the practice and to find a practitioner, go to the National Association of Naturopathic Physicians at www.naturopathic.org.

Three colleges offer degree programs in naturopathic medicine, and about a dozen states license the practice. For information on how to contact the state licensing agencies, go to www.allianceworkbook.com/laws/laws1.htm. You can find out the status of an ND's license through a state agency.

Homeopathy

Homeopathic medicine uses highly diluted solutions of herbs, animal products, and chemicals to treat diseases. Homeopathic treatments may include arsenic and snake venom, but in minuscule doses. This practice was once hugely popular in the United States, until it was pushed aside by today's mainstream medicine. It's still big with Britain's royal family.

Finding an alternative practitioner

Practitioners of alternative medicine come with a wide variety of credentials. You should choose them as carefully as you would choose your mainstream physician.

Many states license practitioners who provide alternative therapies, such as acupuncture, chiropractic services, naturopathy, herbal medicine, homeopathy, and massage therapy. State licensing agencies may be able to provide information about a specific practitioner's credentials and background.

You may also locate practitioners by asking your healthcare provider or by contacting a professional association or organization. These organizations can provide names of local practitioners and provide information about how to determine the quality of a specific practitioner's services.

The National Center for Complementary and Alternative Medicine offers an online pamphlet, "Considering Complementary and Alternative Therapies" (nccam.nih.gov/nccam/fcp/faq/considercam.html), which lists questions to consider when choosing an alternative healthcare practitioner.

The agency urges you to:

✔ Speak with people who have undergone the treatment, preferably both those who were treated recently and those treated in the past. Find people with the same health condition that you have and who have received the treatment.

✔ Remember that patient testimonials used alone do not adequately assess the safety and effectiveness of an alternative therapy, and should not be the exclusive criterion for selecting a therapy. Controlled scientific trials usually provide the best information about a therapy's effectiveness and should be sought whenever possible.

✔ Examine the practitioner's expertise. You may want to take a close look into the background, qualifications, and competence of any potential practitioner, whether a physician or a practitioner of alternative and complementary healthcare.

✔ Visit the practitioner's office, clinic or hospital. Ask the practitioner how many patients he or she typically sees in a day or week, and how much time the practitioner spends with the patient. Look at the conditions of the office or clinic.

✔ Consider the costs. Costs are an important factor to consider, as many complementary and alternative treatments are not currently reimbursed by health insurance. Many patients pay directly for these services. Ask your practitioner and your health insurer which treatments or therapies are reimbursable.

✔ Consult your health provider. Most importantly, discuss all issues concerning treatments and therapies with your healthcare provider whether a physician or practitioner of complementary and alternative medicine. Competent healthcare management requires knowledge of both conventional and alternative therapies for the practitioner to have a complete picture of your treatment plan.

Medical doctors, osteopathic physicians, chiropractors, and naturopathic physicians may use homeopathic approaches. And these days, your neighborhood drugstore or health food store is likely to sell homeopathic remedies for allergies, headaches, indigestion, colds, flu, and so on. For background on homeopathy and to find a practitioner, go to the National Center for Homeopathy at `www.homeopathic.org`.

Massage therapy

Massage therapy is one of the more popular alternative techniques. It helps with muscle pain, back pain, headaches, as well as other ailments. Massage therapy aims to get the blood moving and the muscles relaxed. It's a great stress reliever.

You can find out more about massage therapy through the American Massage Therapy Association at `www.amtamassage.org`. Look in the ATMA Online Massage Room (which you can access by clicking the <u>Massage Room</u> link) to find a therapist. Also, take a break there with some relaxing pictures and music. Ah, we feel better already.

Massage therapists undergo special training for certification. About 30 states license practitioners. To find out which states regulate massage therapists, go to Massage Practice Laws Information Guide at `www.amtamassage.org/about/lawstateguide.htm`. You can contact a state agency to find out the status of a therapist's license.

Herbal medicine

Herbal medicine has one of the longest traditions the world over. Herbal practitioners come in a lot of varieties, such as naturopathic physicians and Chinese medicine practitioners. You can get some leads for finding herbal practitioners by looking at the Web sites listed in the "Chiropractic," "Acupuncture," "Naturopathy," and "Homeopathy" sections, earlier in this chapter. You can find out more about herbalists at the American Herbalists Guild's Web site at `www.healthy.net/herbalists`.

Here are a few additional sites that offer information on herbal medicine:

 ✔ **Ask Dr. Weil** (`www.drweil.com`): Dr. Andrew Weil, a leading proponent of integrative medicine, offers tips on using herbs — based on the seasons — at his Web site. To take a peek inside Dr. Weil's Herbal Medicine Chest, click the <u>Herbal Medicine Chest</u> link under the Self-Help heading on the left side of the home page.

 The Herbal Medicine Chest page, shown in Figure 8-5, identifies the herbs that Dr. Weil recommends for a particular season, such as summer. You can click any bottle in the medicine chest for in-depth information about the herb. Links to other seasonal medicine chests are available under Related Links on the right-hand side of the Herbal Medicine Chest page.

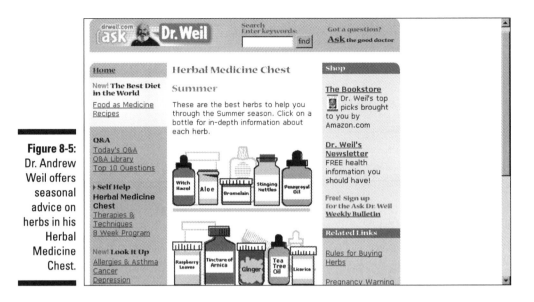

Figure 8-5: Dr. Andrew Weil offers seasonal advice on herbs in his Herbal Medicine Chest.

✔ **The Alternative Medicine Foundation's HerbMed** (www.herbmed.org): This site, shown in Figure 8-6, presents scientific evidence on the therapeutic benefits and adverse effects of herbs as well as other information on herbs.

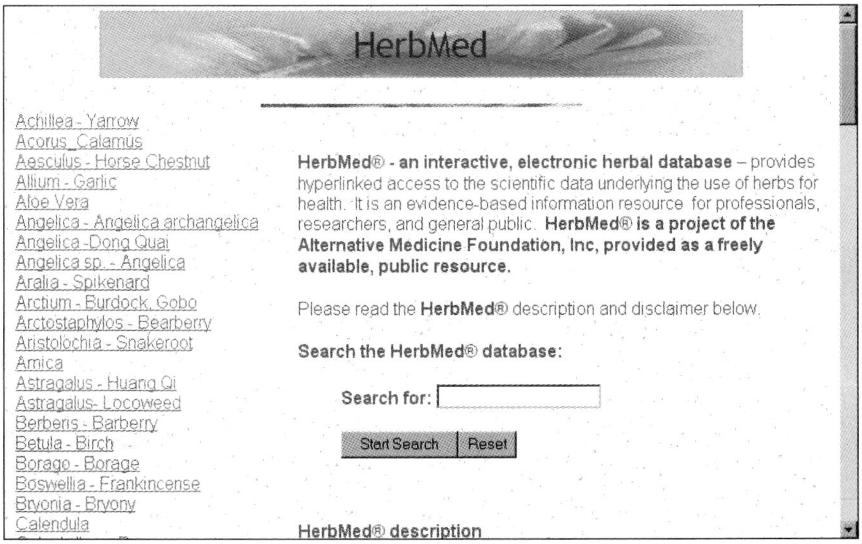

Figure 8-6: You can find out about commonly used medicinal herbs at HerbMed.

✔ **The University of Washington Medicinal Garden** (`www.nnlm.nlm.nih.gov/pnr/uwmhg/index.html`): This site provides listings of herbs by common and botanical names, images and information on what is known about the plants, and links to the U.S. Department of Agriculture's Ethnobotany and Medicinal Plants of North America online databases.

✔ **Botanical.com** (`www.botanical.com`): This site contains a hypertext version of *A Modern Herbal,* originally published in 1931.

Uncle Sam and Alternative Health

Even Uncle Sam is getting in on the act. The National Institutes of Health, the federal government's premier research organization, has established the National Center for Complementary and Alternative Medicine. NCCAM (`nccam.nih.gov`), shown in Figure 8-7, is exploring complementary and alternative health by using the scientific method, something sorely lacking in the past.

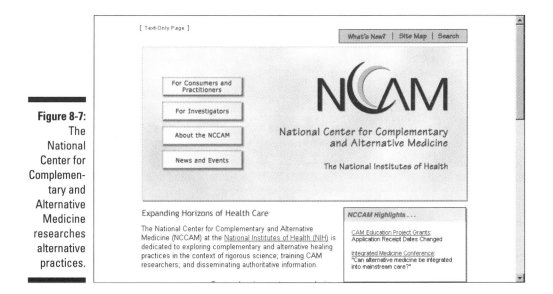

Figure 8-7: The National Center for Complementary and Alternative Medicine researches alternative practices.

On the site's main page, click the For Consumers and Practitioners button to go to the For Consumers and Practitioners page. From here, you may want to check out these links:

✔ **Fact Sheets:** Fact sheets on acupuncture, hepatitis C, and St. John's wort

✔ **Complementary & Alternative Medicine Databases (CAM):** Direct links to search for information in the scientific literature on alternative medicine topics

✔ **Clinical Trials:** Studies on alternative medicine

The National Center for Complementary and Alternative Medicine isn't the only federal agency looking into alternatives. The National Cancer Institute, NCCAM's sister agency, has its own Office of Cancer Complementary and Alternative Medicine (OCCAM) at occam.nci.nih.gov, as shown in Figure 8-8.

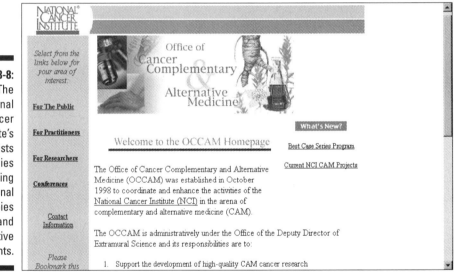

Figure 8-8: The National Cancer Institute's OCCAM lists studies comparing conventional therapies and alternative treatments.

Click the For The Public link to find a listing of some studies using alternative therapies to treat cancer, such as a comparison of treatment with shark cartilage versus combined chemotherapy and radiation therapy for lung cancer. Toward the middle of the page, click the CAM Cancer Physician Data Query (PDQ) Summaries link to see summaries of the research on treating cancer with coenzyme Q10; 714-X; Laetrile; and mistletoe. We'll kiss off with that last one.

A skeptical eye on alternative medicine

Checks and balances are healthy things. They create a tension that ultimately should lead to the truth — that's the goal anyway. Throughout medicine, mainstream or alternative, there is controversy and heresy. It's said that for every M.D., there is an equal and opposite M.D.

You'll find that the critics of alternative medicine have a lot to say. And it's always worthwhile to get a second opinion when you can. Here are some sites that cast a skeptical eye on alternative medicine:

✔ **THE ENTIRELY ON-LINE ALT MED PRIMER at www.seanet.com/~vettf/Primer.htm:** This site has links to articles that look critically at acupuncture and traditional Chinese medicine, aromatherapy and Bach flower remedies, homeopathy, herbal medicine, and energy field medicine.

✔ **Healthcare Reality Check at www.hcrc.org:** Click the Encyclopedia link on the left side of the home page to see The HCRC Encyclopedia, with critical articles ranging from AIDS quackery to the Zone diet. If the spirit moves you, click the Dictionary link on the left-hand side of the HCRC Encyclopedia page or the home page to see *The Expanded Dictionary of Metaphysical Healthcare,* which describes over 1,200 health-care methods with a mystical bent, ranging from Ayurveda to Zulu Sangoma bones.

While on the skeptic's tour, stop by Dr. Stephen Barrett's Quackwatch Web site (www. quackwatch.com). The Quackwatch Web site has advice on how to avoid being quacked. Barrett also takes on chiropractic at his Chirobase site (www.chirobase.com). Barrett has made a career of warning people about health fraud and taking on those he considers to be flimflam artists. Though some of his critics think that he goes overboard, you should decide for yourself.

Part IV
Using the Web to Research Major Illnesses

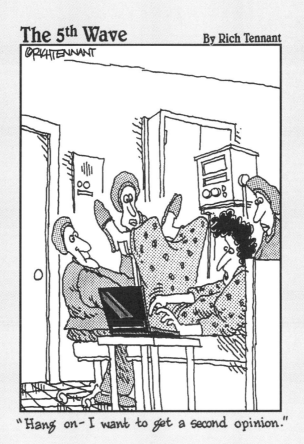

The 5th Wave   By Rich Tennant

"Hang on — I want to get a second opinion."

In this part . . .

*I*n this part, we do the work for you. We show you where to research major health concerns, how to find online and offline support groups, how to find research studies, and how to locate medical journal articles. The major health concerns covered in this part include heart disease and stroke (Chapter 9); cancer (Chapter 10); diabetes (Chapter 11); arthritis (Chapter 12); and HIV/AIDS, hepatitis, and other infectious diseases (Chapter 13).

Chapter 9

Heart Disease and Stroke

. . . .

In This Chapter

▶ Getting the big picture on heart disease and stroke

▶ Finding medical specialists who specialize in cardiac or stroke care

▶ Getting support

▶ Locating clinical trials

. . . .

*H*eart disease and stroke are major health threats. Respectively, they're the first- and third-largest killers of Americans. According to the Centers for Disease Control and Prevention, more than 59 million Americans have some form of cardiovascular disease, including high blood pressure, coronary heart disease, stroke, or congestive heart failure.

This chapter, in effect, is two chapters for the price of one. It has sections on both heart disease and stroke. You find the best online sources for information about these conditions plus information on how they're diagnosed and treated, how to determine if you're at risk and what you can do about it, and where you can find support. In some cases, the resources apply to both heart disease and stroke. In others, they're specific for one condition or the other. We let you know which is which as we go along.

You've got a lot of clicking ahead. So warm up your index finger, grab your mouse, and get ready to click.

The Big Picture on Heart Disease

Many of the medical megasites have excellent resources on heart disease. Here are a few that you may want to check out:

- ✔ **MayoClinic.com** (`www.mayoclinic.com`) has a Heart and Blood Vessels Center with information on the circulatory system, including diseases and conditions, and steps that you can take to keep your heart healthy. To go to the Heart and Blood Vessels Center, select it from the drop-down text box under Condition Centers on the opening page.

- ✔ **WebMD Health** has a heart disease section at `my.webmd.com/condition_center/cvd`. Look for the Related Links area where links take you within the site to Overview, Treatment, Complementary Therapies, Diagnosis, and Self Care. You can also follow links to an illustrated guide to heart disease, to information for the newly diagnosed, and to an article on a heart-healthy diet. Scroll down the page to find a link to articles from *The Yale University School of Medicine Patient's Guide to Medical Tests* that describe tests used in diagnosing heart disease and a link to support through message boards.

Many other sites on the Web have information on heart disease. The next two sections introduce you to a few we recommend, starting with those that give you the big picture.

American Heart Association

The Web site of the American Heart Association (`www.americanheart.org`) is an excellent place to begin researching heart disease. It's also home to the American Stroke Association, a division of AHA.

Among the features you can find at this Web site are the following:

- ✔ **Heart and Stroke A–Z Guide:** This gives you easy access to information on a number of related topics, including congestive heart failure, congenital cardiovascular disease, cardiomyopathy, mitral valve prolapse, cholesterol problems, and hypertension.

- ✔ **Family Health:** This area has links to AHA's heart and stroke patient information, heart-healthy nutrition, cookbooks and recipes, exercise tips, and information on cholesterol, blood pressure, and children and heart disease.

- ✔ **Risk Awareness:** This has an excellent section that explains how the heart works. It also has a thorough discussion of the risk factors for heart disease and suggestions for what you can do about those risks you can do something about, such as weight, smoking, high blood pressure, and cholesterol. This section also has links to the association's easy-to-understand explanations of heart disease, heart attack, and coronary bypass surgery.

Coronary heart disease risks

Treatment for heart disease has come a long way, but the key to prevention is controlling risk factors where you can. According to the National Heart, Lung, and Blood Institute at www.nhlbi.nih.gov/health/public/heart/other/chdfacts.htm, the controllable risk factors for developing heart disease are

✔ High blood pressure

✔ High blood cholesterol

✔ Smoking

✔ Obesity

✔ Physical inactivity

✔ Diabetes

✔ Stress

(Although stress may be a risk factor for coronary heart disease, scientists still do not know exactly how stress might be involved in heart disease.)

You can find out your risk for heart attack and stroke by taking a quiz at the American Heart Association site at www.americanheart.org/risk/quiz.html.

Until recently, heart disease was regarded as a problem exclusive to men. Not so. Heart attack, stroke, and other cardiovascular diseases are devastating to women, too. According to the American Heart Association, coronary heart disease, which causes heart attacks, is the leading cause of death for American women.

To help focus on the situation, the American Heart Association site has a special section called Take Wellness to Heart (women.americanheart.org/wellness/index.html) devoted to women's heart health. In this section, you find basic information on heart disease and stroke, questions to ask your doctor, a women's online forum, and the A Lighter Heart area with practical tips on heart-healthy lifestyle changes you can make.

You can also find a large Self-Care section for women at women.americanheart.org/self_care/index.html. With a drop-down text box at the bottom of the page, you can select articles on such topics as contraception, pregnancy, menopause, smoking, physical fitness, nutrition, blood pressure, and diabetes.

While we're on the subject, the National Heart, Lung, and Blood Institute has an online book, *Healthy Heart Handbook for Women,* at www.nhlbi.nih.gov/health/public/heart/other/hhw/hdbk_wmn.pdf. This 105-page book covers such areas as hormone replacement therapy, cholesterol, healthy eating, and heart-smart recipes.

Coronary heart disease symptoms

The National Heart, Lung, and Blood Institute (NHLBI) at www.nhlbi.nih.gov/health/public/heart/other/chdfacts.htm lists the following symptoms of coronary heart disease:

✔ Chest pain (angina) or shortness of breath may be the earliest signs

✔ Heaviness, tightness, pain, burning, pressure, or squeezing, usually behind the breastbone, but sometimes also in the arms, neck, or jaws.

NHLBI says these signs usually bring the patient to a doctor for the first time. Nevertheless, some people have heart attacks without ever having any of these symptoms.

National Heart, Lung, and Blood Institute

The National Heart, Lung, and Blood Institute (NHLBI) is the National Institutes of Health's center that is leading the charge against heart disease. The NHLBI takes you directly to the heart of the matter to matters of the heart at www.nhlbi.nih.gov/health/public/heart/index.htm.

At this site, shown in Figure 9-1, you can find a list of links (arranged by subject) to the Institute's articles on maintaining heart health by lowering your blood pressure, cholesterol, and weight, and by stopping smoking. The Institute also has articles on various heart diseases (such as heart attack, cardiomyopathy, and congestive heart failure) and articles written especially for women, African Americans, and for Spanish-speaking readers.

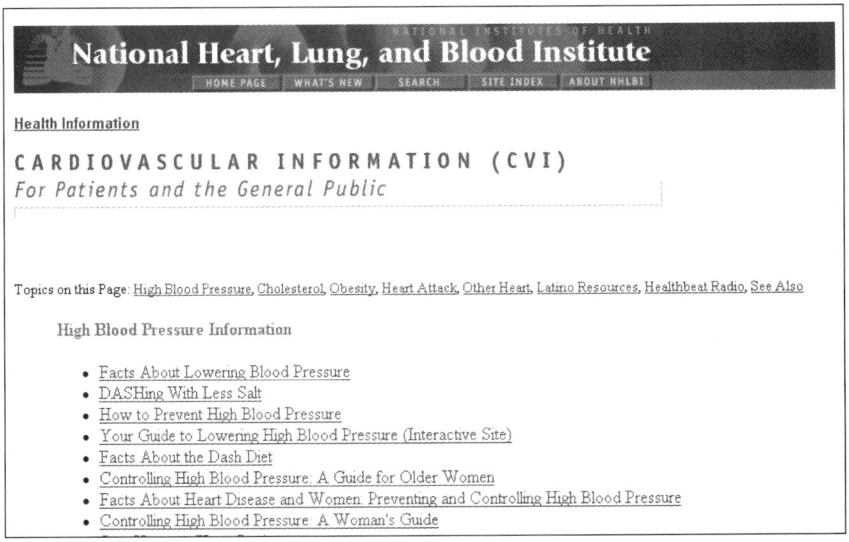

Figure 9-1: The National Heart, Lung, and Blood Institute's Web site covers the basics and more on heart disease.

NATIONAL INSTITUTES OF HEALTH

National Heart, Lung, and Blood Institute

HOME PAGE   WHAT'S NEW   SEARCH   SITE INDEX   ABOUT NHLBI

Health Information

CARDIOVASCULAR INFORMATION (CVI)
For Patients and the General Public

Topics on this Page: High Blood Pressure, Cholesterol, Obesity, Heart Attack, Other Heart, Latino Resources, Healthbeat Radio, See Also

High Blood Pressure Information

- Facts About Lowering Blood Pressure
- DASHing With Less Salt
- How to Prevent High Blood Pressure
- Your Guide to Lowering High Blood Pressure (Interactive Site)
- Facts About the Dash Diet
- Controlling High Blood Pressure: A Guide for Older Women
- Facts About Heart Disease and Women: Preventing and Controlling High Blood Pressure
- Controlling High Blood Pressure: A Woman's Guide

You gotta have heart

We'll never forget that huge heart you could walk through at the Museum of Science and Industry in Chicago. It's been a museum landmark since the 1940s. You got up close and personal with the valves. You could rub elbows with the ventricles. Love that *lub-dub, lub-dub*. Very soothing.

Well, some pretty clever people have created Web sites that you can walk through, virtually anyway, to help you understand what makes the heart tick. Here are a couple of these Web sites that you may want to check out:

✔ **The Heart: An Online Exploration at the Franklin Institute Online at sln2.fi.edu/ biosci/heart.html:** The site offers a multimedia tour of the basics on the heart and heart health and disease, and it also has videos, such as that of a heart bypass operation. On this site, you can listen to a heartbeat and a heart murmur.

✔ **Auscultation Assistant at www.med.ucla. edu/wilkes/inex.htm:** You can listen to the telltale heart sounds that medical students hear through their stethoscopes as they learn to distinguish between a healthy heart and one with problems. By the way, *auscultation* means to listen to sounds arising within organs as an aid to diagnosis and treatment. Go the site for bragging rights at the next cocktail party you go to.

✔ **HeartPoint Gallery at www.heartpoint.com/ gallery.html:** The gallery has more than two dozen multimedia presentations on the heart, including animations on angioplasty, cholesterol formation, and congenital heart disease. It isn't the *Road Runner*, but. . . .

Finally, the Museum of Science and Industry in Chicago shows off its Giant Walk-Through Heart — that's what the museum calls it — at www.msichicago.org/exhibit/heart/ heart.html. The Museum notes that if the heart were real, it would fit into a person 28 stories high. Talk about having a big heart.

Some of the National Heart, Lung, and Blood Institute's links take you directly to the article. Others take you to a page that gives you a variety of choices on how you'd like to read the article. If you'd like to read it online as a regular Web page, click Web HTML Document. If you'd like to read it as a plain text document, click ASCII document. If you'd like to read it online as a brochure, click PDF Document. (If you choose PDF document, you need Adobe Acrobat Reader to read it.)

Here are a couple more Web sites on heart disease that are worth checking out:

✔ **The Heart Information Network** (www.heartinfo.org) has a heart attack guide and a stroke guide, CPR instructions with a printable wallet-size card, heart news, and a chart comparing symptoms of heart attack experienced by men and by women.

✔ **Ask NOAH About: Heart Disease and Stroke** (www.noah-health.org/ english/illness/heart_disease/heartdisease.html) has tons of links to sites covering all aspects of heart disease and stroke.

The Big Picture on Stroke

You can find the big picture on stroke, sometimes called *brain attacks,* at many of the medical megasites, including the following:

✔ **MayoClinic.com** (www.mayoclinic.com) has an excellent stroke section that discusses signs and symptoms, causes, risk factors, when to seek medical advice, screening and diagnosis, treatment, prevention, and coping strategies. To find the stroke information at MayoClinic.com, click the Diseases and Conditions, A–Z link under Find Information on the opening page. Then choose *S* from the alphabetical index and click the Stroke link in the list of choices.

✔ **WebMD Health** has a stroke section at my.webmd.com/condition_center/str with links that take you within the site to Overview, Treatment, Diagnosis, and Self Care and to an illustrated guide to stroke. This site also features links to articles from *The Yale University School of Medicine Patient's Guide to Medical Tests* that describe tests used to diagnose stroke (and to support through message boards).

Many Web sites focus on strokes, but the next three sections describe a few sites that we recommend you start with.

Stroke risks

A stroke is a loss of brain function due to an interruption of blood flow to the brain. The National Institute for Neurological Disorders and Stroke (NINDS) at www.ninds.nih.gov/health_and_medical/pubs/stroke_bookmark.htm says stroke prevention is the best medicine. It lists the following as the most treatable risk factors:

✔ **High blood pressure.** *Treat it.* Eat a balanced diet, maintain a healthy weight, and exercise to reduce blood pressure. Drugs are also available.

✔ **Cigarette smoking.** *Quit.* Medical help is available to help you quit.

✔ **Heart disease.** *Manage it.* Your doctor can treat your heart disease and may prescribe medication to help prevent the formation of clots. If you are over 50, NINDS scientists believe you and your doctor should make a decision about aspirin therapy.

✔ **Diabetes.** *Control it.* Treatment can delay complications that increase the risk of stroke.

✔ **Transient ischemic attacks (TIAs).** *Seek help.* TIAs are small strokes that last only for a few minutes or hours. They should never be ignored and can be treated with drugs or surgery.

American Stroke Association

The American Stroke Association, a division of the American Heart Association (www.strokeassociation.org) is the place to go if you're looking for the big picture on stroke. You can go directly to the site's Consumer section at www.strokeassociation.org/Consumer/consumer.html. On the left-hand side of the page, you see links to stroke-related information on such topics as <u>Prevention & Intervention</u>, <u>Recovery & Support</u>, and <u>Caregiving</u>.

You can find out your risk for stroke by using the American Stroke Association's Stroke Risk Assessment tool at www.strokeassociation.org/Consumer/quiz.html.

The American Stroke Association's Web site also has a Stroke Family Support Network at www.strokeassociation.org/Consumer/support/family.html. This network has contact information for the National Stroke Group Registry, which can help you link up with a stroke support group close to your home.

National Stroke Association

At the National Stroke Association's Web site (www.stroke.org), shown in Figure 9-2, you can find lots of information on stroke, caring for someone who's had a stroke, and links to further information, products, and services for stroke survivors and caregivers.

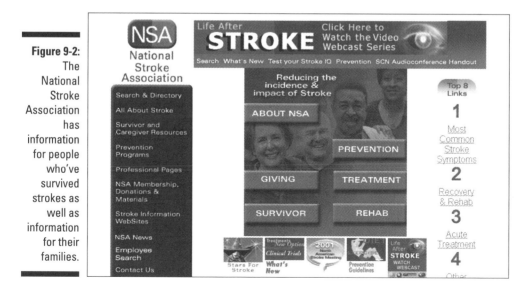

Figure 9-2: The National Stroke Association has information for people who've survived strokes as well as information for their families.

Stroke warning signs

The National Institute of Neurological Disorders and Stroke at `www.ninds.nih.gov/health_and_medical/pubs/stroke_bookmark.htm` lists the following symptoms of a stroke:

✔ Sudden numbness or weakness of face, arm, or leg, especially on one side of the body.

✔ Sudden confusion or trouble speaking or understanding speech.

✔ Sudden trouble seeing in one or both eyes.

✔ Sudden trouble walking, dizziness, or loss of balance or coordination.

✔ Sudden severe headache with no known cause.

Treatment can be more effective if given directly. Every minute counts!

If you see or have one or more of these symptoms, don't wait, call 9-1-1 right away.

Here are some shortcuts to parts of the National Stroke Association Web site that you may find particularly useful:

✔ **All About Stroke:** Go to `www.stroke.org/about.cfm`. From here, you can choose from a menu of topics, which include What Is a Stroke?, Recognizing Symptoms, Prevention — Reducing Risks, Types of Stroke, Effects of Stroke, and Recovery & Rehabilitation. This page also has a link to a stroke glossary.

✔ **Regional Resources:** Go to `www.stroke.org/regional.cfm`. From this page, you can click the <u>Regional Stroke Support Groups</u> link to search for a support group in your area. Or click the <u>Life at Home</u> link for a helpful discussion on issues survivors and caregivers may face, including how to help the survivor with depression, memory loss, communication problems, pain, and daily care.

✔ **Stroke Information Web Sites:** Go to `www.stroke.org/web.cfm`. This page features links to Web sites for products and services for stroke survivors and caregivers, such as adaptive clothing, exercise equipment, wheelchairs, scooters and walkers, reading and writing aids, and bathing aids. You can also find links to additional stroke-related Web sites if you scroll down the Stroke Information Web Sites page.

Some listings on the National Stroke Association Stroke Information Web Sites page are paid ads. Those that are, are labeled as such.

National Institute of Neurological Disorders and Stroke

The National Institute of Neurological Disorders and Stroke (NINDS) is the federal government's lead agency on researching disorders of the brain and nervous system. You can get down to the basics on stroke at the NINDS Stroke Information Page at www.ninds.nih.gov/health_and_medical/disorders/stroke.htm (see Figure 9-3). This easy-to-navigate, easy-to-understand page answers the following questions for you:

- ✔ What is stroke?
- ✔ Is there any treatment?
- ✔ What is the prognosis?
- ✔ What research is being done?

Figure 9-3:
The NINDS Stroke Information Page at the National Institute of Neurological Disorders and Stroke fills you in on stroke.

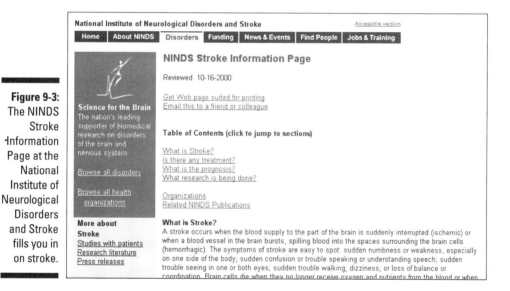

Scrolling down the page, you also find a list of related organizations with contact information and Web addresses, where available. These related organizations include the Brain Aneurysm Foundation, Stroke Clubs International, and the National Aphasia Association. These organizations can provide you with information and support.

At the bottom of the NINDS Stroke Information page are links to more than a dozen informational online booklets on stroke prevention, risk factors and symptoms, research, and post-stroke rehabilitation and support, as well as information on *transient ischemic attacks* (mini-strokes) and *multi-infarct dementia* (a common cause of dementia in the elderly, which occurs when blood clots block small blood vessels in the brain and destroy brain tissue).

On the left-hand side of the NINDS Stroke Information page, under the More about Stroke heading, you get direct links to information on <u>Studies with Patients</u> and to stroke <u>Research Literature</u>.

Look It Up, Quick

If you don't need the big picture on heart disease and stroke, many Web sites can get you answers to your questions with a minimum of clicks. Here are some useful sites.

Heart and stroke dictionaries

If you need to look up terms relating to heart disease or stroke, go to the following Web sites:

- A–Z Glossary from the Heart and Stroke Foundation of Canada at `hsf.ca/az/atoz-a.htm`
- Heart Information Network Glossary of Terms at `www.heartinfo.org/home/glossary.htm`
- Speaking the Language of Stroke from the National Stroke Association at `www.stroke.org/pages/about.cfm`

If you need more information on a heart or stroke term than you can find in a glossary, use the American Heart Association's "Heart and Stroke A–Z Guide" at `www.americanheart.org/Heart_and_Stroke_A_Z_Guide`, which is like a mini-encyclopedia.

Finding a doc or treatment center

If you're looking for a doctor or treatment center specializing in cardiac or stroke care, these Web sites are here to help.

Heart disease

To find a *cardiologist,* a specialist in heart disease, use Physician Select from the American Medical Association at `www.ama-assn.org/aps/amahg.htm`. For a step-by-step guide to this tool, see Chapter 3.

U.S. News lists its picks for best cardiology programs at teaching hospitals at `www.usnews.com/usnews/nycu/health/hosptl/speccard.htm`. You can find more on checking out hospitals in Chapter 4.

General internal medicine specialists, family physicians, and pediatricians also care for people with heart problems.

Stroke

To find a *neurologist,* a doctor specializing in brain and nervous system disorders such as stroke, go to the American Academy of Neurology's Find A Neurologist page at `www.aan.com/roster_f.html`.

Physiatrists, or physical and rehabilitative medicine specialists, help people who are recovering from strokes. The American Academy of Physical Medicine and Rehabilitation has a Find a PM&R Physician feature at `www.aapmr.org/pmaps.html`. You can search by state by clicking a map, or you can choose the Alternate Search Methods link to search by last name, city, area code, and zip code.

Neurosurgeons, or brain surgeons, perform surgery to treat stroke patients. To find a neurosurgeon, go to the Web site for the American Association of Neurological Surgeons at `www.neurosurgery.org/health/findaneurosurgeon.html`.

U.S. News lists its picks for the best neurology and neurosurgery programs at teaching hospitals at `www.usnews.com/usnews/nycu/health/hosptl/specneur.htm`. You can find the *U.S. News* picks for the best rehabilitative programs at `www.usnews.com/usnews/nycu/health/hosptl/specreha.htm`. You can read more about finding a hospital in Chapter 4.

Medications for heart disease and stroke

The American Heart Association Web site features a Compliance Action Program at `www.americanheart.org/cap/patient/splash_con.html`. This program has tips and tools to make it easier for you or your family member to keep track of and take the medications prescribed to prevent or treat heart disease or stroke.

Highlights of the Compliance Action Program include the following:

- ✔ **Medication Information and Drug Classification at** www. americanheart.org/cap/patient/con_classification.html: This section provides you with a short summary of some of the major types of commonly prescribed cardiovascular medications.

- ✔ **Tips for Taking Charge at** www.americanheart.org/cap/patient/ con_tctips.html: This section includes lots of links to quick tips for compliance (ideas on how to remember to take your medications and make lifestyle changes), special information for caregivers (which includes self-care), and a compliance quiz you can take to see how you're doing.

- ✔ **Tools for Taking Charge at** www.americanheart.org/cap/patient/ con_tctools.html: This feature includes tools that you can print out and use. Tools found here include the following:

  - Medicine Chart

  - Blood Pressure Tips and Chart

  - Cholesterol Tips and Chart

  - Physical Activity Tips and Chart

  - Eating Plan Tips and Chart

  - Weight Management Tips and Chart

Alternative medicine

OneBody.com (www.onebody.com/index.jhtml) has a Heart Disease Care Center with background information, news, and articles on using alternative practices to prevent and treat conditions related to heart disease. To get there, click the Heart Disease link under Care Centers on OneBody.com's opening page.

The Natural Pharmacist (www.tnp.com) also looks at heart disease prevention and treating heart failure with natural methods in its Conditions A–Z link in the *TNP Encyclopedia.*

You can read more about alternative medicine in Chapter 8.

Support

You can find support online at some medical megasites, such as WebMD Health at my.webmd.com. Scroll down the site's front page and look for links under the Talk With People Who Understand heading. Also check out Chapter 2 of this book for more on searching for support.

Heart disease

Mended Hearts (www.mendedhearts.org) can help you find a support group for heart disease patients and their families.

Stroke

The American Stroke Association's Stroke Family Support Network (www.strokeassociation.org/Consumer/support/family.html) offers several ways for finding the support you or a family member may need. The association has a National Stroke Group Registry at www.strokeassociation.org/Consumer/support/registry.html that can put you in touch with a stroke support group in your area.

The American Stroke Association also has a free information and referral service, called the Stroke Family Warmline, which is staffed by stroke survivors and caregivers. You can find out about it at www.strokeassociation.org/Consumer/support/warmline.html. You can call this service toll-free at 888-4STROKE — just ask for the Stroke Family Support Network. The service provides post-stroke information and materials.

The National Stroke Association has a support group search (www.stroke.org/supportsearch.cfm) that can help you find a support group in your area for stroke survivors, families, and caregivers.

The Pediatric Stroke Network (sites.netscape.net/pedstrokenet/index.html) has message boards, chat rooms, and e-mail lists for the families of pediatric stroke survivors.

Clinical trials

When new therapies are being tested, researchers conduct clinical trials. If you're interested in joining a study, you can find out about studies at ClinicalTrials.gov at www.clinicaltrials.gov and CenterWatch at www.centerwatch.com. Be sure to get your doctor's advice on the pros and cons and appropriateness of a study for you. (A step-by-step explanation on searching for a research study appears in Chapter 7.)

The following two sections list additional Web sites where you can search for clinical studies on heart disease and stroke.

Heart disease

The National Heart, Lung, and Blood Institute makes it easy for you to locate a clinical trial on heart disease through its Web site at apps.nhlbi.nih.gov/clinicaltrials. You simply Select a Disease or Condition of Interest from the drop-down text box, use the Select Age Group drop-down text box, and use the Select Current Stage of Trial drop-down text box. After making your choices, click the Submit button. It's as easy as that.

Stroke

If you're looking for a clinical trial related to strokes, you can let the National Institute of Neurological Disorders and Stroke do the search for you. Go to its Web site at `www.ninds.nih.gov/health_and_medical/disorders/stroke.htm`. Under the More about Stroke heading on the left side of the home page, click the <u>Studies with Patients</u> link. This action results in a search for stroke-related research studies at ClinicalTrials.gov. A new browser window will open with your results.

Even if you're not interested in joining a clinical study, such studies can be valuable resources for finding cutting-edge doctors and research centers. The results of a search for a clinical study include contact information for the researchers.

Chapter 10

Cancer

· ·

In This Chapter

▶ Getting the big picture on cancer

▶ Looking up cancer terms and facts

▶ Finding cancer specialists and cancer centers

▶ Getting support

▶ Researching major cancers

· ·

*N*ot many years ago, a cancer diagnosis was considered tantamount to a death sentence. The word was mentioned in whispers. There was a conspiracy of silence. Sometimes, even the patient was kept in the dark.

But attitudes have changed. People with cancer have demanded access to more information on their disease, how it is treated, and where research is being done. They have served as a model for other advocates in changing how the public views their disease and making more tax dollars available for research.

It's still no picnic to get diagnosed with "the Big C." But people receiving that news today, in many cases, can be cured, and in others, can live longer with their symptoms and with side effects from therapy minimized.

What role does the Internet play? That's what this chapter is about. You see how information on cancer is readily available online as are ways to find highly trained physicians and to find the best treatment centers and support groups that can help you or a loved one cope with cancer.

The Big Picture on Cancers

Cancer is a huge subject. More than a hundred different types of cancer exist. We won't be able to write in this book about each one of them, but be assured that online resources can answer your questions or provide you with support no matter how common or uncommon the diagnosis is. You (or your loved one) are not alone.

The best places to start are the American Cancer Society's Web site and CancerNet from the National Cancer Institute.

American Cancer Society

The American Cancer Society has been fighting to eliminate cancer for nearly a century through research, education, advocacy, and service. And now it has taken that fight to the Internet at `www.cancer.org`.

The American Cancer Society's Web site covers all the bases for cancer. There, you can get the big picture on cancer in general, or you can find out about specific types of cancer.

A lot of information appears throughout this site. Here's some of what you can find:

- Overviews on cancer in general as well as on specific types of cancer, including information on symptoms, detection and treatment, and places to get additional information and support.
- Information on coping with cancer day to day, including emotional, legal, and practical concerns.
- Online support groups for people with cancer, and caregivers, through the Cancer Support Network. You have to register to participate.
- Hints on getting help, including homecare, rides to treatment, physical therapy, nursing homes, and hospices.
- Listing of local support groups and links to local cancer society chapters.
- Information on complementary and alternative medicine, including approaches the society feels may help you as well as warning signs of treatments to avoid.

Risk factors associated with cancer

In its online brochure "What You Need To Know About Cancer" at `cancernet.nci.nih.gov/wyntk_pubs/cancer.htm`, the National Cancer Institute lists the following as the leading risk factors that cause cancer:

- Tobacco
- Diet
- Ultraviolet radiation (sunlight)
- Alcohol
- Ionizing radiation (X-rays)
- Chemicals and other substances
- Hormone replacement therapy (HRT)
- Diethylstilbestrol (DES)
- Close relatives with certain types of cancer

CancerNet

The National Cancer Institute (NCI), the nation's premier cancer research organization, hosts CancerNet (`cancernet.nci.nih.gov`), shown in Figure 10-1. This uncluttered site provides top-notch information on all forms of cancer from the experts at the NCI.

Here's a quick tour of what you can find, along with some direct links:

- This is a huge site, so you may want to stop by the visitor's center at `www.cancernet.gov/firsttime.html` to get oriented.

- The different types of cancer are described at `www.cancernet.gov/cancertypes.html`. You can find what you're looking for about a specific type of cancer from a quick list of common cancers, such as cancers of the breast, prostate, colon, lung, and head and neck. An alphabetical list of cancers and a list by body location or system also appear in this area, which also includes an overview on particular cancers along with information on treatment, coping with the disease, and finding support.

- You can find information on tests for cancer at `www.cancernet.gov/testing.html`.

- You can get access to the NCI's PDQ database at `www.cancernet.gov/pdq.html`, with summaries of journal articles on cancer treatment, screening, prevention, genetics, and supportive care, plus a registry of cancer clinical trials from around the world.

Figure 10-1: CancerNet has comprehensive information on the various kinds of cancer.

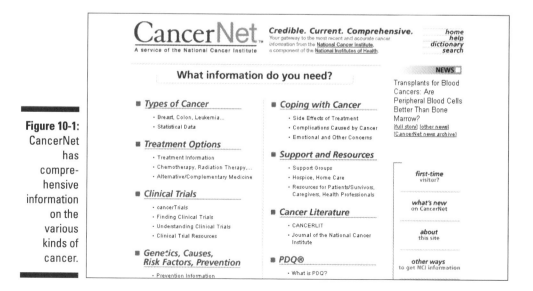

Seven signs of cancer

In its online brochure "What You Need To Know About Cancer" at cancernet.nci.nih.gov/wyntk_pubs/cancer.htm, CancerNet lists the following seven signs of cancer:

- Thickening or lump in the breast or any other part of the body
- Obvious change in a wart or mole
- A sore that does not heal
- Nagging cough or hoarseness
- Changes in bowel or bladder habits
- Indigestion or difficulty swallowing
- Unexplained changes in weight
- Unusual bleeding or discharge

These symptoms are caused by cancer, but also by other conditions, such as infections and benign tumors. See your doctor. You should *not* wait to feel pain: Early cancer usually does not cause pain.

The National Cancer Institute has made available online its "What You Need To Know About" series of brochures at cancernet.nci.nih.gov/wyntk_pubs/index.html. Each booklet has information on specific cancers and how they are diagnosed and treated. The site also includes questions that you should ask your doctor.

Other cancer sites worth checking out

Cancer survivor Steve Dunn offers sage advice on understanding and coping with cancer, alternative medicine, and researching the disease on your own at his CancerGuide Web site at www.cancerguide.org. He provides inspirational stories about patients. We recommend starting with the tour or the table of contents.

Another great site for cancer information is OncoLink from the University of Pennsylvania (www.oncolink.upenn.edu). This site provides comprehensive information about specific types of cancer, updates on cancer treatments and news about research advances.

Look It Up, Quick

If you don't need the big picture, many Web sites can get you answers to your questions right quick. The following few sections list some useful sites.

Dictionaries

CancerNet, from the National Cancer Institute, has a special dictionary of cancer terms at `www.cancernet.gov/dictionary.html`. This dictionary is an A-to-Z index from which you click the first letter of the word you're looking up. If you're looking for a word that begins with a number, such as certain medications, click the A link and scroll up the page.

You also can check out the Cancer Glossary from the Association of Cancer Online Resources at `www.acor.org/glossary/index.html`.

Doctors or treatment centers

To find an *oncologist,* a doctor specializing in cancer care, the American Society of Clinical Oncologists has a Find An Oncologist service at `www.asco.org/people/db/html/m_db.htm`. Scroll down this page and fill in a form. You can search by doctor name, specialty, or geographic location.

The Association of Community Cancer Centers has a Cancer Program Locator at `www.accc-cancer.org/cancercenter/default.asp` to help you find a treatment center specializing in cancer close to your home.

U.S. News lists its picks for the best cancer programs at teaching hospitals at `www.usnews.com/usnews/nycu/health/hosptl/speccanc.htm`.

If you want to know more about checking out doctors and hospitals, check out Chapters 3 and 4.

Support

The American Cancer Society (`www.cancer.org`) has online support groups and information about offline support groups. You may also find some message boards at medical megasites, such as those on breast cancer, lung cancer, and prostate cancer at WebMD Health at `my.webmd.com/roundtable`.

Association of Cancer Online Resources (`www.acor.org`) presents (and helps you sign up for) e-mail lists devoted to cancer.

Clinical trials

You can locate clinical trials online several ways, including ClinicalTrials.gov at `www.clinicaltrials.gov` and CenterWatch at `www.centerwatch.com`, as described in Chapter 7. But CancerNet's Clinical Trials section offers you the fast lane to clinical trials on cancer. Here's how to use it:

1. **Open your Web browser and go to** `cancernet.nci.nih.gov/trialsrch.shtml`.

   The Search for Clinical Trials page at CancerNet appears, as shown in Figure 10-2.

2. **Use the appropriate drop-down text boxes to supply as much information as you can to locate clinical trials. The more specific you are, the more closely the trials will match your needs. When you're finished, click the Search button.**

   At least pick the Type of Cancer and possibly the Location of Trials, if that's important to you. We suggest clicking the Patient radio button for Version of Results so that the trial information will be written in everyday English.

   In our example, we supplied the following information: for Type of Cancer, we selected *Breast Cancer, Female;* for Type of Trial, we selected *Treatment;* for Status of Trial, we selected the Open/Active Trials option button; for Location of Trials, we selected *Washington* from the State drop-down text box; for Country, we selected *U.S.A.;* for Version of Results, we followed our own suggestion and selected *Patient.* Then we clicked the Search button.

   You then see a summary of the results of your search.

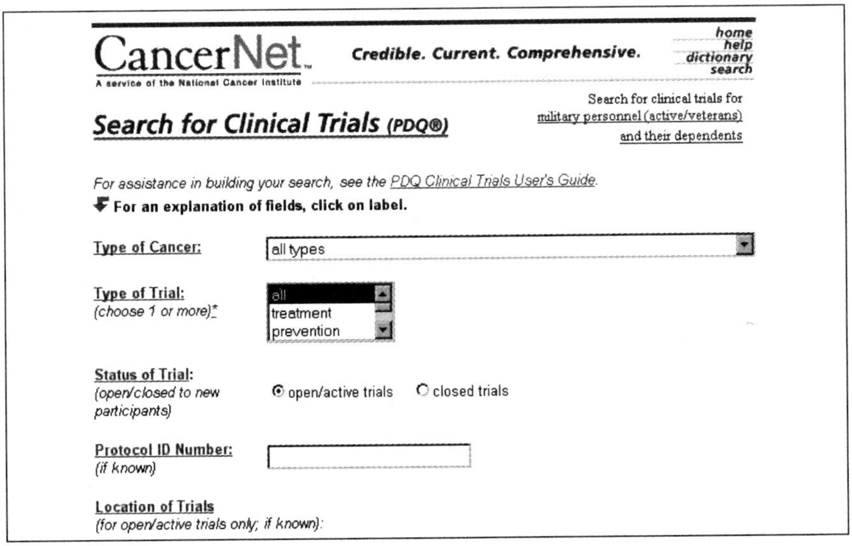

Figure 10-2:
CancerNet, from the National Cancer Institute, can help you quickly locate a clinical trial.

CancerNet™
A service of the National Cancer Institute

Credible. Current. Comprehensive.

home
help
dictionary
search

Search for clinical trials for
military personnel (active/veterans)
and their dependents

Search for Clinical Trials (PDQ®)

For assistance in building your search, see the PDQ Clinical Trials User's Guide.
☛ **For an explanation of fields, click on label.**

Type of Cancer: all types

Type of Trial: all
(choose 1 or more)*   treatment
                               prevention

Status of Trial: ⦿ open/active trials   ○ closed trials
(open/closed to new
participants)

Protocol ID Number:
(if known)

Location of Trials
(for open/active trials only; if known):

3. **You can choose to see your results by clicking the Display These Trials button. Or if you want to refine your search, make selections in such categories as Stage of Cancer, Drug, and Phase of Trial, and then click the Search button at the bottom of the page.**

In our example, the breast cancer search resulted in 17 clinical trials. Clicking the Display These Trials button created a list of the research studies, shown in Figure 10-3.

You can click individual studies to get more information on the purpose of the trial, who's eligible, the treatment being tested, and who to contact about the trial.

Even if you're not interested in participating in a clinical trial, CancerNet's Clinical Trial finder still may come in handy for you. You can use this tool as a way of generating a list of cutting-edge doctors in the field. Each search result describing a study lists the name and contact information of the researchers involved. These researchers could prove to be valuable resources in treating your cancer or that of a loved one.

CancerNet™
A service of the National Cancer Institute

Credible. Current. Comprehensive.

home
help
dictionary
search

Search Results

Your search retrieved 17 clinical trials for:

Type of cancer:	**breast cancer, female**	State:	**WA - Washington**
Type of trial:	**treatment**	Country:	**U.S.A.**
Status of trial:	**open/active**	NIH Clinical Center only:	**no**
Protocol ID:		Version of results:	**patient**
City:			

➤*Display checked documents*

	Title of Clinical Trial	**Protocol ID Number(s)**
1 ☐	<u>Phase I Vaccine Study of HER-2/neu Peptides Incorporated into Polyactide-co-glycolide (PLG) Microspheres in Patients With Advanced Stage HER-2/neu Expressing Cancers</u>	UWASH-103 NCI-V99-1574
2 ☐	<u>Phase II Study of High Dose Combination Chemotherapy and Autologous or Syngeneic Peripheral Blood Stem Cell Rescue Followed by Immunotherapy With Interleukin-2 and</u>	FHCRC-1229.00 NCI-G98-1399

Figure 10-3:
Results of a CancerNet clinical trials search.

Journal articles

CANCERLIT, at www.cancernet.gov/cancerlit.shtml, can help you find citations for medical journal articles on cancer. Here's how to use it:

1. **Type the subject that interests you in the Enter Search Terms box.**

2. **Select the Abstract check box to get a list of articles with short summaries.**

3. **Select the years you want covered.**

4. **Click the Search button to generate a list of relevant citations.**

   The CANCERLIT Search Results page appears.

5. **Click any title that interests you.**

   The summary for that title appears.

You cannot get the complete articles here. You can try to get them through your public library or a local medical library. Another strategy is to run an Internet Grateful Med search from the National Library of Medicine (NLM) at igm.nlm.nih.gov and order copies of the articles through NLM's Loansome Doc service. (You can find more information on medical libraries in Chapter 2 and more on Internet Grateful Med in Chapter 6.)

You probably don't speak medicalese. We don't either. But an awesome tool called Concierge brings a medical dictionary right to the medical article you're wading through on the Web. To use Concierge from the National Cancer Institute, go to research.acor.org/nci/concierge.html, type in or paste in an article's URL in the box provided, pick your favorite color and highlight style, and click the Process button. The *glossified* (Concierge's word) article will appear in your browser with medical terms hyperlinked to their definitions. This concierge does everything but get you tickets to Broadway shows.

Alternative medicine

Often, people with cancer have turned to alternative medicine in hopes of finding a cure or even temporary pain relief. Mainstream medicine's attitudes toward some alternative, or complementary, approaches have been changing. The National Institute of Health has established the National Center for Complementary and Alternative Medicine at nccam.nih.gov to study this increasingly popular area. (Check out Chapter 8 for more on complementary and alternative medicine.)

Even the American Cancer Society (www.cancer.org), in its Alternative & Complementary Medicine section, says that some alternative approaches have something to offer people with cancer. In particular, it sees the following as helpful:

✔ Aromatherapy

✔ Art therapy

✔ Biofeedback

✔ Massage therapy

✔ Meditation

✔ Music therapy

✔ Prayer, spiritual practices

✔ T'ai chi

✔ Yoga

The American Cancer Society advises you to let your doctor know if you are using alternative approaches.

Check out OneBody.com at www.onebody.com for analyses of the scientific evidence for benefits of alternative therapies. For the National Cancer Institute's take on alternative care, go to cis.nci.nih.gov/fact/9_14.htm.

WARNING!

Avoiding dubious therapies

You should remain cautious about quacks. Check out Quackwatch at www.quackwatch. com for tips on dealing with all types of quackery. Also, the American Cancer Society suggests that you ask the following questions to avoid dubious therapies:

✔ Is the treatment based on an unproven theory?

✔ Does the treatment promise a cure for all cancers?

✔ Are you told not to use conventional medical treatment?

✔ Is the treatment or drug a "secret" that only certain providers can give?

✔ Does the treatment require you to travel to another country?

✔ Do the promoters attack the medical/ scientific establishment?

Specific Cancers, Specific Concerns

The following few sections introduce you to some of the best sites devoted to major cancers.

REMEMBER

For virtually any cancer you're interested in, you can find information at CancerNet (www.cancernet.gov/cancertypes.html) or healthfinder (www.healthfinder.gov), a clearinghouse of health information.

Breast cancer

One out of every eight women in the United States will develop breast cancer during her lifetime. And did you know that breast cancer even affects men? The following Web sites have information on the disease:

✔ **Breast health, a service from the Susan G. Komen Breast Cancer Foundation, at** www.breastcancerinfo.com/bhealth: This site has information on the disease and how it is diagnosed and treated, advice about discussing it with family and doctors, and data on its effects on special populations, including lesbians and men.

✔ **Y-Me National Breast Cancer Organization at** www.y-me.org/english. htm: This site has information on the disease as well as lots of links to support groups. Click the Support for All button on the left side of the home page to get to resources for men who are supporting women with breast cancer and listings of support group meetings for women with breast cancer.

✔ **SusanLoveMD.com, The Website For Women, at** `www.susanlovemd.com`: As shown in Figure 10-4, this site from surgeon and author Susan Love helps women make choices about breast cancer treatment and living with the disease. It has electronic bulletin boards and chat rooms. The site has a ShowMe section at `www.susanlovemd.com/showme_frames.html`, which is a gallery of photos from the book *Show Me: A Photo Collection of Breast Cancer Survivors' Lumpectomies, Mastectomies, Breast Reconstructions and Thoughts on Body Image.*

iVillage.com offers a Breast Self-Exam and Mammogram Reminder Service at `www.ivillage.com/auto/ford/windstar/race/self-exam.html`. Complete the site's Web form with your e-mail address to get a monthly breast self-exam and/or annual clinical breast exam and mammogram reminder by e-mail along with expert answers to common questions, tips, and a complete guide to doing a self-exam.

Colon cancer

Colon cancer is the third most common cancer diagnosed in both men and women. Here are some places to find out more about colon cancer online:

✔ **Colon Cancer Alliance at** `www.ccalliance.org`: This site has survivor stories, a colorectal cancer dictionary, news on colon cancer, information on clinical trials, and support for patients and their caregivers through a buddy group and online chats with *cyberhugs*.

✔ **United Ostomy Association at** `www.uoa.org`: This site has information for people who have undergone *colostomies* (surgically created openings in the colon) and similar operations. The site features a glossary, contacts with local ostomy groups, and information about supplies.

Figure 10-4: SusanLoveMD.com provides women with breast cancer the information they need to make decisions.

It's always something

Some say laughter helps cure what's ailing you. We don't know about that, but getting some hearty guffaws couldn't hurt. CancerOnline, a group that aims to improve the lives of people with cancer, has links to cancer jokes, to its CancerOnline Joke Club, and to stand-up comedians who are cancer survivors and do cancer material. Check out these features at `www.canceronline.org/feature/humor-intro.htm`.

Groucho Marx said that he'd never belong to a club that would have him as a member. After comedian Gilda Radner was diagnosed with ovarian cancer, she took it to the next level. She said the cancer gave her a membership in an elite club that she'd rather not belong to.

Gilda Radner's memory lives on in a variety of efforts. The Gilda Radner Familial Ovarian Cancer Registry, at `pci.med.buffalo.edu/departments/gynonc/grwp.html`, offers information and support for women at high risk for ovarian cancer and runs a registry for research purposes. Also, Gilda's Club programs offer support and a Noogieland program for kids. To find out more about Gilda's Club, go to `www.gildasclub.org`. These clubs offer a place for people with cancer not only to cry, but also to laugh.

As Gilda herself said about her own cancer, echoing her classic character from *Saturday Night Live,* the frizzy-haired TV journalist, Roseanne Roseannadana, "Just goes to show ya — it's always something."

Lung cancer

Lung cancer is the most common cause of cancer deaths, with more people dying from this cancer than colon cancer, breast cancer, and prostate cancer put to-gether. Early detection and quit-smoking programs are holding out new hope for people with this disease. You can find out more about lung cancer at these sites:

- **Alliance for Lung Cancer at** `www.alcase.org`: This site lists support groups and phone buddies programs, stories of hope on survivors, links to information on research and the best hospitals and doctors, and new diagnostic options.
- **American Lung Association at** `www.lungusa.org`: This site has facts on diagnosing and treating lung cancer and information about tobacco control.

You can find more on smoking cessation in Chapter 18.

Melanoma skin cancer

If detected early, melanoma can be curable in almost all cases. But if this cancer spreads, it is extremely dangerous. The number of melanoma cases has increased more rapidly than any other type of cancer in the United States and other Western countries in the past ten years. Check out these sites for more on melanoma skin cancer:

- ✔ **Skin Cancer Foundation at** `www.skincancer.org`: This site has information on melanoma and other types of skin cancer, pointers on sun safety, and advice on how to recognize warning signs.

- ✔ **MelanomaNet from the American Academy of Dermatology at** `www.skincarephysicians.com/melanomanet/welcome.htm`: MelanomaNet has the rundown on diagnosing and treating melanoma, a rogue's gallery of photos of melanomas, directions for self-exams, and a melanoma glossary. The American Academy of Dermatology also has a Find a Dermatologist service at `www.aad.org/findaderm_intro.html`.

Prostate cancer

With the exception of nonmelanoma skin cancers, prostate cancer is the most common cancer among American men. It is about twice as common among African American men as white American men. Here are some sites where you can find out more about prostate cancer:

- ✔ **US TOO! International, Inc. at** `www.ustoo.com`: As shown in Figure 10-5, US TOO! is an independent network of support groups for men with prostate cancer and their families. The site has information on treatment options for prostate cancer, a glossary of terms, and contact information to put you in touch with a local support group.

- ✔ **CaP Cure (The Association for the Cure of Cancer of the Prostate) at** `www.capcure.org`: This site has listings of clinical trials, patient profiles, information on living with the disease, and news on prostate cancer.

Figure 10-5:
US TOO!
offers
information
and support
for men with
prostate
cancer.

Chapter 11

Diabetes

. . . .

. . . .

*D*iabetes mellitus is a disorder that prevents the body from effectively converting carbohydrates, which are sugars and starches, into energy. It is a serious, life-long condition.

Sixteen million Americans have diabetes, but one-third of them haven't been diagnosed. And the numbers are increasing at an epidemic rate because of the couch potato/mouse potato lifestyle in the United States. Life in the fast-food lane and in the no-exercise zone has taken its toll: Diabetes is a leading cause of blindness, kidney failure, and amputations. People with diabetes have an increased risk of heart attacks.

There are two main types of diabetes, known as type 1 and type 2:

- ✔ In type 1 diabetes, the pancreas stops producing *insulin,* the hormone that transforms carbs into energy. Type 1 is metabolic disorder that requires the person to take insulin every day.

- ✔ In type 2 diabetes, the body produces enough insulin but does not handle it effectively. Type 2 diabetes is the most common form of the disease, affecting 90 percent or more of people with diabetes. Type 2 is considered largely avoidable through weight control with diet and exercise.

In this chapter, you find the best sites to visit in order to get information about diabetes and support.

The Big Picture on Diabetes

You can get the big picture on diabetes at lots of places on the Web, including medical megasites, such as MayoClinic.com (www.mayoclinic.com) and CBSHealthWatch (www.cbshealthwatch.com).

The following few sections focus on the American Diabetes Association Web site and the National Institute of Diabetes & Digestive & Kidney Diseases Web site.

American Diabetes Association

The American Diabetes Association is a nonprofit organization that has long been a source of information on diabetes. Its Web site (www.diabetes.org), shown in Figure 11-1, is a great place to start your search.

A lot of information is available at this site. Here's some of what you can find in the left-hand column under the Diabetes Info heading:

- **General Information:** Here, you can find information on diagnosing and treating not only type 1 and 2 diabetes but also *gestational diabetes,* a type of diabetes that occurs in pregnant women and can harm developing babies. From here, you can also take the Diabetes Risk Test.

- **Newly Diagnosed:** Here, you can find information specially tailored for people who've just learned that they have diabetes. You can locate a local education program to learn how to cope with diabetes day to day. You also get nutrition and fitness information, a tip of the day for coping, and a recipe of the day.

- **Nutrition:** Here are some tips and articles on healthy eating, including sections on frequently asked questions about nutrition and how you can eat right in popular food chains. After all, you deserve a break today.

- **Exercise:** Here you can find frequently asked questions about exercise and some exercise games you can play.

- **Virtual Grocery Store:** Here's a brief review of the basic principles of meal planning for people who have diabetes.

- **Outreach Programs:** Here are links to special programs aimed at kids, African Americans, and Native Americans.

In the same left-hand column, look under the Recognized Providers heading for links to physicians who specialize in treating diabetes and to diabetes education programs.

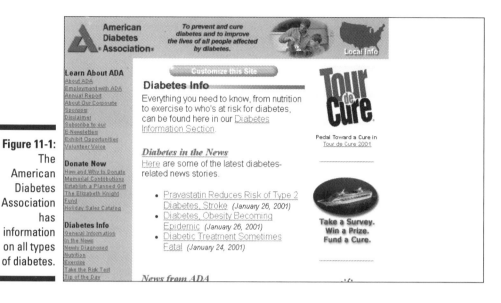

Figure 11-1:
The
American
Diabetes
Association
has
information
on all types
of diabetes.

From the Local Info map in the upper right-hand corner, you can find chapters of the American Diabetes Association that offer local programs and support. The site's main page also has news on diabetes.

If you're interested knowing more about type 1 diabetes, also known as *juvenile-onset diabetes,* you should check out the Juvenile Diabetes Foundation at www.jdf.org. This site features background on the disease, researchers' answers to questions, local chapters for support, news, and clinical trial information.

The warning signs of diabetes

The National Institute of Diabetes & Digestive & Kidney Disease lists these signs for diabetes at www.niddk.nih.gov/health/diabetes/dylb/chap1.htm:

✔ Being very thirsty

✔ Urinating often

✔ Feeling very hungry or tired

✔ Losing weight without trying

✔ Having sores that are slow to heal

✔ Having dry, itchy skin

✔ Losing feeling in the feet or having tingling in the feet

✔ Having blurry eyesight

If you have one or more of these signs, you should see your doctor.

The Institute

The National Institute of Diabetes & Digestive & Kidney Diseases is the National Institutes of Health's center that focuses on diabetes research and education. The Institute has tons of information at its site.

You can find a virtual library of online brochures that cover just about any aspect of diabetes you can think of, and you don't need a library card to access this information. Just go to www.niddk.nih.gov/health/diabetes/diabetes.htm, shown in Figure 11-2. Among the titles you can browse are the following:

- Questions to Ask Your Doctor About Blood Sugar Control
- Complications of Diabetes (Eyes, Feet, Heart, Kidneys, Nerves, and Teeth)
- Medicines for People with Diabetes
- Diabetes in African Americans
- Noninvasive Blood Glucose Monitors
- Kidney Failure of Diabetes
- Pancreatic Islet Transplantation

Click the Diabetes Dictionary link to access the site's dictionary of diabetes terms. If you click the Clinical Research link on the left-hand side of the page, you go to a page that can help you find research studies on diabetes. Click the Directory of Diabetes Organizations link to see a list of groups from which you can get more information.

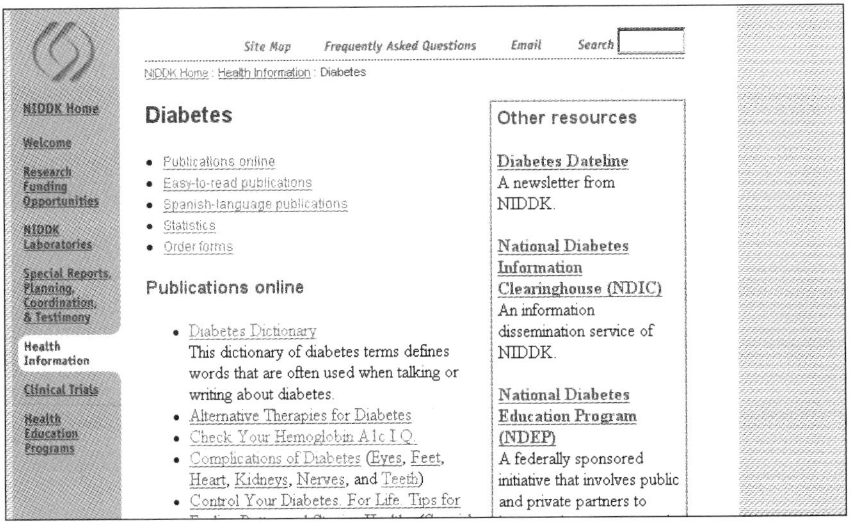

Figure 11-2: The National Institute of Diabetes & Digestive & Kidney Diseases has a virtual library of info on diabetes at its site.

The transplant option

People with type 1 diabetes can have their hands full every day with insulin shots and regular blood sugar monitoring. Transplants of a pancreas or the cells that produce insulin can be an option for people with severe complications of diabetes. These transplants produce insulin and possibly replace the need for insulin shots.

You can find information on these techniques at the United Network for Organ Sharing at `www.patients.unos.org/tpd` and at Insulin-Free World Foundation at `www.insulin-free.org`. A directory of transplant programs is available at `www.insulinfree.org/centers/ uscenters.htm`.

Look It Up, Quick

If you don't need the big picture on diabetes, here are some Web sites that can get you answers to your questions in a jiff.

Dictionaries

A diabetes dictionary is featured at the National Diabetes Information Clearinghouse at the National Institute of Diabetes & Digestive & Kidney Diseases Web site at `www.niddk.nih.gov/health/diabetes/pubs/dmdict/dmdict.htm` (see Figure 11-3).

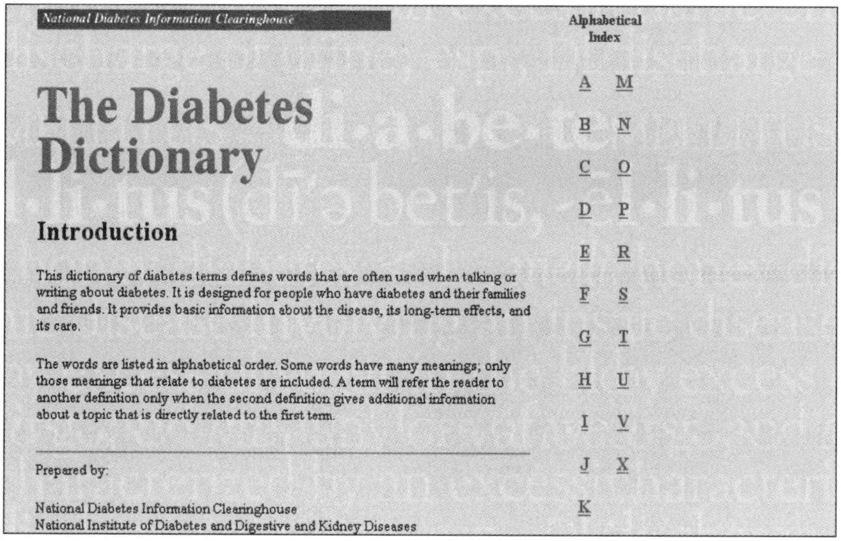

Figure 11-3: The diabetes dictionary at the National Diabetes Information Clearinghouse can help you find the meaning of a diabetes term.

National Diabetes Information Clearinghouse

The Diabetes Dictionary

Introduction

This dictionary of diabetes terms defines words that are often used when talking or writing about diabetes. It is designed for people who have diabetes and their families and friends. It provides basic information about the disease, its long-term effects, and its care.

The words are listed in alphabetical order. Some words have many meanings; only those meanings that relate to diabetes are included. A term will refer the reader to another definition only when the second definition gives additional information about a topic that is directly related to the first term.

Prepared by:

National Diabetes Information Clearinghouse
National Institute of Diabetes and Digestive and Kidney Diseases

Alphabetical Index

A   M
B   N
C   O
D   P
E   R
F   S
G   T
H   U
I   V
J   X
K

The Juvenile Diabetes Foundation, at `www.jdfcure.org/glossary.htm`, has a diabetes glossary.

Medications/devices

Diabetes/Internet maven Rick Mendosa, who has type 2 diabetes and writes a column on diabetes Web sites for the American Diabetes Association Web site, has information on drugs used to treat diabetes at his On-Line Resources for Diabetes site at `www.mendosa.com/drugs.htm`. He lists online resources on insulin at `www.diabetesmonitor.com/insulin.htm`.

People with diabetes use glucose meters to measure blood sugar levels to determine whether they're controlling their insulin. They adjust food intake, insulin, and activity levels accordingly. Mendosa has descriptions of meters for diabetes management and links to manufacturers' Web pages at `www.diabetesmonitor.com/meters.htm`.

You can read Rick Mendosa's column on diabetes resources on the Internet at the American Diabetes Association Web site at `www.diabetes.org/mendosa/default.asp`.

Find a doc/diabetes educator/dietician

You may need a team of health professionals to manage your diabetes. Here are some places that you can find help.

Diabetes doctors

To find a doctor specializing in diabetes care, go to the American Association of Clinical Endocrinologists Search for Endocrinologists site at `www.aace.com/serv/searchindex.htm`. At the site, type in a city or two-letter state abbreviation and select Diabetes Mellitus from the drop-down Select a Specialty text box. Then click the I Need A Doctor button to see the results.

A list, by states, of doctors recognized by the American Diabetes Association appears at `www.diabetes.org/recognition/Physicians/i_prvstate2.asp`.

Family physicians, pediatricians, and general internists also care for people with diabetes. People with diabetes may need to see other specialists, including eye doctors, heart specialists, skin doctors, kidney specialists, and foot doctors. Chapter 3 has more information on how to search for a doctor.

Diabetes programs and diabetes educators

At `www.diabetes.org/education/edustate2.asp`, the American Diabetes Association lists diabetes education programs that meet its standards for excellence.

The American Association of Diabetes Educators (`www.aadenet.org`) lists nurses, dietitians, pharmacists, exercise specialists, doctors, and social workers who specialize in treating people with diabetes. Click the <u>Find an Educator</u> link in the left-hand column of this Web site to see a map on which you can click your state to find an educator.

U.S. News rates the best teaching hospitals for treating diabetes and other hormonal disorders at `www.usnews.com/usnews/nycu/health/hosptl/specendo.htm`. See Chapter 4 for more information on finding a hospital.

Dietitian

You may need to find a dietician to help manage your diet. The American Dietetic Association can assist you with this. Just follow these steps to use the ADA's Find a Registered Dietitian service:

1. **Open your Web browser and go to** `www.eatright.org/find.html`.

2. **Scroll down the page to read the disclaimer and click the <u>I Accept</u> link.**

   The Find a Registered Dietitian page appears.

3. **Click the <u>Consumer Search</u> link.**

   On the next page that appears, you can search for a registered dietitian.

4. **Enter your zip code and the miles you are willing to travel from this zip code, or enter your city and state.**

5. **From the drop-down list boxes, choose the type of services you need (individual or group consultation or programs/workshops), and if you want, select a specialty (such as diabetes).**

6. **When you're finished entering your search specifications, click the Perform Search button.**

   The results of your search for a registered dietician appear.

Support

Diabetes123 (`www.diabetes123.com`), shown in Figure 11-4, and its sister site, Children with Diabetes (`www.childrenwithdiabetes.com`) have unmoderated chats and bulletin boards. They also have a list of e-mail support groups for kids, teens, adults, parents of kids with diabetes, and others at `www.diabetes123.com/people/mailinglists.htm`.

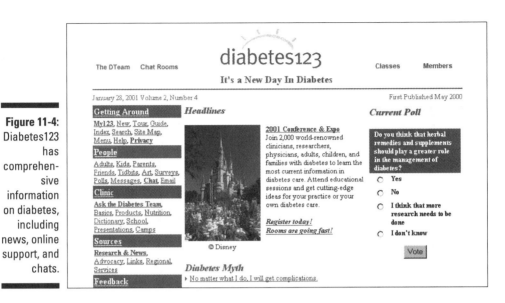

Figure 11-4:
Diabetes123
has
comprehen-
sive
information
on diabetes,
including
news, online
support, and
chats.

A listing of summer camps for kids with diabetes appears at `www.childrenwithdiabetes.com/camps`.

Diabetes123 has an Ask the Diabetes Team feature at `www.diabetes123.com/dteam/d_0d_000.htm`, where you can pose questions to a panel of doctors, nurses, dietitians, psychologists, exercise physiologists, and researchers. The responses are available in an online archive.

Some other sources for support for people with diabetes are the following:

- WebMD Health, at `www.mywebmd.com`, has chat rooms and messages boards for people with diabetes. To find these features, look under the Talk With People Who Understand section on the opening page.

- The American Diabetes Association, at `www.diabetes.org`, has listings for local chapters that sponsor support groups. To find the local chapters, click the map labeled Local Information in the upper-right-hand corner of the opening page. In the small pop-up window that opens, type your zip code and click the Submit button.

- The Juvenile Diabetes Foundation, at `www.jdf.org/chapters`, can help you find local chapters with support groups. You can search by chapter name, city, state, or zip code. Enter your information and click the Search button.

- Google lists a few newsgroups devoted to diabetes. One popular newsgroup for both type 1 and type 2 diabetes is `misc.health.diabetes`. To access this newsgroup, go to Google (`groups.google.com`), enter **diabetes** in the Search Groups search box, and click the Google Search button. On the results page, under the Relevant Groups heading, click the <u>misc.health.diabetes</u> link to read the latest postings to the group.

For more on finding diabetes support online and offline, see Chapter 2.

Clinical trials

When new therapies for diabetes are being tested, researchers conduct clinical trials. If you're interested in joining a study, you can find out about studies at ClinicalTrials.gov at www.clinicaltrials.gov and CenterWatch at www.centerwatch.com. (You can find a step-by-step explanation on searching for research studies in Chapter 7.) Be sure to get your doctor's advice on the pros and cons and appropriateness of a study for you.

Even if you're not planning to join a clinical trial, you can use the results of the searches to find experts in the condition. Descriptions of clinical trials found at ClinicalTrials.gov and CenterWatch include contact information.

Journal articles

If you want to read up on the latest medical research on diabetes, go to the articles written by doctors in the field. A step-by-step explanation on how to find medical journal articles by using Internet Grateful Med from the National Library of Medicine (igm.nlm.nih.gov) appears in Chapter 6.

Alternative medicine

The National Institute of Diabetes & Digestive & Kidney Diseases gives its views on alternative therapies for diabetes at www.niddk.nih.gov/health/diabetes/summary/altmed/altmed.htm. The Institute specifically mentions that among the methods that have been used to manage diabetes and its complications are acupuncture, biofeedback, guided imagery, and vitamin and mineral supplementation. The Institute says that the success of some alternative treatments can be hard to measure. It adds that many alternative treatments remain either untested or unproven through traditional scientific studies.

Alternativediabetes.com (www.alternativediabetes.com), shown in Figure 11-5, is a bit more enthusiastic than that. But it also stresses what is known scientifically about alternatives, including herbal, dietary, and other approaches. The site also offers the *Natural Pharmacist* encyclopedia.

Other alternative health sites, including WholeHealthMD.com (www.wholehealthmd.com), have information on diabetes. See Chapter 8 for more on alternative care.

Figure 11-5:
alternativedi
abetes.com
explores the
connection
between
alternative
and
mainstream
approaches
to diabetes
care.

You should be careful to avoid quack therapies for diabetes or anything else. The American Diabetes Association warns what to look out for at `www.diabetes.org/DiabetesCare/Supplement198/S85.htm`. It cautions, among other things, about exaggerated and unrealistic claims, misapplication of scientific research, and results communicated outside the regular channels of scientific communications.

Also, check out Quackwatch at `www.quackwatch.com`.

Chapter 12

Arthritis

Arthritis is one of the major diseases affecting Americans. One in six Americans has one form or another of this inflammatory joint disease, which is the leading cause of disability in this country. And with the Baby Boom generation aging, an accompanying boom in the number of cases of *osteoarthritis,* the degenerative joint disease and most common form of arthritis, is anticipated.

In this chapter, you find the best online sources of information on arthritis and find out where you or your loved one can get support.

The Big Picture on Arthritis

More than 100 types of arthritis exist. We don't have the space to write about them all in this book, but you can get the big picture on arthritis from the Web sites of the Arthritis Foundation and from the National Institute of Arthritis and Musculoskeletal and Skin Diseases. Medical megasites, such as MayoClinic.com (www.mayoclinic.com) and InteliHealth (www.intelihealth.com), also can provide you with the basics on diagnosing and treating arthritis.

In the next few sections, we give you information on the two top online sources for arthritis information.

Arthritis Foundation

A great starting place to find out about things relating to arthritis online is the Arthritis Foundation's Web site (www.arthritis.org), shown in Figure 12-1. This site offers a lot of information for visitors to read. Fortunately, the Arthritis Foundation has provided a few easy ways to navigate the site, starting from the opening page.

Starting points

Under the Information banner on the left-hand side of the opening page, click the Starting Points link to find information that has been organized for you based on your situation. Choose from this list of categories:

- ✔ I've just been told I have arthritis
- ✔ I've had arthritis for years
- ✔ I'm a parent of a child with arthritis
- ✔ I'm a young adult with arthritis
- ✔ Someone in my family has arthritis
- ✔ My employees have arthritis
- ✔ I work in health care with people who have arthritis

Figure 12-1: The Arthritis Foundation's Web site has comprehensive information on the many types of arthritis.

Clicking these choices brings you to lists of links to information within the Web site. These links include a guide on medications, a chapter locator (to find local groups offering support and other services), online brochures, information on alternative and complementary therapies, and message boards tailored to your needs.

Arthritis answers

Under the Information banner on the left-hand side of the opening page, click the Arthritis Answers link. Scroll down the Arthritis Answers page to see a list of links on a variety of topics. Click the Disease Center link for information on the various types of arthritis. Click the Medications link to access *Arthritis Today*'s Drug Guide. Links to information on arthritis in children, water exercise, self-care, and complementary and alternative medicine approaches all appear here, too.

Quick hits

Here's how to access some of the features within the Arthritis Foundation's Web site directly:

- ✔ **Disease Center:** Go to www.arthritis.org/answers/disease_center. asp to find an A-to-Z index of arthritis types. Click the first letter of the type of arthritis you're interested in and then click the name of the arthritis type to find out this information:

  - What it is

  - What causes it

  - What its symptoms are

  - How it is diagnosed

  - Treatment options

  - Who is at risk

  - Resources, including Web sites, and suggestions

- ✔ **Message Boards:** Go to www.arthritis.org/forums to find forums devoted to Coping Skills, Fibromyalgia, Women and Arthritis, and Parents/Parenting.

- ✔ **Chapter Locator:** At the bottom of the left-hand column on the opening page, you find a Chapter Locator by Zip search box. Enter your zip code to get contact information for the nearest Arthritis Foundation chapter, where you can find local services and programs.

The Institute

The National Institute of Arthritis and Musculoskeletal and Skin Diseases —
that mouthful is one of the parts of the National Institutes of Health — is the
leading research organization on arthritis. It's a good place to get clued in
online on arthritis. Go to www.nih.gov/niams, shown in Figure 12-2.

If you click the <u>Health Information</u> link on the opening page, you go to the
Health Information page, where you can access online brochures on a variety
of arthritis topics, including Behçet's disease, fibromyalgia, gout, juvenile
rheumatoid arthritis, lupus, osteoarthritis, and psoriasis. Here are a few of
the links you find on this page:

- ✔ **Resource Directory-NIAMS Coalition:** Click this link for a listing of
  patient and professional groups with information on various types of
  arthritis.

- ✔ **NIH Clinical Trials Database** and **NIAMS Clinical Studies at the
  National Institutes of Health (NIH):** Click either of these links to find
  research studies.

- ✔ **MEDLINE:** Click this link to track down medical journal articles.

Figure 12-2:
The
National
Institute of
Arthritis and
Musculo-
skeletal and
Skin
Diseases
has online
pamphlets
with helpful
information
on arthritis.

Warning signs of osteoarthritis

How do you know whether you might have osteoarthritis? In its online pamphlet, "Handout on Health: Osteoarthritis," available at www.nih.gov/niams/healthinfo/osteoarthritis, the National Institute of Arthritis and Musculoskeletal and Skin Diseases lists the warning signs for osteoarthritis:

- ✔ Steady or intermittent pain in a joint

- ✔ Stiffness after getting out of bed

- ✔ Joint swelling or tenderness in one or more joints

- ✔ A crunching feeling or sound of bone rubbing on bone

If you have a joint that is hot or tender, you probably do not have osteoarthritis, but you could have rheumatoid arthritis. Check with your doctor.

Osteoarthritis does not always cause pain. Only one-third of people with evidence of osteoarthritis on X-rays experience pain or other symptoms.

Look It Up, Quick

If you don't need the big picture on arthritis, several Web sites can give you answers to your questions right quick. The following sections list some useful sites.

Dictionaries

Check out these sites for arthritis dictionaries and glossaries:

- ✔ **ArthritisInsight.com** — an Australia-based patient-support group — has an arthritis dictionary at www.arthritisinsight.com/resources/dictionary.

- ✔ **Merck** has an arthritis glossary at www.merck.com/disease/arthritis/glossary.html.

- ✔ **Arthritis.com** has a glossary at www.arthritis.com/tools/health_library/basics/glossary.html.

Medications

Arthritis Today's Drug Guide, from the Arthritis Foundation at www.arthritis.org/Answers/DrugGuide/default.asp, profiles more than 200 medications used by people with arthritis, provides advice on avoiding stomach damage from nonsteroidal anti-inflammatory medications, and offers other useful information.

Find a doc or hospital

To find a *rheumatologist,* a doctor specializing in arthritis care, go to American College of Rheumatology's Find a Rheumatologist service at www.rheumatology.org/directory/geo.html. You can look for a rheumatologist based on geographic location by using the drop-down text box provided on this Web site.

Family physicians, pediatricians, and general internists also care for people with arthritis. Chapter 3 has more on how to search for a doctor.

The American College of Rheumatology also has online fact sheets for consumers on arthritis (www.rheumatology.org/patients/factsheets.html), covering such conditions as gout, psoriatic arthritis, osteoarthritis, and juvenile arthritis.

U.S. News gives its rating on top hospitals for treating arthritis at www.usnews.com/usnews/nycu/health/hosptl/specrheu.htm. You can find more on locating hospitals in Chapter 4.

Support

The Arthritis Foundation has message boards where patients and family members can discuss their concerns at www.arthritis.org/forums/default.asp. Special message boards are devoted to coping with arthritis, parenting a child with arthritis, and fibromyalgia. The foundation also has contact information for local chapters at www.arthritis.org/ChapDirectory.asp.

WebMD Health (www.mywebmd.com) and other medical megasites have chats and message boards for people concerned with various types of arthritis. See Chapter 2 for more information on finding support online.

Clinical trials

When new therapies for arthritis are being tested, researchers conduct clinical trials. If you're interested in joining a study, you can find out about them at ClinicalTrials.gov at www.clinicaltrials.gov and CenterWatch at www.centerwatch.com. Be sure to get your doctor's advice on the pros and cons and appropriateness of a study for you. (Chapter 7 features a step-by-step explanation on searching for a research study.)

It's a pain

The word *arthritis* means joint inflammation. And inflammation of the joint lining and tendons and ligaments (along with muscle strain and fatigue) contribute to the pain of the most common types of arthritis: *osteoarthritis,* a degenerative disease of the joints, and *rheumatoid arthritis,* an autoimmune disease.

The National Institute of Arthritis and Musculoskeletal and Skin Diseases has an online brochure, "Questions and Answers About ARTHRITIS PAIN" (www.nih.gov/niams/healthinfo/arthpain.htm), that discusses how pain is measured and various types of medications used to control pain. It also recommends these steps to help manage arthritis pain:

✔ Eat a healthy diet

✔ Get 8 to 10 hours of sleep at night

✔ Keep a daily diary of pain and mood changes to share with your physician

✔ Choose a caring physician

✔ Join a support group

✔ Stay informed about new research on managing arthritis pain

---

Even if you're not planning to join a clinical trial, you can use the results of the searches to find experts on the condition. Descriptions of clinical trials found at ClinicalTrials.gov and CenterWatch also include contact information.

Journal articles

If you want to read up on the latest medical research on arthritis, go to the articles written by doctors in the field. You can find a step-by-step explanation in Chapter 6 on how to find medical journal articles by using Internet Grateful Med from the National Library of Medicine at igm.nlm.nih.gov.

Alternative medicine

The Arthritis Foundation gives its take on using alternative and complementary medicine to treat arthritis at www.arthritis.org/AltTherapies/Default.asp. The foundation says some alternatives can help ease some symptoms, including pain, stiffness, stress, and anxiety, and also improve the quality of life. However, the foundation also says that alternatives do not replace conventional care.

Resources for coping with pain

Here are some online resources on pain:

- **American Academy of Pain Medicine** has a Membership Directory (www.painmed.org/membership) that lists physicians specializing in pain management.

- **The American Academy of Physical Medicine and Rehabilitation** (www.aapmr.org) provides information on physical and rehabilitative medicine specialists. Such specialists are also known as physiatrists (fizz-eeAT-trists). They help treat such problems as osteoarthritis, fibromyalgia, and back pain. Click the Find a PM&R Physician link on the academy's home page

to find one of these specialists in acute and chronic pain.

- **International Center for the Control of Pain in Children and Adults** (adultpain.nursing.uiowa.edu/index1.htm) has information on medications and alternative medical means of controlling pain.

- **Pain.com** (www.pain.com) promises "A World of Information on Pain." And it delivers with information on arthritis, headaches, cancer pain, postoperative pain, and others. Forums, chat rooms, and an online library are also available at Pain.com.

Many alternative medicine sites have information on arthritis. For example, EarthMed.com (www.earthmed.com) has a condition center devoted to alternative health approaches to arthritis care. To find arthritis information, follow these steps:

1. **Open your Web browser and go to** www.earthmed.com/conditions.asp.

   The Find Your Condition page appears.

2. **Choose either *Arthritis* or *Arthritis, Rheumatoid* from the Select a Condition box and then click the Get Info button.**

3. **On the next page that appears, scroll down and select a treatment from the treatment list.**

   A variety of alternative therapies are available in the treatment list, including aromatherapy, herbal medicine, reflexology, therapeutic touch, and traditional Chinese medicine. (See Chapter 8 for more on alternative care.)

4. **Click the Find Treatment Info button to see the results.**

 The Arthritis Foundation says that many types of complementary medicine practitioners are regulated and have ethical standards. However, arthritis is one of the conditions that has attracted a lot of quack treatments. To help protect you, the Arthritis Foundation has two articles on avoiding quackery. You can read "Seven Danger Signs About a Therapist" at www.arthritis.org/AltTherapies/SevenDangers.asp and "Tip-Offs to Rip-Offs" at www.arthritis.org/AltTherapies/TipOffs.asp. Also check out Quackwatch at www.quackwatch.com.

Arthritis-Related Conditions

The following few sections list some of the best sites devoted to arthritis-related conditions.

For virtually any condition related to arthritis you're interested in, you can find information at the Arthritis Foundation (www.arthritis.org) or go to healthfinder (www.healthfinder.gov), a government clearinghouse of health information.

Fibromyalgia

Fibromyalgia involves widespread musculoskeletal pain and fatigue. Fibromyalgia affects up to six million Americans, primarily women of child-bearing years.

You can find more on fibromyalgia at these Web sites:

- **The Fibromyalgia Network** (www.fmnetnews.com) has basic information on the disease, coping tips, and other information.
- **The Arthritis Foundation** (www.arthritis.org/forums/default.asp) has a message board for people with fibromyalgia.

Lyme disease

Lyme disease is a bacterial infection transmitted by the bite of an infected tick. Lyme disease can cause such medical conditions as arthritis, nerve problems, such as weakness and paralysis, or heart problems, such as irregular heartbeats and chest pain.

Here are two online resources for Lyme disease:

- **LymeNet** (www.lymenet.org) has information on the disease and listings of support groups.
- **The American Lyme Disease Foundation, Inc.** (www.aldf.com) has information and news on Lyme disease and other tick-borne conditions. To find information about referrals to physicians with expertise in treating Lyme disease, go to www.aldf.com/templates/PhysicianReferral.cfm, where you find an e-mail form with which to request names of local Lyme-literate physicians.

Lupus

As many as 1.5 million Americans have been diagnosed with some form of lupus. *Lupus* is a chronic inflammatory disease that can affect the skin, joints, blood, and kidneys. Women of childbearing years are affected more than any other group.

Check out these Web sites for more on lupus:

✔ **The Lupus Foundation of America** (`www.lupus.org`) has background on the disease, current developments in research, and a list of local chapters.

✔ **Lupus Around the World** (`www.mtio.com/mclfa`) has quick facts on lupus, a buddy list program, forums, and chats.

Scleroderma

About 300,000 Americans have *scleroderma,* an autoimmune-system disorder that attacks the connective tissue. The Scleroderma Foundation (`www.scleroderma.org`), shown in Figure 12-3, has scleroderma facts, a list of support groups, and schedules of online chats at AOL and at iVillage Women's Network allHealth channel.

Figure 12-3: The Scleroderma Foundation Web site has facts, support, and news for people with the arthritic condition.

Sjogren's syndrome

Sjogren's syndrome is an autoimmune disease that attacks moisture-producing glands and causes dry eyes and a dry mouth. It affects up to 4 million Americans, mostly women. The Sjogrens Foundation (www.sjogrens.org) has information on symptoms and treatment, a listing of centers specializing in treating the condition, and news about the condition.

Spondylitis

Ankylosing spondylitis and related conditions, such as *Reiter's syndrome,* are types of arthritis that affect the spine and other joints. The American Spondylitis Association (www.spondylitis.org) has information on these disorders, news, and message boards.

Chapter 13

HIV/AIDS, Hepatitis, and Other Infectious Diseases

*W*hat a difference a century makes. One hundred little years.

Back at the turn of the last century, the leading causes of death were pneumonia, tuberculosis, and diarrhea. Each one is an infectious disease spread by bacteria, viruses, or parasites. And then there was the flu, also an infectious disease. It was as frightening as the black plague in its time. The Spanish flu epidemic of 1918–1919 killed 20 million people worldwide, including 500,000 in the United States, in less than a year. That's more than have ever been killed in such a short time during any war or famine.

Today, the top three killers are heart disease, cancer, and stroke. All three, for the most part, are considered lifestyle diseases, rather than bacterial or viral diseases. With the advent of effective vaccines and antibiotics, some doctors predicted that, in the second half of the last century, infectious disease would be history. Turned out they were wrong. New threats, such as Human Immuno-deficiency Virus (HIV), the virus linked to Acquired Immunodeficiency Syndrome (AIDS) and hepatitis C, and old ones, such as tuberculosis (TB), emerged at the end of the century.

As we begin the new century, infectious diseases, including flu/pneumonia and AIDS, remain major killers. In this chapter, we start with a look at the Web sites of two major infectious disease fighters, the Centers for Disease Control and Prevention and the National Institute of Allergy and Infectious Diseases. Then, we present some sites with information on the major infectious diseases, including HIV/AIDS, hepatitis, the flu, and pneumonia.

CDC

Infectious disease is the Centers for Disease Control and Prevention's *raison d'être*. (Pardon our French.) The federal government's centers, best known as the CDC, are the cops on the beat, fighting all manner of infectious disease from HIV/AIDS and Ebola hemorrhagic fever on to the flu (and *E. coli* infections from burgers).

And the CDC has taken its disease-preventing efforts online at its Web site (`www.cdc.gov`), as shown in Figure 13-1. The site has a wealth of information on preventing, diagnosing, and treating infectious diseases.

Starting on the left-hand side of the CDC site's home page, here are some of the highlights that you may want to check out:

✔ **Health Topics A–Z:** This section (`www.cdc.gov/health/diseases.htm`) is an A-to-Z index of diseases and health topics found on the CDC Web site. Subjects covered with fact sheets run the gamut from adolescents, African sleeping sickness, chemical weapons, child development, fifth disease (a mild rash in children), firearm-related injuries, and foodborne illnesses, to safety on the job, smoking, violence, and zoonotic diseases (diseases spread from animals to people).

Alphabetically, this huge list goes from *Acanthamoeba,* a parasitic infection, to *zoster,* the virus that causes chickenpox and shingles. Only the letters *K* and *X* are not represented — but we know that those intrepid CDC disease sleuths are working on it 24/7.

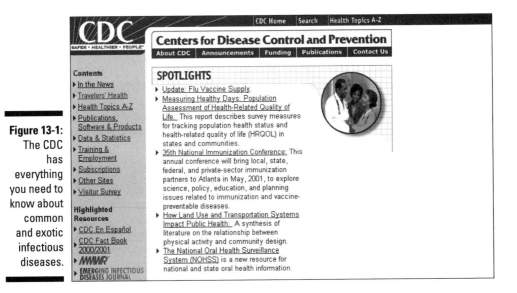

Figure 13-1: The CDC has everything you need to know about common and exotic infectious diseases.

✔ **Travelers' Health:** This superb section, shown in Figure 13-2, has the resources the complete traveler needs in order to be healthy and safe in foreign lands.

On the Travelers' Health page, under Destinations, a drop-down text box on regions of the world appears. Pick your spot, and you'll get the scoop on health concerns and on the vaccinations you'll need to travel in those parts. Also, on the Travelers' Health page, under Outbreaks, you can find the latest news of disease outbreaks around the world.

The site also has information for special travelers, such as children, pregnant women, the disabled, and people with HIV/AIDS. And if you're planning a cruise in international waters, you can check out your ship's sanitation inspection records at `www.cdc.gov/travel/cruiships.htm`.

You can find more on travel health in the *Healthcare Online For Dummies Internet Directory.*

✔ **Hoaxes and Rumors:** This section of the CDC Web site (`www.cdc.gov/hoax_rumors.htm`) deals with rumors about infectious diseases that spread on the Net like a cold in a preschool.

The disease fighters at the CDC debunk these rumors and urban legends, such as the rumor about HIV being spread from needle sticks in phone booth coin return slots, movie theater seats, and gas pump handles. The CDC says that these rumors are not true. (See Chapter 1 for more on discrediting Internet rumors.)

Figure 13-2:
The CDC's Travelers' Health pages offer a guide to the ills that can befall travelers and point out how to avoid them.

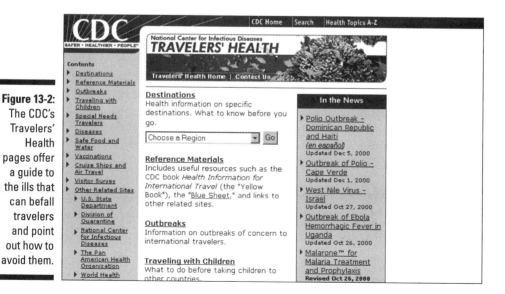

Hooray for public health!

As Paul Simon wrote in the song, "The Boy in the Bubble," these are the days of *miracles and wonder*. Indeed, medical marvels (such as operations performed on babies in the womb and multiple organ transplants) make the nightly news, with doctors being hailed as conquering heroes.

But the major health breakthroughs of the last century often have been overlooked. These breakthroughs are public health measures, such as vaccination campaigns, water clean-up projects, improved care for mothers and babies, and campaigns to help people kick their smoking habits. And the life expectancy of Americans increased 30 years in the last century. Not to knock the medical breakthroughs, but 25 of those years are attributable to public health.

The Centers for Disease Control and Prevention at its Web site at www.cdc.gov/epo/mmwr/preview/mmwrhtml/00056796.htm lists the "Ten Great Public Health Achievements — United States, 1900–1999," which follow:

- ✔ Vaccination
- ✔ Motor-vehicle safety
- ✔ Safer workplaces
- ✔ Control of infectious diseases
- ✔ Decline in deaths from coronary heart disease and stroke
- ✔ Safer and healthier foods
- ✔ Healthier mothers and babies
- ✔ Family planning
- ✔ Fluoridation of drinking water
- ✔ Recognition of tobacco use as a health hazard

Thanks to all you public health types!

The CDC makes it easy for you to find your state health department, which has information about infectious diseases (such as the flu), local programs to test for and treat sexually transmitted diseases, and ways to get birth and death records. Go to wwww.cdc.gov/travel/namerica.htm#state and click the state (or, in some cases, the county agency) you want to reach. The CDC also has a search engine for information within state sites at www.cdc.gov/search2.htm.

National Institute of Allergy and Infectious Diseases

The National Institute of Allergy and Infectious Diseases is the federal government's lead agency on researching infectious diseases. Its Web site (www.niaid.nih.gov) has information on HIV/AIDS, hospital-associated infections, Lyme disease, hantavirus, multidrug-resistant tuberculosis, tropical diseases, and others.

Here's what we suggest that you look at:

- **Publications:** On the opening page, scroll down to the Information section and click the <u>Publications</u> link. (Or go directly to the page at www.niaid.nih.gov/publications.)

  In the list of topics that appears, click the links that interest you to find online brochures and fact sheets on a wide array of infectious diseases, what they are, how to avoid them, and how they are diagnosed and treated. On those pages, you also find links to news and to related sites.

  Topics covered include AIDS, hepatitis, influenza and colds, pneumonia, sexually transmitted diseases, emerging infectious diseases, fungal diseases, and food-borne diseases.

- **Clinical trials:** When researchers want to find out whether a new treatment works, they conduct clinical trials. The National Institute of Allergy and Infectious Diseases Clinical Trials Database at www.niaid.nih.gov/clintrials/niaidsearch.asp has information on research on experimental treatments and vaccines for infectious, immunologic, and allergic diseases.

  You can search for studies by typing the name of a disease in the search box. Or, scrolling down, you can reach a topic by choosing a disease from the drop-down text box and by setting other parameters.

  You can also search ClinicalTrials.gov at www.clinicaltrials.gov and CenterWatch at www.centerwatch.com to find studies. For more on locating studies, see Chapter 7.

A dirty little secret revealed

The American Society for Microbiology says many folks — we're sure, dear reader, that you're not among them — don't wash up after using the, uh, facilities. The society's research has shown that, although 95 percent of people say that they wash their hands, only 67 percent actually do. The society had people planted in bathrooms to *discretely* observe nearly 8,000 people scrub up — or not.

We're proud to say that Chicago, our hometown, rated the cleanest hands — with 83 percent of people washing up. (We almost always listen to Mom.) New Yawkers had the dirtiest paws: Only 49 percent of 2,283 people observed washed their hands after using a restroom in Grand Central/Penn Station. *Eeyew.*

America's dirty little secret has some serious potential consequences in this age of antibiotic-resistant superbugs and emerging infectious diseases. The Society for Microbiology has launched its Clean Hands Campaign to get people to wash up. Get the facts, including a downloadable brochure with instructions on hand washing, at www.washup.org. The society urges potential handwashers to use soap, water, and elbow grease. Who knew? (We live in Chicago, so we already knew that.)

The site also has a downloadable poster — suitable for framing — to hang in your own bathroom. Maybe someone will hang one up in Grand Central/Penn Station.

Infectious Threats

In the following few sections, you find out about some online resources for specific infectious diseases.

HIV/AIDS

Human Immunodeficiency Virus is passed from one person to another in several ways, such as the following:

- Through bodily fluids (such as through unprotected sex without a condom)
- Through the sharing of contaminated needles by drug users
- Through transmission to babies by infected mothers during childbirth and breastfeeding

HIV destroys immune system cells that ordinarily fight off disease, resulting in AIDS (Acquired Immunodeficiency Syndrome). Gay men, drug abusers, and hemophiliacs are among the groups that have been hardest hit by HIV/AIDS in the United States.

The CDC estimates that up to 900,000 Americans are living with HIV and AIDS. Worldwide, the United Nations AIDS program estimates that 47 million people have been infected with HIV, and 22 million have died worldwide. Treatment has made major advances, though expensive therapies aren't commonly available in poorer counties.

A lot of good information about HIV/AIDS appears online. Here are some places to look.

The basics

You can get the basic facts on HIV/AIDS at the following sites:

- The Centers for Disease Control and Prevention's "Living with HIV/AIDS" online brochure is available at www.cdc.gov/hiv/pubs/brochure/livingwithhiv.htm.
- The National Institute of Allergies and Infectious Diseases, at www.niaid.nih.gov/publications/aids.htm, has online brochures and fact sheets on HIV/AIDS.
- Gay Men's Health Crisis, at www.gmhc.org, has background on the infection and sound advice on testing for and living with the disease.

Glossary

For a glossary of HIV/AIDS terms, go to www.hivatis.org/glossary/?list.

One-stop shop

The U.S. Department of Health and Human Services' AIDS Clinical Trials Information Service (www.actis.org), shown in Figure 13-3, is a central resource for current information on federally and privately funded clinical trials for people with AIDS and with HIV infections.

In addition, you can use the site to search for information on HIV/AIDS drugs, vaccines, and treatment guidelines. It also links to AIDSLINE from the ACTIS Search Other Databases page at www.actis.org/otherdata.html, where you can find journal articles through the National Library of Medicine's Internet Grateful Med.

The Body (www.thebody.com) has some unusual HIV/AIDS tools and information. On the site's home page, click the <u>AIDS Basics & Prevention</u> link and follow the link for an interactive questionnaire you can use to determine your risks for HIV/AIDS. Confidentiality is promised.

At www.thebody.com/quality.html, The Body has inspiring stories, book reviews, and even humor. At www.thebody.com/experts.shtml, the site has forums on such topics as fatigue, spiritual support, workplace issues, oral health, and diet. Experts moderate the forums.

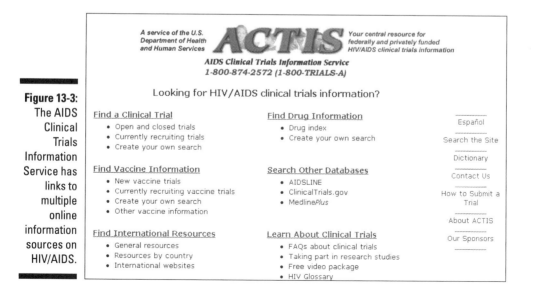

Figure 13-3: The AIDS Clinical Trials Information Service has links to multiple online information sources on HIV/AIDS.

AIDS clock

HIV/AIDS is a big problem in the United States. But it's also a huge problem worldwide, with 95 percent of cases occurring in poor countries. New HIV infections topped 14,500 a day in the year 2000, for a record-breaking 5.3 million new infections in 2000, according to the United Nations.

To dramatize the situation, the UN has an AIDS clock, at `www.unfpa.org/modules/aidsclock`, with images that change 11 times per minute to represent the number of new HIV cases occurring. You need Shockwave software to view the clock. (Click the <u>Requires Shockwave</u> link on the page to download the free software.)

Testing

More than 200,000 Americans are estimated to be infected with HIV and don't know that they have it. At `HIVTEST.org`, the CDC answers questions about who should undergo testing. The site has a clickable map (`HIVTEST.org/locate/index.htm`) featuring local places where HIV testing is available.

Treatment

The HIV/AIDS Treatment Information Service (`www.hivatis.org`) has a run-down on federally approved treatment guidelines for HIV and AIDS.

Services/support

You can find a variety of services for people with HIV/AIDS through the CDC National Prevention Information Network's Resources and Services Database at `www.cdcnac.org/db/public/rsmain.htm`. The site also includes services for other sexually transmitted diseases and tuberculosis. The database lists more than 19,000 programs providing counseling and testing, outreach, health care, support, housing, and legal services.

The JAMA HIV/AIDS Information Center (`www.ama-assn.org/special/hiv`) lists support groups and helplines and has other information on treatment.

Lots of online support is available for people with HIV/AIDS:

✔ Yahoo! Groups (at `groups.yahoo.com`) features numerous e-mail lists concerned with HIV/AIDS.

✔ Two newsgroups dealing with HIV/AIDS are `misc.health.aids` and `sci.med.aids`. You can read these groups at Google Groups by going to `groups.google.com`. Type **AIDS** in the Search Groups box and click the Google Search button. You see the two groups listed under Revelant Searches on the results page. Click the link to either group to read the latest postings. Chapter 2 has more on finding and using online support.

Alternative medicine

People with HIV/AIDS have used lots of alternative therapies to try to improve their health. Here are some places to find out about such alternative therapies:

- ✔ The Alternative Medicine Homepage's AIDS & HIV: Alternative Medicine Resources page (`www.pitt.edu/~cbw/hiv.html`) has lots of links to information on alternative medicine resources for people with HIV and AIDS. It also has links to anti-quackery information.

- ✔ EarthMed.com (in its Conditions area at `www.earthmed.com`) notes that many people with HIV/AIDS try alternative therapies, such as nutritional therapy, herbal medicine, and homeopathy.

- ✔ The Body, at `www.thebody.com/treat/altern.html`, reviews alternative and complementary therapies for people with HIV/AIDS, including yoga, massage, meditation, and diet.

- ✔ TheNaturalPharmacist (`www.tnp.com`) in its Conditions A–Z section says that no well-documented natural treatments for HIV infection are available. But it does talk about some proposed therapies and others to avoid.

Chapter 8 has more on alternative medicine.

Sellers of quack remedies have preyed on people with HIV/AIDS. The U.S. Food and Drug Administration has formed a network of AIDS Health Fraud Task Forces to combat these rip-offs. For information, go to `www.fda.gov/oashi/aids/eval.html`.

News

HIVInSite (`hivinsite.ucsf.edu`), shown in Figure 13-4, has the latest news on HIV/AIDS developments along with patient information and many links to other sites.

The American Foundation for AIDS Research (AMFAR), which has backed research on the disease, has daily news reports on HIV/AIDS and also treatment updates at `www.amfar.org`, as shown in Figure 13-5.

The NPIN Prevention News Update, at `www.cdcnac.org/db/public/dnmain.htm`, includes more than 26,000 summaries, or *abstracts,* of articles about HIV/AIDS-, STD-, and TB-related events in the news and research findings from major newspapers, wire services, medical journals, and newsmagazines.

New & Noteworthy

HIV/AIDS and Young People: Recent Research and Reports, 10/00.

40th ICAAC Conference Summary L. Peiperl, MD, 9/26/00.

HIV/AIDS in Sub-Saharan Africa: Post-Durban Analysis L. Garbus, MPP, 9/00.

Mother-to-Child Transmission Topic Documents and links. Updated 9/00.

HIV/AIDS Prevention and Treatment in Developing Countries An HIV InSite international roundtable discussion with AIDS doctors from Brazil, China, Peru, and Thailand, 8/00.

No Time to Lose: Getting More from HIV Prevention IOM Report on HIV Prevention in the US, 9/28/00.

Figure 13-4:
HIVInSite has the latest news on HIV/AIDS.

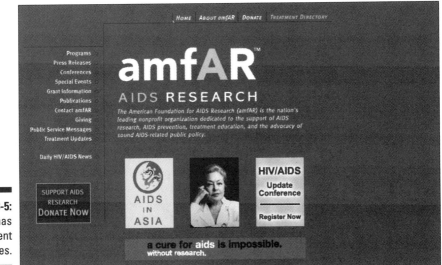

Figure 13-5:
AMFAR has treatment updates.

Other STDs

HIV/AIDS isn't the only *STD* (sexually transmitted disease).

One in five people in the United States has an STD. Two-thirds of all STDs occur in people 25 years of age or younger. STDs are a major cause of infertility and even can cause certain types of cancer.

Here are some sites that offer information and help:

✔ The American Social Health Association, at www.ashastd.org/ stdfaqs/index.html, has information on a dozen STDs, including HIV/AIDS, hepatitis A and B, herpes, syphilis, chlamydia, gonorrhea, trichomoniasis, and pediculosis pubis, or *crabs*. It also has links to fact sheets on the conditions with information on symptoms and treatment. The site also has a link to a Sexual Health Glossary.

Go to www.ashastd.org/hotlines/index.html for a listing of hotline numbers at which you can talk to a counselor.

✔ Iwannaknow.org (www.iwannaknow.org) is an information service on sexual health and STDs aimed at teens. The American Social Health Association sponsors the site, which has a 411 Basic Info Fast section. The site also features a supervised chat room where teens can talk with a sexual health counselor and other teens.

✔ The National Institute of Allergy and Infectious Diseases (www.niaid. nih.gov/publications/stds.htm) and the CDC's National Prevention Information Network (www.cdcnpin.org/std/ common.htm) have information on symptoms of and treatment for other STDs, including chlamydia, genital herpes, gonorrhea, human papillomavirus, genital warts, and syphilis.

Tuberculosis

Tuberculosis, the infectious lung disease, was the leading killer at the beginning of the last century. Its resurgence in recent years has been linked with HIV. In fact, TB is the leading cause of death in people who test positive for HIV. The TB picture has been complicated by the emergence of strains that are resistant to multiple medications.

The CDC has information on tuberculosis at www.cdc.gov/nchstp/tb/ faqs/qa.htm. Also check out the American Lung Association fact sheet on TB at www.lungusa.org/diseases/tbhivfac.html.

Liver infection

The liver is a remarkable organ. It serves as the body's filter and is an amazing chemical factory. It is the only organ in the body that can regenerate itself.

Your liver also can be affected by a number of diseases, including the infectious ones. For an overview on liver diseases, go to the Liver Foundation at www.liverfoundation.org. The site has background on various liver conditions and links to online support.

The Centers for Disease Control Viral Hepatitis site has an overview on hepatitis types — from A to E — at `www.cdc.gov/ncidod/diseases/hepatitis` (see Figure 13-6).

Hepatitis B

Hepatitis B is an inflammation of the liver that is more common and much more infectious than AIDS. The condition, which chronically infects more than 1 million Americans, can lead to scarring of the liver, known as *cirrhosis,* and to liver cancer.

Hepatitis B can be spread sexually and in other ways similar to the ways in which HIV is spread. You can protect yourself with a hepatitis B vaccine.

The Hepatitis B Foundation (`www.hepb.org`) has background on the disease, a medical specialist finder (including the doctors' research projects), and also a listing of online support groups.

Hepatitis C

An estimated 4 million Americans are infected with hepatitis C, which can damage the liver and result in death. Risks include using intravenous drugs, having a history of blood transfusions, being on kidney dialysis, and working in healthcare. Transmission may also occur through sexual contact.

You can find out more about testing, symptoms, and treatment at the Hepatitis C: The Epidemic for Everyone Web site at `www.epidemic.org/index2.html`. The site has links to support groups.

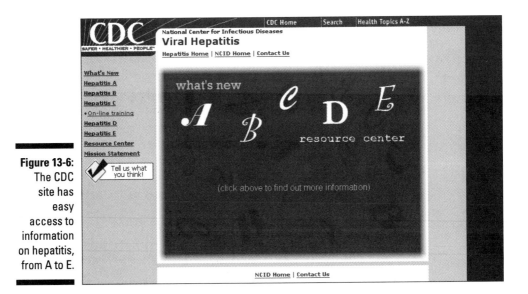

Figure 13-6: The CDC site has easy access to information on hepatitis, from A to E.

Ulcers as infection

Have you been blaming spicy foods and stress for a stomach ulcer? If so, get thee to a doctor. You may actually have an infection brewing.

In most cases, scientists have confirmed in recent years that ulcers are caused by infection from a bacterium, *Helicobacter pylori (H. pylori)*. This spiral-shaped bacterium is a *survivor*. This bad boy outwits, outlasts, and outplays all those digestive juices to attack the stomach lining, and you can't vote it out at the Tribal Council. But most people infected with the bacteria can be readily cured with a course of antibiotics.

Researcher Dr. Barry J. Marshall is a survivor, too. He had to fight against conventional views and the medical establishment to prove his theory. Way to go, Dr. M. He established the Helicobacter Foundation with information on the condition and its diagnosis and treatment at www.helico.com.

The National Digestive Diseases Information Clearinghouse has an online brochure on *H. pylori* at www.niddk.nih.gov/health/digest/pubs/hpylori/hpylori.htm#2.

If you've got one of those curable infections, you soon could be chowing down on some tom yum soup or green curry chicken. Yum.

Pneumonia and the flu

What's the most deadly infectious disease in the United States? No need to ask Regis to query the audience. If you answered AIDS, you'd be wrong. It's pneumonia.

Pneumonia, an inflammation of the lungs, can result from more than 30 causes. One of the more serious types of pneumonia is a complication of the flu. So getting flu shots can help you not only duck the flu, but also avoid pneumonia. Combined with the flu, pneumonia is the sixth leading killer of Americans. Most deaths from pneumonia and the flu occur in people over 65.

Pneumonia

Until the mid-1930s, pneumonia was the leading killer of Americans, according to the American Lung Association. The association has information on pneumonia at www.lungusa.org/diseases/lungpneumoni.html. In many cases, pneumonia is a complication of infection with the flu, a virus.

Another major cause of pneumonia is a type of bacteria, known as *Streptococcus pneumoniae.* These bacteria can cause pneumonia and others serious infections that kill thousands of toddlers and seniors. The *Streptococcus pneumoniae* bacterium is the most deadly of bacteria, but the infections can be avoided with immunizations.

The National Coalition for Adult Immunizations (www.nfid.org/ncai) has everything you need to know about pneumonia and flu, including schedules for when adults should be immunized.

The flu

Some people may dismiss influenza, or *the flu,* as a trifle. It isn't.

The viruses that cause respiratory tract infections, accompanied by fever, headache, muscle ache, and fatigue, have caused some of the most deadly epidemics in history, including the Spanish flu outbreak in 1918–1919 and the Asian flu outbreak in 1957–1958.

At its site at www.cdc.gov/ncidod/diseases/flu/fluvirus.htm, the Centers for Disease Control and Prevention has background on the flu and information on avoiding it and treating it with antiviral medications.

Who's who for flu shots

Flu shots help protect you from the flu. But the CDC recommends that only people at high risk for complications from the flu get the shots. The CDC recommends, at www.cdc.gov/ncidod/diseases/flu/fluvac.htm, that the following people be immunized annually:

✔ All people aged 50 years or older

✔ People of any age with chronic diseases of the heart, lung or kidneys, diabetes, immunosuppression, or severe forms of anemia

✔ Residents of nursing homes and other chronic-care facilities housing patients of any age with chronic medical conditions

✔ Women who will be more than 3 months pregnant during the influenza season

✔ Children and teenagers who are receiving long-term aspirin therapy and who may therefore be at risk for developing Reye syndrome after an influenza virus infection.

By the way, the CDC insists that flu shots prevent the flu and *don't* cause it.

The Healthcare Online
For Dummies
Internet Directory

The 5th Wave

By Rich Tennant

"...and whoever finds a cure for Mr. Pheeb's athletes foot gets extra credit."

In this directory . . .

*P*lanning a cruise and worried about the health conditions on the ship? Wonder where you can get your medications cheaper? Looking for an online support group for a chronic condition? Want to figure out how many calories you're burning right this very minute?

Well, bunkie, you've come to the right place. These screaming yellow pages are where you can find these goodies and a boatload of other useful, interesting, even quirky, health-related Web sites.

We've packed more than 400 sites into this space — we wish we could fit more — and arranged them into tidy alphabetic categories.

But don't rest on formalities. As always, browsing and random page turning are tolerated — even encouraged. So what are you waiting for? Dive in.

About This Directory

To use this directory, all you need to do is browse through it, read the descriptions that appeal to you, and then visit those sites.

To help you judge at a glance whether a site may be useful to you, this directory includes some handy miniature icons (otherwise known as *micons*). Here's an explanation of what each micon means:

Find a practitioner.

This site requires registration to use some or all information.

Online and/or offline support groups or information on local groups is available.

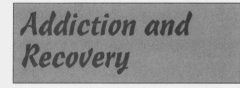

Addiction and Recovery

A variety of online groups offer assistance to people recovering from addictions. Here are few.

Recovery Works

www.addictions.org/recoveryworks

Addiction center: This Web site has statistics and links for these addictions: alcohol, drugs, sex, gambling, food, work, grief, and the Internet. Click the Support Groups button to find online support. This site also has tips aimed at adolescents.

Substance Abuse Treatment Facility Locator

findtreatment.samhsa.gov

Find a treatment program: Click the Here link and then use the map to locate the drug and alcohol abuse treatment programs nearest you.

Alcohol

Adult Children of Alcoholics World Service Organization, Inc.

www.adultchildren.org

Al-Anon/Alateen

www.al-anon.alateen.org

Alcoholics Anonymous

www.alcoholics-anonymous.org

National Institute on Alcohol Abuse and Alcoholism

www.niaaa.nih.gov

Co-dependency

Co-Dependents Anonymous

www.codependents.org

Drugs

Chemically Dependent Anonymous

www.cdaweb.org

Cocaine Anonymous

www.ca.org

Marijuana Anonymous

www.marijuana-anonymous.org

Narcotics Anonymous World Services

www.wsoinc.com

National Institute on Drug Abuse
www.drugabuse.gov/NIDAHome1.html

Nicotine Anonymous
www.nicotine-anonymous.org

Food

Overeaters Anonymous
www.overeatersanonymous.org

Gambling

Gam-Anon
gam-anon.org

Gamblers Anonymous
www.gamblersanonymous.org

National Council on Problem Gambling
www.ncpgambling.org

Sex

Survivors of Incest Anonymous, Inc.
www.siawso.org

Sex Addicts Anonymous
www.sexaa.org

Sexaholics Anonymous
www.sa.org

Sexual Compulsives Anonymous
www.sca-recovery.org

Sexual Recovery Anonymous
sexualrecovery.org

Work

Workaholics Anonymous
people.ne.mediaone.net/wa2/index.html

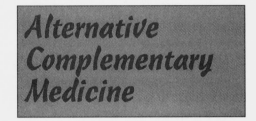

Alternative Complementary Medicine

Chapter 8 is devoted to alternative and complementary medicine. Here are a few more Web sites on the topic.

Alexander Technique
www.alexandertechnique.com

Healthy moves: Alexander Technique teaches you how to balance the body to increase energy and reduce tension in everyday movements.

American Music Therapy Association
www.namt.com

The sounds of music: Music therapy uses music and rhythm to ease a variety of mental and physical conditions. This site answers basic questions about music therapy and its use with specific populations.

American Holistic Medical Association (AHMA)
www.holisticmedicine.org

The holistic picture: Holistic medicine aims to treat the whole person: body, mind, and spirit. The AHMA lists a series of questions you can ask practitioners to determine whether they follow this philosophy. You can order a copy of AHMA's Doctor Finder at the site.

Ayurvedic Foundations

www.ayur.com

Original recipe: Holistic medicine is a hot topic these days. But Ayurvedic physicians in India have been practicing this approach to healing and life for more than 6,000 years. This site explains the approach and hosts an electronic bulletin board. May the Tridoshas be with you.

Biofeedback Certification Institute of America

www.bcia.org

What's your body telling you?: Biofeedback is a method of learning to use your body's signals to improve your health. This site covers the basics and suggests questions you should ask a practitioner.

ChiroWeb.com

www.chiroweb.com

Getting adjusted: Chiropractic is the fastest growing form of alternative care. This site from *Dynamic Chiropractic* newspaper gives the facts on what chiropractic is and what to look for in selecting a practitioner. The site also has an Ask a Doctor of Chiropractic Forum.

Feldenkrais Guild

www.feldenkrais.com

Get it moving: Moshe Feldenkrais, a multi-talented engineer and judo expert, developed this gentle approach to improve movement and human functioning.

Fragrant World: The Guide to Aromatherapy

www.fragrant.demon.co.uk

Catch a whiff: This site is a guide to aromatherapy. It includes a glossary and a description of oils — from *ajowan* to *zanthoxylum* — and information on how to use them and where to buy them.

HealthWorld Online

www.healthy.net

Consider the alternatives: Lots of info on nutrition, fitness, self-care, wellness, natural health, and alternative medicine.

Homeopathy Home

www.homeopathyhome.com

Homeopathic remedies: This site has comprehensive homeopathic information, including articles, lists of practitioners and suppliers, chats, and discussion boards.

Macrobiotics Online

www.macrobiotics.org

Living in harmony: Macrobiotics is a way of life that encourages living in harmony with nature by eating a balanced whole-foods diet, engaging in an active lifestyle, and respecting the environment. This site includes articles on macrobiotics, recipes, and illness recovery stories.

The Rolf Institute of Structural Integration

www.rolf.org

Rolf and roll: Named for its inventor, Dr. Ida P. Rolf, Rolfing is a system of soft tissue manipulation and movement education. People use Rolfing as a way to ease pain and stress. The site has information about Rolfing in general — its history, theory, and principles — and on Rolfing's effect on back pain, repetitive stress, and athletic performance.

If you know where to look, the Web can help you understand how you tick.

Gray's Anatomy of the Human Body

www.bartleby.com/107

Searchable classic: This 1918 classic of anatomy has more than 1,200 illustrations and 13,000 entries, ranging from the Antrum of Highmore to the Zonule of Zinn. Check it out by using the site's search engine.

Visible Human

www.exploratorium.edu/bodies/ vhuman.html

See-through man: Convicted murderer Joseph Paul Jernigan left his body to science, and science put him to good use through the National Library of Medicine's Visible Human Project. Jernigan was encased in gelatin and carved into 1,862 horizontal slices. Surgeons have used these slices and those from a woman to plan surgery. You can find out a bit about anatomy at this site as well as from other sites that are linked to the project. You need the Shockwave plug-in, which you can download from this site.

Seventy percent of the population at some time experiences back pain. Here are some sites that will help.

American Academy of Orthopaedic Surgeons (AAOS)

www.aaos.org

Back track: The AAOS gives tips on preventing back pain; a lesson on spinal anatomy; lifting techniques for caregivers; information on low back pain, sciatica, scoliosis, spinal fusion, and kids and backpacks; and exercises you can do to relieve back pain.

How to Prevent Back Pain

www.nlm.nih.gov/medlineplus/tutorials/ backpain.html

Interactive tutorial: The National Library of Medicine's MEDLINE*plus* makes available this tutorial with sections on anatomy, causes of back pain, disks and their problems, back pain, preventing back pain, and good back techniques for back safety. To see and hear this animated tutorial, click the Go to Module button.

Spine-Health.com

www.spine-health.com

Spine megasite: Information on the common causes of back pain, diagnosis, non-surgical and surgical treatment, and basic anatomy. The site has interactive animations and a Getting Started section for newcomers.

As medicine crosses new frontiers in cloning and genetics, new organ transplantation techniques, and the like, ethical issues are raised daily. You can find out more about them online.

Bioethics.net

www.med.upenn.edu/bioethics

Commentary on medical issues: Top medical ethicists Glenn McGee and Art Caplan from the University of Pennsylvania Center for Bioethics and others discuss issues in medicine, such as genetics and cloning.

Cancer

Chapter 10 is devoted to cancer. Here are a few more Web sites on the topic.

CancerSourceKids.com

www.cancersourcekids.com

Cancer info for kids: Dealing with cancer is tough, especially for kids. Run in partnership with the Association of Pediatric Oncology Nurses, this site offers information on cancer aimed at kids, teens, and parents. Kids can plug in the type of cancer that they or a sibling has and get the facts.

Children's Cancer Web

www.cancerindex.org/ccw

Quick facts: This site is designed to make it easier to find online information about childhood cancer. Also, check out the index of some of the key cancer-related sites and pages.

Imaginis: The Breast Health Specialists

www.imaginis.com

Breast cancer help: Imaginis has info on breast cancer diagnosis and treatment and reconstructive surgery, as well as a breast cancer glossary. The site also provides information on other breast conditions and other types of women's cancer.

Shared Experience Cancer Support Knowledgebase

www.sharedexperience.org

Sharing stories: The premise of this site is that it helps you share with others what you've gone through as a cancer patient. Patients can post diaries of their experiences at the site. The Shared Experience community has links to sites where patients and their families can chat online.

Caregivers Support

Being a full-time caregiver can be difficult. You may experience anger, isolation, and guilt. Here are some places to get support.

Family Caregiver Alliance

www.caregiver.org

Caring for caregivers: You can find online support groups, fact sheets on diseases, and more at this site.

National Family Caregivers Association (NFCA)

www.nfcacares.org

Caregiver support: NFCA's Web site offers inspiration and tips for caregivers, including advice on how to deal with doctors.

National Respite Locator Service

www.chtop.com/locator.htm

Get a break: This service helps you find respite services. The site provides links by state for respite and crisis care contacts.

Cut Medication Costs

Many Americans can't afford the drugs they need to stay healthy. Here are some leads to better prices and even free meds.

Drug company assistance

Drug companies have assistance programs to help the needy.

American Foundation for AIDS Research (AMFAR)

www.amfar.org

AIDS drug aid: AMFAR, in its Treatment Directory, provides information about AIDS Drug Assistance programs. It contains Medicaid contact information, a drug index, a listing of patient assistance programs, and other general information.

Directory of Prescription Drug Patient Assistance Programs

www.phrma.org/searchcures/dpdpap

Industry's own listing: The Pharmaceutical Research and Manufacturers of America lists company programs that provide drugs to physicians whose patients could not otherwise afford them.

Needy Meds

www.needymeds.com/MainPage.html

Drug company programs: This site lists medications and provides links to information on assistance programs that can help you purchase those medications.

Prescription Drug Assistance Programs

www.medicare.gov/Prescription/ Home.asp

Medicare cares: The federal Medicare program has databases you can search for programs that offer discounts or free medication to individuals in need. The search includes prescription drug assistance programs, Medicare managed care plans, and Medigap plans that offer prescription drug coverage in your area.

RxHope.com

www.rxhope.com

Industry pitches in: Physicians and certain patient advocate organizations can use this site to get low-cost or no-cost medications for patients in need. In the Patients section, a database provides state-by-state information on programs to help specific groups, including veterans, the elderly, children, Medicare patients, pregnant teens, and others.

O, Canada

Some seniors have been taking advantage of lower drug prices in Canada. In fact, they've ridden buses to Canada, where there's a favorable exchange rate and cheaper generic medications that are not sold in the United States. With the help of the Net, you can get similar savings without crossing the border. The Food and Drug Administration has looked the other way on this issue.

Prescription Drug Pricing Reform

bernie.house.gov/bustocanada/index.asp

For those who want to get on the bus: Vermont Congressman Bernie Sanders has led bus trips to Canada to purchase medications there. For information on his campaign, check out this Web site.

Other Sites to Check Out

You can save the bus fare and go to Canadian drugstores online to order prescriptions at up to 50-percent savings:

Canadameds.com
   www.canadameds.com

CanadaRX.net
   www.canadarx.net

TheCanadianDrugStore.com
   www.TheCanadianDrugstore.com

Dental Care

American Dental Association
www.ada.org/public/index.asp

Brusha, brushsa, brusha: The American Dental Association has information on caring for your teeth and gums.

Disabilities

The Internet has a wealth of resources to help people with disabilities to find information, help, and support.

A Blind Net
www.blind.net/blindind.htm

Net help for blind: This site's motto is: Blind People Need Equality, Not Random Acts Of Senseless Kindness." You can find lots of information and links about blindness, including organizations *for* rather than *of* the blind (there's a difference), information on courtesy rules when dealing with people who are blind, listings of companies that make products for the blind, and information on the causes of blindness.

American Foundation for the Blind
www.afb.org

Continuing Helen Keller's work: Every seven minutes, someone goes blind in the United States. The foundation aims to help these people online with information and services.

Americans with Disabilities (ADA) Act
www.eeoc.gov/facts/fs-ada.html

Act and facts: The ADA prohibits job discrimination against people with disabilities. The U.S. Equal Employment Opportunity Commission provides a quick rundown on ADA, which has a big impact on the lives of the disabled.

Amputee Coalition of America On-Line Resource Center
www.amputee-coalition.org

Help for amputees: Fact sheets to help amputees cope, listings of support groups, and the National Limb Loss Information Center.

Best Hospitals: Rehabilitation
www.usnews.com/usnews/nycu/health/hosptl/specreha.htm

Best rehab centers: U.S. News lists the most highly rated rehabilitation centers in the United States.

disAbility.gov
www.disability.gov

One-stop-shop government resource: The federal government offers a wide array of information for people with disabilities. You can find out how to prepare for natural disasters as well as find information aimed at children. In addition, you can find links to these topics on the site's main page: tax credits, employer information, civil rights, education, technology advances, recreation and travel, and transportation.

Disabled Sports USA
www.dsusa.org

Disabled jocks: This movement aims to help people with disabilities rehabilitate themselves through sports. Winter skiing, water sports, summer and winter competitions, fitness, and special sports events are available. Participants include people with visual impairments, amputations, spinal cord injuries, dwarfism, multiple sclerosis, head injuries, cerebral palsy, and other neuromuscular and orthopedic conditions. Local chapters are listed at the site.

HandSpeak

www.handspeak.com

Sign language online: Learn American and international sign languages. Pick a word to see a video demo.

The Home Ramp Project

www.wheelchairramp.org

Ramping up the home: Information on how to construct ramps to make homes wheelchair accessible.

March of Dimes

www.modimes.org

Birth defects info: This site includes information on the effects of medications, cocaine, alcohol, and smoking on fetuses as well as provides fact sheets on a variety of birth defects, including clubfoot, Down syndrome, oral-facial clefts, Marfan syndrome, phenylketonuria, Rh disease, sickle cell anemia, spina bifida, Tay-Sachs disease, and thalassemia. The site also has information on finding local chapters as well as provides information on how to have a healthy baby.

Microsoft Accessibility Technology for Everyone

www.microsoft.com/enable

Microsoft helps: The leading software maker offers tips, hints, guides, and more on how to make computing more accessible to people with vision impairments, hearing impairments, mobility impairments, and cognitive and language impairments.

National Association of the Deaf (NAD)

www.nad.org

Accessibility and civil rights: NAD looks out for the rights of the 28 million Americans who are deaf or hard of hearing. The site's Info Center answers questions important to the deaf and hard-of-hearing community, including what educational opportunities are available, why deaf people prefer not to be called hearing impaired, how long it takes to learn sign language, and so forth.

Social Security Online Disability Programs

www.ssa.gov/disability

Benefits for disabled: A 20-year-old worker has a 3-in-10 chance of becoming disabled before reaching retirement. The Social Security Administration explains disability benefits at this site.

Spinal Cord Injury Resources

www.makoa.org/sci.htm

Full gamut of info for spinal cord injured: This site has a comprehensive listing of online resources for people with spinal cord injuries, including rehabilitation centers, e-mail lists, bulletin boards/chat rooms, stores that sell products for the disabled, articles, and pamphlets.

Women with Disabilities

www.4women.gov/wwd/index.htm

Women's view: Twenty-six million women are coping with disabilities. This site offers information for these women from a variety of angles. The site's main page provides access to these areas: Abuse, Access to Health Care, Parenting, Sexuality, Substance Abuse, and more.

Disease, Health, and Art

Sometimes the best way to cope with a disease is through art. Here are some sites linking art and diseases.

American Art Therapy Association, Inc.

www.arttherapy.org

Healing arts: Art therapists use art as a healing force. The American Art Therapy Association explains how the therapy works and provides links to additional information.

American Council for Headache Education Art Museum

www.achenet.org/museum

Painful expression: People with severe headaches express their pain through their paintings.

Breastfeeding.com's Art Gallery

breastfeeding.com/artgallery.html

Breastfeeding through the centuries: This gallery looks at images of breastfeeding from ancient to modern times.

Confronting Cancer through Art

www.upenn.edu/ARG/CCTA/intro.html

Coping with cancer: The University of Pennsylvania Cancer Center and the Arthur Ross Gallery have pulled together nearly 200 works by cancer survivors or friends and family of people with cancer.

Cunningham Dax Collection of Psychiatric Art

www.ozemail.com.au/~ecdax/ artworks.html

Psychiatric art: This gallery includes art by people with neuroses, depression, mania, and schizophrenia. The goal is to increase public understanding of these illnesses.

Tobacco Advertising Gallery

tobaccofreekids.org/adgallery

Smokin' images: The Campaign for Tobacco-Free Kids has a gallery of tobacco ads from around the world. See how creativity is put to work to promote this life-threatening product.

Disease Info and Support

Virtually any disease you can think of is represented by an organization with an online presence. These Web headquarters typically offer information about the condition as well as provide links to related sites, support groups, and sometimes a physician finder.

Here are a few sites that can help you locate these groups. And following this list of sites is a sampling of these online organizations.

DIRLINE: Directory of Health Organizations

dirline.nlm.nih.gov

LII.org's Health and Medicine: Diseases & Conditions

www.lii.org/search/file/ diseases_and_conditions

Yahoo! All Diseases and Conditions

dir.yahoo.com/Health/ Diseases_and_Conditions/ All_Diseases_and_Conditions

Allergy, asthma, and lung diseases

American Lung Association
www.lungusa.org

Asthma and Allergy Foundation of America
www.aafa.org

National Emphysema Foundation
emphysemafoundation.org

Arthritis and related conditions

American Behcet's Disease Association
pweb.netcom.com/~mharting

Arthritis Foundation
www.arthritis.org

Fibromyalgia Network
www.fmnetnews.com

Lupus Foundation of America
web4.xor.com/lupus

National Marfan Foundation
www.marfan.org

Scleroderma Foundation
www.scleroderma.org

Spondylitis Association of America
www.spondylitis.org

Autoimmune Disorders

American Autoimmune Related Diseases Association
www.aarda.org

Chronic Fatigue and Immune Dysfunction Syndrome Association of America
www.cfids.org

Jeffrey Modell Foundation: National Resource Center for Primary Immune Deficiency
www.jmfworld.org

Sjogren's Syndrome Foundation
www.sjogrens.org

Birth defects

Alpha 1 Association
www.alpha1.org

American Cleft Palate-Craniofacial Association
www.cleftline.org

American Pseudo-obstruction and Hirschsprung's Disease Society
www.tiac.net/users/aphs

Angelman Syndrome Foundation
www.angelman.org

Birth Defects Research for Children Inc.
www.birthdefects.org

Cornelia de Lange Syndrome (CdLS) Foundation
www.cdlsoutreach.org

Hydrocephalus Foundation
www.hydrocephalus.org

Klinefelter Syndrome and Associates
www.genetic.org/ks

March of Dimes
www.modimes.org

National Association for Down Syndrome
www.nads.org

National Foundation for Ectodermal Dysplasias
www.nfed.org

National Fragile X Foundation
www.fragilex.org

National Urea Cycle Disorders Foundation
www.nucdf.org

Nevus Network
www.nevusnetwork.org

Polycystic Kidney Disease Foundation
www.pkdcure.org

Spina Bifida Association of America
www.sbaa.org

Support Organization for Trisomy 18, 13, and Related Disorders
www.trisomy.org

Twin to Twin Transfusion Syndrome Foundation
www.tttsfoundation.org

Wide Smiles: Cleft Lip and Palate Resource
www.widesmiles.org

Williams Syndrome Association
www.williams-syndrome.org

Blood diseases

American Sickle Cell Anemia Association
www.ascaa.org

Cooley's Anemia Foundation
www.thalassemia.org/home/ net_op/h3.htm

National Hemophilia Foundation
www.hemophilia.org/home.htm

Bone disorders

National Osteoporosis Foundation
www.nof.org

Osteogenesis Imperfecta Foundation
www.oif.org

Paget Foundation
www.paget.org

Brain and neurological disorders

ALS Association
www.alsa.org

Alzheimer's Association
www.alz.org

American Council for Headache Education
www.achenet.org

American Stroke Association
www.strokeassociation.org

Brain Injury Association
www.biausa.org

Children's Hemiplesia and Stroke Association
www.hemikids.org

Epilepsy Foundation
www.efa.org

Huntington's Disease Society of America
www.hdsa.org

Migraine Awareness Group: A National Understanding for Migraineurs (M.A.G.N.U.M)
www.migraines.org

Multiple Sclerosis Association of America
www.msaa.com

Muscular Dystrophy Association
www.mdausa.org

Myasthenia Gravis Foundation
www.myasthenia.org

National Neurofibromatosis Foundation
www.nf.org

National Stroke Association
www.stroke.org

Parkinson's Disease Foundation
www.parkinsons-foundation.org

Restless Legs Syndrome Foundation
www.rls.org

Cancer

Alliance for Lung Cancer
www.alcase.org

American Brain Tumor Association
www.abta.org

American Cancer Society
www.cancer.org

BreastCancerinfo.com
www.breastcancerinfo.com

Kidney Cancer Association
www.kidneycancerassociation.org

The Leukemia & Lymphoma Society
www.leukemia-lymphoma.org

Lymphoma Research Foundation of America
www.lymphoma.org

Multiple Myeloma Research Foundation
www.multiplemyeloma.org

(Prostate Cancer) US TOO! International, Inc.
www.ustoo.com

Skin Cancer Foundation
ww.skincancer.org

Testicular Cancer Resource Center
www.acor.org/diseases/TC

ThyCa: Thyroid Cancer Survivors' Association
www.thyca.org

Women's Cancer Network
www.wcn.org

Y-Me National Breast Cancer Organization
www.y-me.org

Diabetes and digestive diseases

American Diabetes Association
www.diabetes.org

American Liver Foundation
www.liverfoundation.org

Celaic Disease Foundation
www.celiac.org

Crohn's & Colitis Foundation of America
www.ccfa.org

Cyclic Vomiting Syndrome Association
www.beaker.iupui.edu/cvsa/index.html

Hepatitis Foundation International
www.hepfi.org

Juvenile Diabetes Foundation
www.jdf.org

National Kidney Foundation
www.kidney.org

National Pancreas Foundation
www.pancreasfoundation.org

Pediatric Crohn's & Colitis Foundation
pcca.hypermart.net

Polycystic Kidney Research Foundation
www.pkdcure.org

United Ostomy Association
www.uoa.org

Developmental and learning disorders

Asperger Sydrome Coalition of the United States
www.asperger.org

Autism National Committee
www.autcom.org

Autism Society of America
www.autism-society.org

Children and Adults with Attention Deficit/Hyperactivity Disorder
www.chadd.org

International Dyslexia Association
www.interdys.org

National Attention Deficit Disorder Association
www.add.org

Eating disorders

Anorexia Nervosa and Related Eating Disorders
www.anred.com

Eating Disorder Referral and Information Center
www.edreferral.com

Empowered Parents: A Family Approach to the Prevention and Treatment of Eating Disorders

www.empoweredparents.com

National Association of Anorexia Nervosa and Associated Disorders

www.anad.org

Something Fishy Website on Easting Disorders

www.something-fishy.org

Eye diseases

The Foundation Fighting Blindness

www.blindness.org

Glaucoma Foundation

www.glaucoma-foundation.org

Macular Degeneration Foundation

www.eyesight.org

National Keratoconus Foundation

www.nkcf.org

Heart diseases

Adult Congenital Heart Association

www.achaheart.org

American Heart Association

www.americanheart.org

Children's Health Information Network on Congenital Heart Disease

www.tchin.org

Mitral Valve Prolapse Research & Support

www.mvpsupport.com

Hormone disorders

American Thyroid Association

www.thyroid.org

Human Growth Foundation

www.hgfound.org

Little People of America

www.lpaonline.org

National Adrenal Diseases Foundation

www.medhelp.org/nadf

National Graves' Disease Foundation

www.ngdf.org

Pituitary Tumor Network Association

www.pituitary.org/default.htm

HIV/AIDS

American Foundation for AIDS Research

www.amfar.org

American Red Cross African American HIV/AIDS Program

www.redcross.org/services/hss/hivaids/afam.html

American Red Cross Hispanic HIV/AIDS Program

www.redcross.org/services/hss/
hivaids/hispanic.html

Elizabeth Glaser Pediatric AIDS Foundation

www.pedaids.org

Gay Men's Health Crisis

www.gmhc.org

National Association of People with AIDS

www.napwa.org

National Native American AIDS Prevention Center

www.nnaapc.org

Project Inform

www.projectinform.org

Mental illnesses

Anxiety Disorders Association of America

www.adaa.org

Children & Adolescent Bipolar Foundation

www.bpkids.org

National Alliance for Research on Schizophrenia and Depression

www.mhsource.com/narsad

National Alliance for the Mentally Ill

www.nami.org

National Depressive and Manic-Depressive Association

www.ndmda.org

Obsessive-Compulsive Foundation

www.ocfoundation.org

Sidran Traumatic Stress Foundation

www.sidran.org

World Fellowship for Schizophrenia and Allied Disorders

www.world-schizophrenia.org

Movement disorders

Ataxia-Telangiectasia Children's Project

www.atcp.org

Tourette Syndrome Association

www.tsa-usa.org

We Move

www.wemove.org

Wilson's Disease Association

www.wilsonsdisease.org

Sensory disorders

Acoustic Neuroma Association

www.ANAUSA.org

Alexander Graham Bell Association for the Deaf and Hard of Hearing

www.agbell.org

American Association of the Deaf-Blind
www.tr.wosc.osshe.edu/
DBLINK/aadb.Htm

American Tinnitus Association
www.ata.org

Association of Late-Deafened Adults
www.alda.org

Ear Foundation
www.earfoundation.org

Vestibular Disorders Association
www.teleport.com/~veda

Sexually transmitted diseases

American Social Health Association
www.ashastd.org

Skin diseases

National Alopecia Areata Foundation
www.alopeciaareata.com

National Eczema Association
www.eczema-assn.org

The National Organization for Albinism and Hypopigmentation
www.albinism.org

National Psoriasis Foundation
www.psoriasis.org

National Vitiligo Foundation
www.nvfi.org/menu.htm

Sleep disorders

American Sleep Apnea Association
www.sleepapnea.org

Hair Loss Information Center
www.hairloss.com

Narcolepsy Network
www.websciences.org/narnet

Sleep Foundation
www.sleepfoundation.org

Spinal cord injuries

Christopher Reeve Paralysis Foundation
www.apacure.com

National Spinal Cord Injury Association
www.spinalcord.org

Urologic diseases

American Foundation for Urologic Disease
www.afud.org

Interstitial Cystitis Association
www.ichelp.org

Prostatitis Foundation

www.prostatitis.org

Simon Foundation for Continence

www.simonfoundation.org/html

Voice

National Aphasia Association

www.aphasia.org

National Spasmodic Dysphonia Association

www.dystonia-foundation.org/NSDA

Recurrent Respiratory Papillomatosis Foundation

www.rrpf.org

Environmental Health

As they say in the musical *Hair*, "the air, the air is everywhere" — and sometimes, so is the pollution. Here are some places where you can find out more about environmental health.

National Institute of Environmental Health Sciences

www.niehs.nih.gov

Something in the air: This federal agency offers some online pamphlets on topics involving the environment and health, including asthma, lead, and ozone. Find out how *Pfiesteria piscicida* (fee-STEER-ee-uh pis-kuh-SEED-uh) is affecting fish. The site also includes a page for kids.

Office of Children's Health Protection

www.epa.gov/children

Air, water, and so on: The U.S. Environmental Protection Agency's Office of Children's Health Protection looks at what can be done to protect kids from threats in the water, air, and food. Childhood cancers, asthma, and neurological disorders also are addressed.

Also, check out the EPA for health-related information on pollutants and toxins at `www.epa.gov/epahome/topics.html`.

TOXLINE

igm.nlm.nih.gov

Chemical lookup: If you want to check out the literature on a particular chemical, go to Internet Grateful Med (`igm.nlm.nih.gov`) and click the <u>TOXLINE</u> link in the left-hand column.

Ergonomics

Ergonomics is the science that seeks to adapt work or working conditions to suit the worker.

ErgAerobics

www.ergaerobics.com

Ergonomically speaking: This site provides information on exercises to avoid repetitive stress injuries (RSI) as well as product reviews. It makes the point that even the best-designed equipment won't help prevent RSI unless it is used properly.

Occupational Safety and Health Administration (OSHA)

www.osha-slc.gov/SLTC/ergonomics/
   index.html

Twenty-five tons: If you are typing away, you may be exerting up to 25 tons of force a day. In addition, you may be exposing yourself to the strain of poor lighting and back pain from using a poorly designed chair. OSHA, a federal agency, provides its standards for ergonomics and recommendations for computer workstations. Also, the site offers recommendations for baggage handling, sewing, and other work environments.

A Patient's Guide to Carpal Tunnel Syndrome

www.sechrest.com/mmg/ reflib/ctd/cts/cts.html

Tunnel of pain: This fact sheet explains what carpal tunnel syndrome is, how it's diagnosed, and various treatment options.

Typing Injury FAQ (Frequently Asked Questions)

www.tifaq.com

Oops, I did it again: Prevention, treatment, links, and support for RSI (Repetitive Stress Injury). The site includes an extensive glossary, basic ergonomic information and suggested resources, medical and alternative health articles, as well as disability and workers' compensation information.

Eye Care

American Academy of Ophthalmology: The Eye M.D. Association

www.medem.com/MedLB/ bufferpage_aao.cfm

Eye, eye: The Eye M.D. Association presents the facts on cataracts, detached/torn retinas, diabetes-related eye disease, glaucoma, macula problems, vision corrective surgery, and more.

American Optometric Association

www.aoanet.org

Look at eye care: Read the facts on children's eye care, low vision problems, contact lenses, and corrective eye surgery.

First Aid

Chapter 1 has some Web sites on first aid and injury prevention. Here are some more.

American Association of Poison Control Centers

www.aapcc.org

Be prepared: Why not locate the nearest poison control center now and jot that number down to keep by the phone? Click the Find Your Poison Center link on the left-hand side of the page and choose between three options for finding your local center.

Emergency Treatment of Burns

www.shrinershq.org/Prevention/ BurnTips/treatment.html

Burn treatment: This fact sheet tells you the steps to take if someone receives a thermal burn from a fire, a hot liquid, or a hot surface, or a chemical or electrical burn.

First Aid For Electrical Accidents

www.cdc.gov/niosh/nasd/ docs3/me97006.html

What a shock: What to do if someone receives an electrical shock or burn.

MayoClinic.com's First-Aid & Self-Care Guide

www.mayohealth.org/home?id=SP5.6

May(o) you never need this:
MayoClinic.com comes to the rescue with practical and easy-to-follow advice on what to do in all sorts of medical emergencies. The topics range from how to treat a sunburn, how to recognize the signs of a heart attack, how to avoid back injuries, to how to treat everyday aches and pains. This online guide also has a self-care section.

Venomous Snake Bites

www.cdc.gov/niosh/nasd/ docs/as31600.html

Snakebite safety and first aid: Seven thousand venomous snakebites are reported each year in the United States. Here's what to do and what not to do with snakebites from the National Ag Safety Database. This site also has prevention tips.

Fitness

You can find more on fitness in Chapter 18. And be sure to check out these sites, too.

FitnessLink

www.fitnesslink.com

Shape up: This comprehensive site shows you how to shape up your body. It includes the Exercise Encyclopedia to help you pick the best workout for you and pointers on using exercise gear in the Virtual Gym.

FitnessZone

www.fitnesszone.com

Find a gym: On the road and need to find a gym? This site has a Gym Locator database that enables you to find a gym based on zip code or city. More than 13,000 gyms and health clubs are listed. The site also offers personalized exercise profiles.

JustMove.org

www.justmove.org

Get movin': The American Heart Association provides the tools and information that will enable you to get an exercise program underway. You can keep an exercise diary online and join in on communities that help motivate you and enable you to share exercise tips.

MEDFACTS' SportsDoc

www.medfacts.com/sprtsdoc.htm

Jock doc: This sports medicine Web site has a sports medicine glossary and library.

Shape Up America!

www.shapeup.org

Drop 10: This site provides interactive tools and programs designed to help you to shape up, including a fitness center with online and offline tests to determine how ready you are to start working out and recommendations of what you should do based on your goals and lifestyle. The site also offers nutrition information. Check out the Shape Up & Drop 10 program that integrates healthy eating and increased physical activity to meet weight-loss goals.

Total Fitness Guide

www.totalfitnessguide.com

Find a trainer: Personal trainers can help inspire you and guide you to reach your fitness goals. Total Fitness Guide's UStrainersearch.com database can help you locate a certified personal trainer close to home.

Also, the American Council on Exercise, which certifies trainers, has a database with lists of trainers at www.acefitness. org. Click Find a Health Pro link and use your city or zip code to locate a trainer.

Other Sites to Check Out

Whatever your exercise or sports interest, you can get loads of information, support, tips, gear, and advice online.

Aerobics and Fitness Association of America
www.afaa.com

AikiWeb: The Source for Aikido Information
www.aikiweb.com

American Bodybuilding
www.getbig.com

Asimba
www.asimba.com

Atozfitness
www.atozfitness.com

Bicycling
www.bicyclingmagazine.com

Bike-Zone.com
www.bike-zone.com

CoolRunning
www.coolrunning.com

CyberPump!: Home of High Intensity Training
www.cyberpump.com

Dr. Squat
www.drsquat.com

FitnessOnline
www.fitnessonline.com

Inside Triathlon
www.insidetri.com

Jazzercise.com
www.jazzercise.com

MarathonTraining
www.marathontraining.com

Martialinfo.com
www.martialinfo.com

Muscle 101
www.muscle101.com

MyDailyYoga
www.mydailyyoga.com

Pilates Studio
www.pilates-studio.com

Powerlifting.com
www.powerlifting.com

Racewalk.com
www.racewalk.com

Reebok University
www.reeboku.com

Runner'sWorld Online
www.runnersworld.com

Run The Planet
www.runtheplanet.com

Skating.com
www.skating.com

Speedskating.com
www.speedskating.com

Spinning.com
www.spinning.com

SportsForWomen.com
www.sportsforwomen.com

SwimInfo
www.swiminfo.com

The Tennis Server
www.tennisserver.com

Turnstep.com
www.turnstep.com

The Walking Connection
www.walkingconnection.com

WorkOutsForWomen.com
www.workoutsforwomen.com

Yang Style Tai Chi
www.chebucto.ns.ca/Philosophy/Taichi

YogaCentral
www.yogaclass.com/central.html

Foot Care

American Podiatric Medical Association

www.apma.org

Feet to stand on: This podiatrist Web site provides foot-health information as well as fun foot facts. Did you know that the 52 bones in the feet make up about one-quarter of the bones in your body? The site also has information on foot disorders, such as bunions, corns, and athlete's foot.

Government Health Publications (Free Stuff)

The federal government is giving it away. Here's your chance to scoop up reliable information on a wide variety of health and medical topics.

Online Consumer Health Publications

www.nih.gov/health/consumer/
conkey.htm

Fact sheets, pamphlets: This is the subject index for the publications from the institutes that make up the National Institutes of Health. Find the health topic you're interested in and click away. In most cases, you can read 'em online as Web pages.

Other Sites to Check Out

Agency for Healthcare Quality and Research
www.ahrq.gov/consumer

Federal Consumer Information Center — Health
www.pueblo.gsa.gov/health.htm

U.S. Food and Drug Administration Publications
www.fda.gov/opacom/catalog/alpha.html

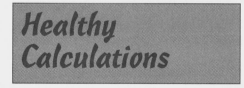

Healthy Calculations

Harness the power of the Web to figure out all sorts of stuff for you.

Activity Calorie Calculator

www.primusweb.com/fitnesspartner/
jumpsite/calculat.htm

How many calories do you burn?: Enter your weight and the length of your usual workout to get a customized chart listing the number of calories you'll use for 158 activities.

If you enter your weight and one minute for the duration, you get your basic chart. Then you can multiply the one-minute number by the length of time you actually worked out.

Blood Alcohol Level

health.discovery.com/tools/calc/alcohol/
blood_alcohol_content.html

Estimate your blood alcohol content under different circumstances: Enter the type of drink, your gender, the number of drinks, and the time you spent drinking those drinks. Then click the Enter button to see your estimated blood alcohol level.

BMR Calculator

www.global-fitness.com/BMR_calc.html

Figures your basal metabolic rate (BMR): This calculator tells you how many calories your body burns when it's at rest. You enter your age, height, and weight and click Enter to see the BMR for both men and women.

Body Fat Estimator

www.stevenscreek.com/goodies/pi.shtml

Find your estimated percentage of body fat: Enter your height, weight, and waist size. The estimator then uses two different methods, one based on height and weight, and the other based on waist size and weight, to estimate your body fat. Take the estimates with a *very* large grain of salt.

Calorie Calculator

www.caloriescount.com/calculator.html

Look up calories and fat grams for the foods you eat: Click the Enter Calculator button, type in the food items with or without a description, and click the Search button. The results show you the serving size, fat grams, and calories for the food you're interested in.

The Web site also has an Enhanced Calorie Calculator that helps you keep a running list of what you eat during the day and your calorie total and, if you want, your fat grams. Go to www.caloriescount.com and click the Enter Calculator button. Then type in the food in the Keyword text box and click Submit Food Item. On the results page, supply the number of servings and click Add Items to My List. By clicking the appropriate buttons, you can also calculate the fat grams and the percentage of fat in your list.

Children's Growth Calculator

www.healthatoz.com/atoz/growthdiary/
growthcalculators.asp

Children's height and weight: Find out how your child's growth compares to other kids of the same age. You can use this calculator for infants to children up to 20 years old.

Cost of Smoking Calculator

health.discovery.com/tools/calc/
smoke/cost_of_smoking.html

How much money could you save if you quit smoking?: Enter the number of cigarettes you smoke a day and the price you pay per pack. Then select whether you want the answer to reflect what you spend in a week, a month, or a year. Then click Enter to see your how much smoking is costing you.

Customize an Immunization Chart for Your Child

www.parentsplace.com/health/vaccinate

Interactive immunization chart: Supply your child's birth date (and name, if desired) and click the Generate Table button to create a customized chart for your child, showing recommendations for the date and age for your child's immunizations. You can click a link above the chart to create a printable form of the chart, which includes space to record the date each vaccine is given.

Due Date Calculator

www.babycenter.com/calculators/
duedate

Find out when your baby is due: Enter the date of your last period and your adjusted cycle length and then click the Submit button. In addition to giving you your baby's due date, the results tell you what week of pregnancy you're in and provide links to information for that week of pregnancy and to support.

Health Calculator

www.ivillage.com/healthcalc

Multipurpose tool: This site is really ten calculators in one. Choose any or all of the weight, daily requirement, or height calculators, select your measurement preference and your gender, and then click Next. On the next page that appears, supply the information requested and click Calculate to see your results.

How Well Are You Eating Calculator

homearts.com/helpers/
calculators/ddiary.htm

How do your meals stack up against the pyramid?: Enter the number of servings you've eaten from each of the major food groups and click the Tell Me How Well I'm Eating button. Your diet is then compared to the recommendations.

Longevity Game

www.northwesternmutual.com/ games/longevity

How long can you expect to live?: To play, click the Longevity Game link and answer each of the questions. If you keep an eye on the Age Tabulator in the upper-right-hand corner of the page, you'll see the effect each of your answers has on your predicted longevity.

Ovulation Calculator

www.babycenter.com/ calculators/ovulation

When's the best time to conceive a baby?: Fill in the date of your last period and the length of your cycle, and then click Submit. The results indicate when you're most likely to be fertile and what the resulting due date would be.

Pregnancy Calendar

www.babycenter.com/calendar/getinfo

Generate a day-by-day calendar of your pregnancy: Supply a date, your cycle length, and then click the Build My Calendar button. This generates a customized chart with links to information, tips, quizzes, and articles to keep you company while you're waiting for *Baby*.

RealAge

www.realage.com

Getting real: There's your chronological age based on your birthday. And then there's your real or biological age based on your diet, exercise, whether you smoke and wear seatbelts, your personal and family health history, and other factors. The comprehensive RealAge Test helps you gauge your real age and then recommends what you can do to change your lifestyle to

lower it. The site offers a variety of other health risk assessments to determine your risk for allergies, anxiety, depression, menopause, osteoporosis, prostate problems, and others.

Sleep Calculator

www.drkoop.com/tools/ calculator/sleep.asp

Are you getting enough sleep?: Stay awake long enough to answer a series of eight questions to rate your level of sleep deprivation.

Target Heart Rate Calculator

my.webmd.com/heartrate

Are you in the zone?: Enter your weight and click Calculate. The results show you your target heart rate expressed as a range of the number of heart beats per minute that are considered safe for exercising. You can also have the rate expressed in terms of 6, 10, 15, and 30 seconds.

Vision Strength Calculator

www.drkoop.com/tools/ calculator/vision.asp

Do you need glasses?: Follow the directions to determine the correct settings for your computer; then stand 10 feet from the screen and type the letters you see. You can test each eye separately.

Weight Maintenance Calculator

www.caloriecontrol.org/calcalcs.html

How many calories does it take to maintain your weight?: This site provides separate calculators for men and women, but for each, you enter your height, weight, age, and activity level. Then you click the Determine Calories button to see the number of calories you need to maintain your weight.

Other Sites to Check Out

Calculators at drkoop.com
   www.drkoop.com/tools/calculator

Hearing Health

American Academy of Audiology

www.audiology.org/consumer

Now hear this: The American Academy of Audiology has online guides to hearing loss, information on how to understand your hearing test, and advice on buying a hearing aid.

American Academy of Otolaryngology – Head and Neck Surgery

www.entnet.org/patient.html

Head and neck: These docs have the head and neck covered, including allergies, snoring, balance, and hearing problems.

Hotlines

Sometimes, you need to get help on the phone. These sites have the *4-1-1.*

Domestic Violence Hotlines

www.feminist.org/911/crisis.html

Hotlines and resources: This page, which is part of the Domestic Violence Information Center site, provides contact information for state coalitions and national organizations dealing with domestic violence.

Health Hotlines from the National Library of Medicine

newsis.nlm.nih.gov/hotlines

Toll-free phone numbers: You can search this online database of health-related organizations by keyword or by browsing a subject list. If you click an organization name, you see the full record, including the Web site address, if there is one.

Toll-Free Numbers for Health Information

www.health.gov/nhic/Pubs/
2000healthobserv/toll.htm

Hotlines: This U.S. Department of Health and Human Services list, which is organized by health concern, contains the toll-free numbers of organizations you can call for information, education, and support.

Injury Prevention

Here are some Web sites that look at what you can do to prevent injuries.

Childhood Sports Injuries and Their Prevention: A Guide for Parents with Ideas for Kids

www.nih.gov/niams/healthinfo/
childsports/child_sports.htm

Keeping the young athlete safe: If your child participates in football, baseball, soccer, gymnastics, or track and field, this Web site has suggestions on how you can prevent and treat sports-related injuries in children. It also has links to related information.

Fire Prevention in the Home

www.cdc.gov/niosh/nasd/docs3/
me97014.html

Fight fire with prevention: Tips on what you can do to keep your house safe from fires and how to make a fire escape plan.

Injury Prevention Web Site

www.chp.edu/besafe/index.html

An ounce of prevention: This site is filled with child safety tips for kids and parents. Topics covered include staying safe while playing sports, playing at the playground, playing with dogs, riding bikes, riding school buses, lighting fireworks, and crossing the street. Included are animated videos for the kids and fact sheets that Mom and Dad can print and use, including a babysitter's guide.

Mad Cow Disease

In Europe, there has been increasing evidence of a relationship between ongoing outbreaks of a disease in cattle, known as bovine spongiform encephalopathy (BSE, or "mad cow disease"), and a disease in humans, called new variant Creutzfeldt-Jakob disease (nvCJD). No cases have been reported in the United States, but you may want to keep an eye on this developing story.

Bovine Spongiform Encephalopathy (BSE) and Creutzfeldt-Jakob Disease (CJD)

www.cdc.gov/ncidod/diseases/cjd/cjd.htm

Federal case: The Centers for Disease Control and Prevention, the federal government's leading disease fighter, provides a fact sheet on the mad cow disease problem.

Monthly CJD Statitical Figures

www.doh.gov.uk/cjd/cjd_stat.htm

Keeping tabs: England has been the epicenter of the mad cow disease epidemic. The Department of Health provides the latest tallies on cases that have been found in Britain.

The Official Mad Cow Disease Home Page

www.mad-cow.org

How now mad cow: This site has thousands of links to articles on the growing mad cow problem.

Medical Forms

Following are some forms you can download and print out.

Adult Immunization Record Card

www.nfid.org/ncai/schedules/card

Shots for all seasons: The National Coalition for Adult Immunization has a form that you can use to keep track of all those immunizations — from hepatitis A to tetanus.

Advance Directives: Living Wills, Durable Power of Attorney for Health Care

www.partnershipforcaring.org/ad.htm

Legal papers: Partnership for Caring offers living wills and durable powers of attorney that you can print out. Information is available on a state-by-state basis.

Emergency Medical Forms

www.acep.org/index.cfm/pid/14.htm

Form fitting: The American College of Emergency Physicians provides you with forms that contain information that you may need in an emergency. These forms include a Personal Medical History Form to bring to the emergency room and a Consent to Treat Form that grants permission for your child to be treated. The latter is available in Spanish.

Health Record Forms

www.ahima.org/consumer/index.html

Adult and child forms: Print out a five-page adult form or a three-page child form for keeping track of your family's medical history. Click the Patient Health Record Forms link in the left-hand column to access the forms. The forms are provided by the American Health Information Management Association.

Organ & Tissue Donor Initiative

organdonor.gov/signup1.html

Print 'n carry: You can download a copy of an organ donor card from this federal government site. Sign the card and carry it at all times.

Medical Museums

Sometimes, you just gotta' take a break and get cultured. So why not visit a few online museums with medical themes?

Emerging Diseases: Ancient Scourge, Modern Menace

www.collphyphil.org/emerging_dis/emdsmain.htm

Something old, something new: The Dermatology Section of the College of Physicians of Philadelphia presents an illustrated and interactive exhibit on ancient and modern diseases. The site tells some Philadelphia stories, such as on the Legionnaires' disease outbreak in 1976 and the yellow fever outbreak in 1793, as well as stories about the black plague and smallpox outbreaks in ancient Egypt.

International Museum of Surgical Science

www.imss.org

Old-timey medicine: Get a taste of 1860-style medicine in this online exhibit. After you enter the site, click the Interactive Antique Illness link. Watch out for the oil of turpentine.

Museum of Menstruation and Women's Health

www.mum.org

Offbeat look at that time of the month: The exhibits at this online museum are devoted to all aspects of menstruation.

The Quackatorium

radiantslab.com/quackmed

Quack, quack, quack: Take a gander at the pictures of the Radio Disease Killer, Electropoise, and other contraptions once promised as cures for whatever ailed you.

The Virtual Museum — John Q. Adams Center for the History of Otolaryngology – Head and Neck Surgery

www.entnet.org/museum/exhibits.html

Stick it in your ear: The ear, nose, and throat specialists take you on a tour of their brand of medicine from ancient Rome to the present day.

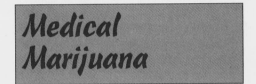

Medical Marijuana

One of the more hotly debated issues is whether marijuana should be made available for medical purposes, such as to relieve pain for people with AIDS and cancer as well as for other purposes. The U.S. Supreme Court is hearing the issue. Here are Web sites that offer some pros and cons.

Alliance for Cannabis Therapeutics

www.marijuana-as-medicine.org/alliance.htm

Marijuana Rx: The Alliance for Cannabis Therapeutics presents fact sheets on using marijuana to help people with cancer, AIDS, muscle spasticity, and glaucoma.

Cannabis Research Library

www.druglibrary.org/crl/default.htm

Library search: Articles from medical journals researching the medical use of marijuana.

U.S.A. Hemp Museum

hempmuseum.org

History of marijuana: The Hemp Museum takes an online look at marijuana in a variety of ways, including as a medicine.

The Use of Marijuana for Glaucoma

www.nei.nih.gov/news/marij.htm

Marijuana eye care: The National Eye Institute reviews the use of marijuana to treat glaucoma, the eye disease that can increase pressure in the eye and cause vision loss. The Institute says that marijuana does lower pressure, but no more so than other medications.

What's Up with Marijuana?

www.usdoj.gov/dea/pubs/ straight/mari.htm

G-man's view: The Drug Enforcement Administration warns of the dangers of "weed," including its effects on the immune system, the heart, and the ability to make judgments.

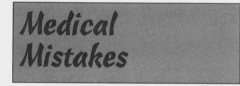

The first rule of medicine is: First, do no harm. But it doesn't always happen that way. The Institute of Medicine has estimated that as many as 98,000 people die in U.S. hospitals each year as the result of medical errors. More people die from medical errors than from motor vehicle accidents, breast cancer, or AIDS.

20 Tips to Help Prevent Medical Errors

www.ahrq.gov/consumer/20tips.htm

Help yourself avoid medical injuries: The Agency for Healthcare Research and Quality outlines what you can do to

minimize your chances of becoming a victim of a medical mistake in a hospital, doctor's office, nursing home, and other settings.

In Chapter 2, we list some medical news sites online. Here are a bunch more:

ABCNEWS.com
  abcnews.go.com/sections/living/
    index.html

Achoo
  www.achoo.com/news/default.asp

BBC
  news.bbc.co.uk/hi/english/sci/tech/default
    .htm

Boston Globe
  www.boston.com/globe/healthscience

Chicago Sun-Times
  www.suntimes.com/index/health.html

Chicago Tribune
  www.chicago.tribune.com/leisure/family/
    printedition

Detroit Free Press
  www.freep.com/index/health.htm

Discover Magazine
  www.discover.com

latimes.com
  www.latimes.com/health

Minneapolis startribune.com
  www.startribune.com/health

NandoTimes
  www.nandotimes.com/healthscience

NPRonline
  www.npr.org/news/healthsci

PBS HealthWeek
  www.pbs.org/healthweek

Philly.com
  health.philly.com

San Francisco Chronicle
  www.sfgate.com/health

Time.com Health
  www.time.com/time/health

U.S. News
www.usnews.com/usnews/nycu/health/hehome.htm

WhyFiles
whyfiles.org

YourHealthDaily
www.yourhealthdaily.com

Also, for news releases from research institutions and journals, check out this site:

EurekAlert!
www.eurekalert.com

Medical Records Online

Do you want access to your medical records wherever you go? You can enter your data online yourself.

PersonalMD

www.personalmd.com

Manage your medical records online: This site allows members to store and retrieve personal medical information online, including lab results and X-rays. Privacy is promised.

WebMD Health

www.mywebmd.com

On the record: You can keep your medical history, immunization records, and so on here. Click the MyHealthRecord link.

Medical Schools

Medical schools can be great resources for information, care, and research. You often can use your local medical school's library.

Yahoo! Medical Schools

dir.yahoo.com/Health/Medicine/Education/Medical_Schools

School directory: Yahoo! lists links to Web sites for more than 250 medical schools in the United States and abroad.

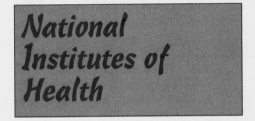

National Institutes of Health

The National Institutes of Health (NIH) is the federal government's premier research organization. It has 18 individual institutes specializing in specific health concerns. You can find online brochures for individual illnesses and research information at the various institutes' Web sites. The NIH also has offices focused on particular health issues. Following are the Web addresses for the NIH institutes and offices.

National Cancer Institute (NCI)
www.nci.nih.gov

National Center for Complementary and Alternative Medicine (NCCAM)
nccam.nih.gov

National Eye Institute (NEI)
www.nei.nih.gov

National Heart, Lung, and Blood Institute (NHLBI)
www.nhlbi.nih.gov/index.htm

National Human Genome Research Institute (NHGRI)
www.nhgri.nih.gov

National Institute on Aging (NIA)
www.nih.gov/nia

National Institute on Alcohol Abuse and Alcoholism (NIAAA)
www.niaaa.nih.gov

National Institute on Allergy and Infectious Diseases (NIAID)
www.niaid.nih.gov

National Institute on Arthritis and Musculoskeletal and Skin Diseases (NIAMS)
www.nih.gov/niams

National Institute of Child Health and Human Development (NICHD)
www.nichd.nih.gov

National Institute on Deafness and Other Communication Disorders (NIDCD)
www.nidcd.nih.gov

National Institute of Dental Craniofacial Research (NIDR)
www.nidr.nih.gov

National Institute of Diabetes and Digestive and Kidney Disorders (NIDDK)
www.niddk.nih.gov

National Institute on Drug Abuse (NIDA)
www.nida.nih.gov

National Institute of Environmental Health Sciences (NIEHS)
www.niehs.nih.gov

National Institute of General Medical Sciences (NIGMS)
www.nigms.nih.gov

National Institute of Mental Health (NIMN)
www.nimh.nih.gov

National Institute of Neurological Disorders and Stroke (NINDS)
www.ninds.nih.gov

National Institute of Nursing Research (NINR)
www.nih.gov/ninr

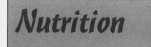

Nutrition

You are what you eat. Find out more about nutrition at these sites.

Food Finder

www.olen.com/food

Fire up the fryer: Find out how much fat, how many calories, how much salt, and so forth are in your Whopper, Big Mac, or other fast food. This service is based on a book by the Minnesota Attorney General's Office.

FoodFit.com

www.foodfit.com

All the food that fits: FoodFit.com has the recipes and tools to help shape up your diet and plan healthy menus. The online community, to which registration is required, offers recipe swaps and online encouragement.

Interactive Menu Planner

hin.nhlbi.nih.gov/menuplanner

Seeing those calories add up: The National Heart, Lung, and Blood Institute helps you figure out and control your calories, fat, and carbs with this calculator.

TheDietChannel.com

www.thedietchannel.com

Loads of links: This site has more than 600 links to all sorts of diet information, including critical analysis of fad diets, diet-related online calculators, diet news, and ways to make menus healthier.

Chapter 12 has information on pain management. Here are a few more pain-related Web sites.

American Chronic Pain Association (ACPA)

www.theacpa.org

You are not alone: The ACPA provides support for people with chronic pain through education in pain management skills and self-help-group activities. Don't miss the Pain Management section of this Web site for tips and wisdom about living with chronic pain.

American Academy of Pain Management

www.aapainmanage.org

Pain information: The Patient Information area of this Web site has articles on dealing with pain in general as well as pain related to specific conditions such as arthritis, back problems, cancer, digestive diseases, endocrine conditions, headaches, musculoskeletal conditions, neurological conditions, and women's health problems. The Web site also has an extensive list of links to other pain-related resources.

www.library.ucla.edu/libraries/biomed/his
/PainExhibit/index.html

Online exhibit: This exhibit takes a look at the history of pain research and modern pain treatment from the 1800s on.

Pet Health

Healthcare expenditures on pets are skyrocketing. Pet care is getting to be as high-tech as human care. Here are some sites for pet care.

Animal Poison Control Center

www.napcc.aspca.org

Animal rescue: Though most dog owners don't know it, chocolate, onions, macadamia nuts, and bread dough can be fatal to their pet. Likewise, Easter lilies can kill cats. This site has tips on how to prevent your dog or cat from being poisoned both indoors and outdoors.

Definitions & Abbreviations of Veterinary Terms

www.vetmed.wsu.edu/glossary/
glossary.asp

Talk to the animals: Human doctors speak medicalese. Vets speak their own version. This A to Z glossary from the Washington State University College of Veterinary Medicine spells it all out.

The Green Book

www.fda.gov/cvm/greenbook/

Pet meds: The U.S. Food and Drug Administration's database lists doses, side effects, and more for medicines used to treat pets and livestock. This is the PDR for animals.

NetVet

netvet.wustl.edu/vspecial.htm

Bow wow: This site from a professor at Washington University's Division of Comparative Medicine offers links to everything you could think of concerning veterinary medicine, including alternative medicine (acupuncture, chiropractic, and so forth), ethics, infectious disease, nutrition, and sports medicine (for canine athletes). This site is the Yahoo! of the pet world.

OncoLink Vet

www.oncolink.upenn.edu/
specialty/vet_onc

Pet cancer: OncoLink, one of the top Web sites for cancer in humans, has a section devoted to cancer in pets. You can find answers to the most common questions about cancer in pets. The site also provides links to veterinary oncologists, vets specializing in cancer treatment.

Other Sites to Check Out

AltVetMed: Alternative and Complementary Veterinary Medicine
www.altvetmed.com

Feline Diabetes
felinediabetes.com

Pets with Diabetes
www.petdiabetes.org

Reference Books

Many useful medical references are available online for free.

Columbia University College of Physicians and Surgeons Complete Home Medical Guide

cpmcnet.columbia.edu/texts/guide

Clickable medical guide: This online medical guide has information on how the medical system works, as well as information on wellness, diseases, medications, prevention, and first aid.

Merck Manual Home Edition

www.merckhomeedition.com

Famed medical reference: The Merck Manual has been a standby for doctors for a century. Now a patient-friendly version of the book is available online for free. In addition to text, the site has photos, animations, videos, pronunciations, and illustrations. The interactive book has information on diseases, medications, common tests, and more. It also has a guide to resources, which includes contact information and Web sites for patient groups.

Self-Care Flowcharts

www.familydoctor.org

Charts to help you decide when to see the doc: The American Academy of Family Physicians' site contains online flowcharts on symptoms from its *AAFP Family Health and Medical Guide*. The site also has handouts on conditions, information on medications, herbal and alternative remedies, and brochures on family health topics.

The World Book – Rush-Presbyterian-St. Luke's Medical Center – Medical Encyclopedia

www.rush.edu/worldbook

Searchable encyclopedia: You can search this book by symptom and by age. It also has first-aid and prevention information.

The Yale University School of Medicine Patient's Guide to Medical Tests

my.webmd.com/yale_books

Guide to diagnostic tests: From ateriography to X-rays, you can find out what medical tests are used for, how long they take, what discomfort you may encounter, what the risks are, how the results are interpreted, how quickly you can expect the results, and how much the tests cost.

Organ Transplantation

Every 14 minutes, another name is added to the national organ transplant waiting list. Here are some sites on transplants and related services.

AirLifeLine

www.airlifeline.org

Wings of mercy: AirLifeLine is a charitable organization of over 1,000 private pilots who provide transportation or other services for ambulatory patients who can't afford the cost to travel to medical centers for diagnosis and treatment.

Children's Organ Transplant Association (COTA)

www.cota.org

Helping hand: COTA aims to ensure that no American child is denied a life-saving transplant and to educate the public about the need for organ donation.

Organ & Tissue Donor Initiative

organdonor.gov/signup1.html

Transplant questions answered: This federal government site has answers to frequently asked questions about transplants, addresses urban legends such as myths about the black market in organs, and also provides a glossary of transplant terms.

Transplant 101

www.patients.unos.org

Scoop on transplants: The United Network for Organ Sharing (UNOS) offers a primer called Transplant 101. UNOS explains how the waiting list works and how to evaluate transplant programs. The site also contains a glossary and information about financing a transplant.

Other Sites to Check Out

American Association of Kidney Patients
www.aakp.org

American Organ Transplant Association
www.a-o-t-a.org

Bone Marrow Transplant Support Online
www.bmtsupport.org

Insulin-Free World Foundation
www.insulin-free.org

Kidney Directions
www.kidneydirections.com

Marie "Mitzi" Singel Foundation for lung transplantation
www.mitzisingelfoundation.org

National Kidney Foundation
www.kidney.org

National Marrow Donor Program
www.marrow.org/index.html

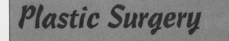

Plastic Surgery

Cosmetic surgery is increasingly popular among Americans. Find out more at this site.

American Society of Plastic Surgeons

www.plasticsurgery.org

Cosmetic/aesthetic: Information on the various types of plastic and reconstructive surgery, including costs.

Rare Diseases

Medical research often has focused on the major diseases to the detriment of people who have rare conditions. Efforts are being made to level the playing field.

NORD

www.rarediseases.org

Nothing so rare: National Organization for Rare Disorders (NORD) is a federation of voluntary health organizations dedicated to helping people with rare diseases, which are sometimes referred to as *orphan diseases*. The site has databases of over 1,000 rare diseases, of over 900 *orphan drugs* (drugs that have been neglected by drug companies because the potential market is small), and of organizations to help people with these conditions.

Search Engines That Can

Our top picks for search engines and online directories are Google, healthfinder, and MEDLINE*plus*. But other sites can help you find what you want, too. Check 'em out.

AltaVista
www.altavista.com

Ask Jeeves
www.askjeeves.com

Excite
www.excite.com

Google
www.google.com

Hardin Meta Directory of Internet Health Sources
www.lib.uiowa.edu/hardin/md

healthfinder
www.healthfinder.gov

Hotbot
hotbot.lycos.com

Medhunt
www.hon.ch

MEDLINEplus
www.medlineplus.gov

MedWeb@Emory University
www.medweb.emory.edu/MedWeb

NOAH
www.noah-health.org

Yahoo!
www.yahoo.com

Your skin is your body's largest organ. Find out more about it at this site.

American Academy of Dermatology
www.aad.org/patient_intro.html

Get the skinny: The skin docs present information on hair and skin problems. The site also provides links to AcneNet, EczemaNet, MelanomaNet, PsoriasisNet, and Kids Connection sites.

Translator

Language can be a barrier in getting medical attention.

AltaVista
www.altavista.com

Translator: Click the <u>Translate</u> link to get help translating words or Web sites.

Multilingual Glossary of Technical and Popular Medical Terms in Nine European Languages
allserv.rug.ac.be/~rvdstich/eugloss/welcome.html

Viva la difference: In plain English, it's called a headache. In English medicalese, it's cephalalgia. In plain Italian, it's dolore di testa. In plain French, it's migraine. In plain Dutch, it's hoofdpijn. However you say it, language can be a headache when you're seeking medical care. This site has scaled the Tower of Babel with translations of everyday healthcare terms and their technical forms in nine European languages.

When you go on a trip, whether you're rafting on the Amazon (as in the river) or sampling truffles in France, you don't want to bring back a disease as a souvenir.

Here are some Web sites that provide information to help keep you out of harm's way.

Cruise Ships

www.cdc.gov/travel/cruiships.htm

Check out that cruise ship: Cruises are more popular than ever. If you want to check out the sanitation reports on a cruise ship you're interested in, the Centers for Disease Control and Prevention offers this database of sanitation inspections, where you can find out if the Minnow or Albatross was in shipshape.

Foreign Entry Requirements

travel.state.gov/foreignentryreqs.html

Official entry requirements for getting into countries: Sometimes the wanderlust gets to be too much, and we have to get up from the computer and see the offline world — hard to believe. Find out what official papers and shots you need to cross borders.

HealthLinks.com

healthlink.mcw.edu/travel-medicine

Online travel clinic: The Medical College of Wisconsin offers articles of interest to travelers, ranging from a piece on altitude sickness to one on West Nile encephalitis.

International Society of Travel Medicine (ISTM)

www.istm.org/clinic_frame_redirect.html

Travel docs: You can use this site to find a member of the society who is an expert in travel medicine. The site has links to news from the Centers for Disease Control and Prevention and the World Health Organization.

Medical Emergencies Involving U.S. Citizens Abroad

travel.state.gov/acs.html#medical

Body politic: The U.S. State Department's site lists emergency contacts around the world, including hospitals and doctors. We suggest bringing a printout of this information with you on your trip.

MedicinePlanet.com

www.medicineplanet.com

Worldwide health information: This site helps you locate a clinic specializing in travel medicine. You can get information about which vaccinations are recommended for overseas travel, as well as find out how to avoid getting sick. The site has a Healthy Travel Store, where you can pick up a first-aid kit for the road or travel health insurance.

Travelers' Health

www.cdc.gov/travel

The ultimate travel health authority: The Centers for Disease Control and Prevention (CDC) provides a comprehensive guide to everything you need to know about health risks all over the world. Choose a region from the drop-down list box, and you get a briefing on what diseases are brewing, including news on the latest epidemics. The site has pages devoted to exotic diseases from African sleeping sickness to yellow fever. The CDC site also has special sections containing information on traveling with children or traveling when you're pregnant or have a disability.

Part V
Staying Healthy in All the Seasons of Life

The 5th Wave   By Rich Tennant

CYBERSIZERS

Thigh-Master Laptop

Nordic-Server

Abdominizer Keyboard

In this part . . .

No matter where you are in the circle of life, you have health and wellness concerns. In the chapters in this part, you find online health resources that focus on infants, kids, and teens (Chapter 14); women (Chapter 15); men (Chapter 16); and seniors (Chapter 17).

Chapter 14

Infants', Kids', and Teens' Health

Kids don't come with an operating manual. And parents don't need a parenting license to raise them.

Still, Dr. Benjamin Spock, the pediatrician to the boomer generation, recognized that everything works out fine in most cases if parents follow their instincts. Dr. Spock died at age 94 in 1998, but he's still around in spirit — at drSpock.com. That site and many more offer information and advice to help the Net generation raise its kids.

In this chapter, you find the best Web sites for help and advice on caring for your child. You also discover sites with useful information on major health concerns, such as circumcision, immunizations, allergies, asthma, acne, drug abuse, and more.

Dr. Spock opened his famous book, *Baby and Child Care,* first published in 1946, saying, "Trust yourself. You know more than you think you do." We agree with Dr. Spock that parental instinct is great, but for all those times you need a bit of reassurance or advice, it's a relief to know the Web is out there to help.

The Big Picture on Health Issues for Infants, Kids, and Teens

Our all-time favorite site for health information on infants, kids, and teens is KidsHealth. In the next few sections, we introduce you to this super megasite and you to a few others that you may want to check out.

Taking a look at KidsHealth

You can get the big-screen view of children and teen's health from The Nemours Foundation through its megasite, KidsHealth (www.kidshealth.org), as shown in Figure 14-1.

This site, which is really three sites in one, helps parents, kids, and teens get the answers to their health questions.

KidsHealth for parents

In the KidsHealth for Parents area, which you access by clicking the <u>Enter Parents Here</u> link, you find links to these major topics:

- ✔ **General Health.** Understand aches, pains & caring for your child.
- ✔ **Infections.** Investigate infections, from symptoms to medical care.
- ✔ **Emotions & Behavior.** Explore why kids act a certain way & how they change.
- ✔ **Growth & Development.** Understand how kids grow & change in body & mind.
- ✔ **Nutrition & Fitness.** Learn how to keep kids healthy with diet & exercise.
- ✔ **Pregnancy & Newborns.** Take the best care of yourself & your new baby.
- ✔ **Medical Problems.** Read up on childhood conditions & diseases.
- ✔ **Positive Parenting.** Ramp up on parenting tips & explore tough subjects.
- ✔ **First Aid & Safety.** Be prepared to care inside and outside the home.
- ✔ **Medical Care & The Health Care System.** Learn about hospitals, tests, insurance & medicines.
- ✔ **Newsroom.** Get the latest news in children's health, hot off the press!

Figure 14-1:
KidsHealth
provides
easy access
to health
information
for parents,
kids, and
teens.

KidsHealth

The KidsHealth part of the site, which you reach by clicking the Enter Kids Here link, is geared toward, not surprisingly, kids.

KidsHealth has sections, such as Dealing with Feelings, Staying Healthy, Growing Up, and Kid's Health Problems. In addition, you can find these helpful areas:

✔ **Everyday Illnesses & Injuries:** This section discusses topics, such as "Hey! A Tarantula Bit Me!" and "What is Puke?" and also gives kids info on colds, chickenpox, swimmer's ear, fractures, and tonsillitis.

✔ **People, Places & Things That Help Me:** This section helps kids understand the medical world — everything from why they need shots to what to expect from a visit to the doctor, the dentist, and even the hospital.

✔ **Word! A Glossary of Medical Terms:** This area contains a glossary of medical terms for kids.

✔ **Kids' Talk:** If your kid is the curious type, this site can provide answers to classics stumpers, such as "What are boogers?" "What's earwax?" "What causes ice cream headaches?" and "Why do we say that we are sick as a dog or that we have butterflies in the stomach?"

TeensHealth

It's tough being a teen in that border zone between childhood and young adulthood. TeensHealth gives the 4-1-1 on teens' concerns from acne and mono to puberty and dieting. Just click the Enter Teens Here link to enter this area of the site.

Here's a sample of some of the sections you find at TeensHealth:

- ✔ **Body Basics:** What you should know about pimples, hygiene, dieting, body piercings, alcohol, sleep, and smoking and smokeless tobacco.

- ✔ **Mind Matters:** How to cope with body image problems, cancer, an alcoholic parent, divorce, alcohol, and stress. This section also covers suicide.

- ✔ **Sexual Health:** What you should know about menstruation, sex, birth control, and sexually transmitted diseases.

- ✔ **Food & Fitness:** What you should know about nutrition, exercise, and eating disorders. You can also find some easy recipes for teens here.

Additional health sites to check out

Here are some other Web sites on kids' health that are worth a look:

- ✔ **familydoctor.org (www.familydoctor.org):** This site comes from the American Academy of Family Physicians. Click the <u>Children</u> link for information on topics, such as cleft lips and cleft palates, hearing problems, anorexia, mononucleosis, circumcision, scoliosis, attention deficit/hyperactivity disorder, toilet training, croup, runny noses, and more. Click the <u>Self-Care Flowcharts</u> link on the opening page for help in deciding when to see the doctor.

- ✔ **drSpock.com (www.drspock.com):** This site keeps alive the spirit of Dr. Benjamin Spock, whose advice guided the parents of baby boomers. You can find information here on pregnancy and birth, behavior, health, families, and feeding and nutrition. The site also features news headlines, a medical glossary, reports on product recalls, message boards, and an Ask the Experts area.

- ✔ **ParentsPlace.com's Health section (www.parentsplace.com/health):** Here you find news, information, and bulletin boards on health topics concerning infants, children, and teens. The site also covers topics, such as immunizations, breastfeeding, children's dental care, and safety.

- ✔ **American Academy of Pediatrics (www.aap.org):** The AAP, representing the nation's pediatricians, is the leading voice on childcare issues. (See Figure 14-2.) To read the group's policy statements on a variety of major issues, click the <u>Policy Statements</u> link in the right-hand column of the front page. Here, you find the group's positions on hundreds of topics, such as bicycle helmets, children and fireworks, circumcision, learning disabilities, marijuana, suicide in teens, and the varicella (chickenpox) vaccine.

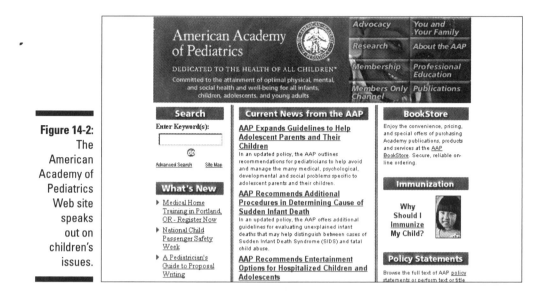

Figure 14-2:
The
American
Academy of
Pediatrics
Web site
speaks
out on
children's
issues.

You can also find valuable information at these sites:

✔ The Children's Health section at InteliHealth (`www.intelihealth.com`)

✔ The Children's Condition and the Family Living Centers at MayoClinic.com (`www.mayoclinic.com`)

✔ The Parenting & Children's Health section at drkoop.com (`www.drkoop.com`)

Locating a hospital or doctor for your child

If you need to find a hospital specializing in care for kids, check out the National Association of Children's Hospitals and Related Institutions' database at `www.childrenshospitals.net/nachri/abouth/profiles_index.html`. From there, click the <u>Search</u> link to search for hospitals based on their specialty or location, or click the <u>Browse</u> link to find hospital profiles in an alphabetical listing by state. You can find out more about finding and evaluating hospitals in Chapter 4.

If your child is not responding to care from your family physician or pediatrician, you may want to consider taking him or her to a specialist close to home or elsewhere in the country. U.S. News lists its picks of the best pediatric programs at U.S. teaching hospitals at `www.usnews.com/usnews/nycu/health/hosptl/specpedi.htm`.

Special Health Concerns for Infants, Kids, and Teens

In the next few sections, we look at Web resources that focus on some of the special health concerns for infants, kids, and teens.

Circumcision

On the eighth day of life, Jewish boys undergo the circumcision ceremony, known as the bris. The mohel, who is specially trained to perform the rite, says some prayers, gives the infant some wine to dull the pain, and then surgically removes the foreskin.

But religious considerations aside, circumcision has caught on among non-Jews in the United States. The operation has been the center of a medical debate: Does it provide health benefits, or is it unnecessary surgery?

The American Academy of Pediatrics (AAP), representing the nation's baby doctors, is on record as saying that circumcision does have some medical benefits, such as a reduced risk for urinary infections and cancer of the penis. The AAP says the benefits aren't sufficient to justify having all baby boys undergo the procedure. However, the organization doesn't oppose circumcision for religious or cultural reasons.

The Circumcision Information and Resource Pages (www.cirp.org) discusses circumcision in detail. Scroll down the page for information on the procedure, the various arguments for and against circumcision, and links to *intactivist* organizations, activists who oppose routine circumcision.

Another topic that has been gaining attention is female circumcision, which is a practice in some African and Middle Eastern cultures. The topic has been brought to light in the United States because of the increasing numbers of immigrants from these parts of the world. Rising Daughters Aware covers the issue at www.fgm.org.

Childhood immunizations

During the early months of their children's lives, parents spend a lot time taking them to the doctor for immunizations. Although the kids may wince and cry, immunizations are important, according to the Centers for Disease Control and Prevention (CDC) and the American Academy of Pediatrics

(AAP). These organizations agree that immunizations protect children from diseases and even death.

Here are a few resources for information about immunizations:

- ✔ The AAP has a chart at `www.aap.org/family/parents/immunize.htm`, showing when your children should have their shots. The chart covers shots from infancy through age 18.
- ✔ The CDC's National Immunization Program covers the benefits of immunization at `www.cdc.gov/nip`.
- ✔ The AAP outlines its arguments for why immunizations prevent disease and deaths, and lists other Web resources on the subject at `www.aap.org/new/immpublic.htm`.

Ear infections

Three out of four children experience an ear infection, known as otitis media, by the age of 4. In fact, ear infections are the most common illnesses in babies and young children and the most common reason that parents take their young children to the doctor. Ear infections can cause temporary hearing loss and language problems, so it's important for your child to see a doctor if he or she has an ear infection.

You can get information about ear infections, their symptoms, and how they're treated from the American Academy of Otolaryngology – Head and Neck Surgery (AAO-HNS) at `www.entnet.org/earache.html`. Otolaryngologists are ear, nose, and throat specialists, and they, along with pediatricians and family physicians, are on the front lines in dealing with ear infections.

Signs of an ear infection

As a parent, it is often difficult to know if your child has an ear infection. Fortunately, the National Institute of Deafness and Other Communication Disorders (`www.nidcd.nih.gov/health/parents/otitismedia.htm`) put together this list of signs to look for in your child:

- ✔ Does she tug or pull at her ears?
- ✔ Does he cry more than usual?
- ✔ Do you see fluid draining out of her ears?
- ✔ Does he have trouble sleeping?
- ✔ Can she keep her balance?
- ✔ Does he have trouble hearing?
- ✔ Does she seem to not respond to quiet sounds?

If you want to locate a specialist, go to the AAO-HNS Patient Info page at `www.entnet.org/patient.html` and click the <u>Find an Otolaryngologist</u> link. The Patient Info page also provides links to information on other health concerns, such as tonsils and adenoids, sinus infections, smokeless tobacco, second-hand smoke and kids, swimmer's ear, nosebleeds, and facial sports injuries.

Asthma and allergies

Asthma and allergies are the most common childhood diseases:

- **Asthma** is a chronic, inflammatory lung disease that causes recurrent breathing problems. Asthma can be triggered by allergens, such as dust and pollen, infection, exercise, cold air, and other factors. About 5 million kids have asthma, which can result in school absences, doctor's office visits, and trips to the emergency room.

- **Allergies** occur when allergens cause your body's immune system to overreact to things that most people's bodies just tune out. Tens of millions of kids — more than 20 percent of American kids all told — have allergies. Those statistics are great for the Kleenex people, but not so great for those of us who suffer through the sneezin' seasons.

Fortunately, you can control asthma and allergies. To find about more about these conditions and how you can control them, check out some of these resources online:

- **Patient information:** The American Academy of Allergy, Asthma & Immunology (AAAAI) provides you with the facts on these conditions, how they're diagnosed, and how they're treated at `www.aaaai.org/public/default.stm`.

- **The lowdown on dust:** A major source of allergies is dust. You can't do much about it at school, but you can control dust at home, especially in your child's bedroom. The National Institute of Allergy and Infectious Diseases' fact sheet at `www.niaid.nih.gov/factsheets/dustfree.htm` tells how you can make your child's bedroom dust-free.

- **Pollen and spore levels:** If you want to check on levels of weed pollen, grass pollen, and mold spores, go to CNN.com's Allergy Report at `www.cnn.com/WEATHER/allergy`. The site also has An Allergy Fact of the Day feature.

- **A glossary of allergy and asthma terms:** The AAAAI's site has a glossary to help translate allergy and asthma terms at `www.aaaai.org/public/fastfacts/glossary.stm`.

- **Locating an allergist:** The AAAAI Physician Referral Service (`www.aaaai.org/scripts/find-a-doc/main.asp`) helps you find an allergist close to home. (See Chapter 3 for more information on how to find a doctor.)

The Asthma and Allergy Foundation of America has a Web site at `www.aafa.org`. Here, you can find information on asthma and allergies, an Ask the Allergist feature, and links to support groups.

Child safety

Accidental injuries are a major concern for children and teens. Here are some Web sites that offer information on how to keep your child safe:

- ✔ **KidsHealth's First Aid & Safety section at** `www.kidshealth.org/parent/firstaid_safe/index.html`: Find out how to babyproof and childproof your house, how to avoid hazards outdoors, and what to do in emergencies.

- ✔ **Car Seat Safety Information from the American Academy of Pediatrics at** `www.aap.org/family/mncrseat.htm`: Here, you find links to a family shopping guide to car seats, a one-minute checkup of your car seat, and more.

- ✔ **Consumer Product Safety Commission at** `www.cpsc.gov`: Find out what products have been recalled and pick up safety tips at this site, such has how to fit a child for a bike helmet and how to avoid scooter hazards. (More than 40,000 people went to the emergency room last year because of scooter accidents.) You can also report an unsafe product online at this site.

- ✔ **The National SAFE KIDS Foundation at** `www.safekids.org`: At this site, you find information on safety issues involving bikes, cars, firearms, poisons, playgrounds, sports, and toys. Click the <u>Car Seat Locator</u> link in the upper right-hand corner to find out where to place a car seat in your car.

    The National SAFE KIDS Foundation has Internet safety rules for kids, too, at `www.safekids.com/kidsrules.htm`.

- ✔ **The American Association of Poison Control Centers at** `www.aapcc.org/findyour.htm`: This site enables you to locate your nearest poison control center.

Dental health

Corny, but true: If you're true to your teeth, they won't be false to you. With proper care, your kids can hold on to their pearly whites for a lifetime.

Here are some places to find out about dental health for kids:

- ✔ **American Dental Association at** `www.ada.org`: This site provides tips for caring for your children's teeth and an Oral Health Topics A–Z index at `www.ada.org/public/topics/parents/index.html`. You can use the Find a Dentist feature at `www.ada.org/public/directory/index.html` to find a pediatric dentist, a general dentist, or an orthodontist.

- ✔ **The American Dental Hygienists' Association at** `www.adha.org/oralhealth/index.html`: Here, you find tips for both child and adolescent oral health care and instructions on proper brushing and flossing.

- ✔ **American Academy of Pediatric Dentistry at** `www.aapd.org`: This site offers a series of 24 brochures and fact sheets on subjects, such as Calming the Anxious Child, Regular Dental Visits, Sealants, Tooth-Colored Fillings, X-Ray Use and Safety, Mouth Protectors, Dental Care for Special Child, Dental Care for Your Baby and Children, Water, and Fluorides.

- ✔ **The American Association of Orthodontists at** `www.aaortho.org`: For the straight talk on braces, check out `www.aaortho.org/consumer.html`. An orthodontics glossary with a mouthful of terms from *acromegaly* to *zygoma* is available at `www.aaortho.org/glossary/index.html`. For help on locating an orthodontist, check out `www.aaortho.org/referral.html`.

- ✔ **KidsHealth at** `www.kidshealth.org/kid/stay_healthy/body/teeth.html`: Here, you get a kid-oriented view of oral health. Guess what people used to use to clean their teeth before today's minty marvels were mass marketed? This site says lemon juice, ashes, and a tobacco-honey mix. Yum.

Teen stuff

Smell like teen spirit? Here are some places where you can get a whiff of teen health issues:

- ✔ **Nicotine, drugs, and lots more:** Go Ask Alice! from Columbia University's Health Education Program (`www.goaskalice.columbia.edu`) covers all the bases: relationships, sexuality, sexual health, emotional health, fitness and nutrition, alcohol, nicotine and other drugs, and more.

  Have a question about tongue brushing, nose picking, ear ringing from loud music? *Whatever.* Don't be bashful — Go Ask Alice!

- ✔ **Acne:** Virtually everyone in his or her teen years develops zits, but every teen feels that he or she suffers alone. The American Academy of Dermatology (AAD), the nation's skin doctors, has a Web site called *AcneNet* (`www.skincarephysicians.com/acnenet`), which is devoted to the skin problem. The site has online brochures, fact sheets on what causes acne and how it can be treated, a Find a Dermatologist feature, and more.

AAD also address sun protection and skin cancer at the Kids' Connection at `www.aad.org/Kids/index.html`.

✔ **Sex and sexually transmitted diseases (STDs):** The American Social Health Association's iwannaknow.org (`www.iwannaknow.org`) has the basics on sexual health and STDs, and offers live chats. You can find out more about STDs, including HIV/AIDS, in Chapter 13.

✔ **Smoking and smokeless tobacco:** Smoking is the leading cause of death in the United States. More Americans die from tobacco-related causes than from AIDS, alcohol, car accidents, murders, suicides, drugs, and fires, combined. And most smokers take their first puffs at age 18 or younger.

The Campaign for Tobacco-Free Kids at `www.tobaccofreekids.org` has the facts on why you shouldn't smoke or chew tobacco.

If you have a strong stomach, go to the ABCs of Tobacco at `www.tobaccofreekids.org/abc` for a list of the many diseases that tobacco causes, along with some graphic images, such as a lung ravaged by cancer. Gross.

Also, check out the Tobacco Advertising Gallery at `www.tobaccofreekids.org/adgallery` for information on how the industry spends $18 million a day in advertising in the United States. You can find out more about tobacco and other addictions in Chapter 18.

✔ **Immunizations and hepatitis B:** Teens aren't little kids, but they still need to be immunized against infectious diseases. The latest vaccination that's recommended for teens fights Hepatitis B, which can be sexually transmitted and can cause liver cancer. The immunization schedule for teens for this vaccine and others is available from the National Coalition for Adult Immunization (`www.nfid.org/ncai/schedules/adolescent`), as shown in Figure 14-3.

Tobacco by the numbers

Every day about 3,000 kids start smoking. Eventually one-third of them will die from tobacco-related diseases.

The Campaign for Tobacco-Free Kids (`www.tobaccofreekids.org`) gives this breakdown on tobacco use and teens:

✔ High school students who smoke: 35%

✔ High school students using smokeless tobacco: 14%

✔ Kids exposed to second-hand smoke at home: 15.5 million

✔ Packs of cigarettes consumed by kids each year: 90 million

✔ Kids alive today who will die from tobacco use: 5 million+

And did we mention that smoking makes your breath smell bad and discolors your teeth?

© 1998-2000 National Coalition for Adult Immunization

Figure 14-3: The National Coalition for Adult Immunization has the scoop on the hepatitis B vaccination and other shots recommended for teens and adults.

The coalition has an online brochure on hepatitis B that's directed to teens at www.nfid.org/factsheets/hbagadol.html. See Chapter 13 for more on hepatitis B.

✔ **Abstinence, sexual orientation, menstruation, pregnancy, abortion, and adoption:** Planned Parenthood has a page devoted to teen issues at www.plannedparenthood.org/teens/index.html. For additional information on pregnancy, check out Chapter 15.

✔ **Alcohol, club drugs, ecstasy, cocaine, steroids, heroin, and more:** The National Clearinghouse for Alcohol and Drug Information at www.health.org/catalog/Index.htm has online pamphlets aimed at teens as well as parents.

✔ **Body piercings:** TeensHealth at kidshealth.org/teen/body_basics/body_piercing_safe.html says body piercings may be trendy, but as they say on the *Sopranos,* "Fogettabout it" — body piercings can lead to infections. The medical establishment gives a green light only to ear piercing.

Chapter 15

Women's Health

*H*elen Reddy's anthem proudly proclaimed in the 1970s and still does today: "I am woman, hear me roar, in numbers too big to ignore."

When it comes to women's health, the numbers are too big to ignore. Women make up 52 percent of the population, and their healthcare influence is even greater. According to national statistics

✔ Women make three-fourths of the healthcare decisions in American households.

✔ Women spend almost two out of every three healthcare dollars, approximately $500 billion annually.

✔ Women make more than 61 percent of physician visits.

✔ Women buy 59 percent of prescription drugs.

✔ Women outlive men by more than seven years.

Women are considered to be more health conscious than men are. Women take better care of themselves. When it comes to healthcare, women rule.

In this chapter, we point you to Web sites where you get the big picture on women's health and wellness and some helpful health tips and tools. We also tell you about sites that focus on specific concerns, such as screening exams, pregnancy, birth control, menopause, infertility, women's cancers, and more.

We know that you're Reddy and roarin' to go. So read on.

The Big Picture on Women's Health

The Web offers a lot of information to help women take care of themselves. In the next few sections, we tell you about some of the major Web sites that cover a broad range of women's health topics.

Medical megasites

All of the medical megasites have women's health sections that give you the big picture on women's health. You're likely to find information on a wide variety of women's health topics, Ask the Doctor features, and support through bulletin boards and chats.

You can't go wrong with any of the medical megasites, but here are a few you may want to try first:

✔ **Women's Health Center at WellnessWeb:** The Women's Health Center at Wellness Web (www.wellnessweb.com/women/women.htm), shown in Figure 15-1, offers information on emergency contraception, violence against women, a variety of illnesses and conditions, medical tests, pregnancy, midwifery, crib death, and breastfeeding. You can also find links to additional Web resources.

Figure 15-1: The Women's Health Center at Wellness Web covers many aspects of women's health.

✔ **Women's Health at iVillage.com's allHealth.com:** You can get to the Women's Health area by going to `www.allhealth.com/womens`, where you can look for information by category, such as birth control, crisis/abuse, fertility, routine care, elder care, menstruation, depression, breast health, heart disease, eating disorders, and female cancers. You can read Daily Article Highlights and take health quizzes.

The Women's Health area also invites you to participate in bulletin board discussions and chats on topics, such as abortion, cystitis, early menopause due to surgery, endometriosis, fibroids, hysterectomy, menopause, osteoporosis, PMS, undiagnosed illnesses, and vulvodynia.

✔ **Women's Health at InteliHealth:** The best way to get to the Women's Health area is to go to the InteliHealth site (`www.intelihealth.com`) and click the Women's Health link at the top of the page.

The Women's Health main page is divided into areas where you can read news about women's health; ask the doc a question; explore related topics, such as fitness, caregiver's health, or weight management; read feature articles; and find out the basics on such topics as menopause, pelvic and pap exams, premenstrual syndrome, and breast cancer screenings.

You may also want to check out the lengthy Just for Women section, which provides links to articles arranged by topic. The topics include Your Health, Specialty Groups (age, ethnicity, sexual orientation), Your Physical Self, Your Appearance, Your Relationships, Your Sex Life, Your Work Life, Your Demons, and Your Heroes.

Although it's not a medical megasite, the New York Times On The Web's Women's Health area (`www.nytimes.com/specials/women/whome/index.html`) is also worth a look. You can find information on over two dozen health topics for women, including incontinence, family violence, urinary tract infections, cosmetic surgery, depression, ovarian cancer, stress, birth control, and hormone replacement therapy. The Women's Health area also provides links to and descriptions of over 100 other places on the Web that offer health information that's geared toward women.

The National Women's Health Information Center

The National Women's Health Information Center (`www.4woman.gov`), shown in Figure 15-2, is a government Web site with news, features, and tons of information on women's health.

Clinical trials — not for men only

In the past, when you heard about the findings of a new research study on the evening news, the "medical breakthrough" applied only to men. For many years, researchers excluded women from their studies because they were fearful of harming women and concerned that they could damage a fetus in a pregnant female. Because new drugs and therapies were tested only on men, it was unclear how they would affect women. Researchers ignored the fact that medications might affect women differently than men because of factors, such as hormones.

Many groups have been working to address gender inequality in clinical studies, and among them is the Society for Women's Health Research (www.womens-health.org). At its Some Things Only a Woman Can Do page (www.womancando.org), the Society provides information on medical research, facts and figures about how women can make a difference, links to information on clinical studies, and a glossary of terms commonly used in medical research. (See Chapter 6 for more information on finding clinical trials.)

The Society for Women's Health Research Web site also provides this information for women:

- **Health Facts & Links (www.womens-health.org/healthfactsheet2.html):** This page contains a huge list of links to information on many of the diseases and conditions that affect women, such as breast cancer, lung and gynecological cancers, eating disorders, menopause, mental illness, STDs, osteoporosis, and violence.

- **Internet Myths and Women's Health (www.womens-health.org/myths.html):** This page gives examples of false information about women's health that have been making the rounds on the Internet. For example, the site debunks the claims that wearing bras or using antiperspirants causes cancer and that tampons contain asbestos and/or dioxin. This page also includes links to sites where you explore the myths, hoaxes, and rumors you've heard. (You can read more about urban-legend-debunking Web sites in Chapter 1.)

Figure 15-2: The National Women's Health Information Center has information on all aspects of women's health.

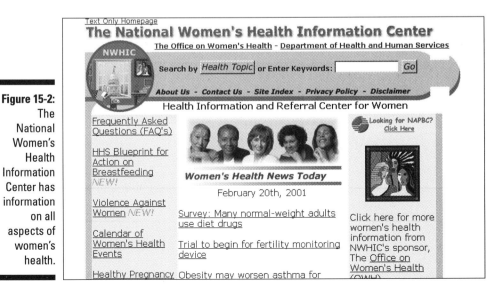

Here are some highlights of what you find at this site (you can access all of these areas by clicking the appropriate link on the site's main page):

- **Frequently Asked Questions (FAQ's):** This FAQ is an extensive index of topics of interest to women. Each link in the index leads to a brief, to-the-point, question-and-answer overview on the topic, with links to further information. The index is arranged alphabetically. Here are some of the topics you find just in the *A*'s: Acne, African American Women's Health, Aging, Alcohol Abuse and Treatment, Allergies, Alternative Medicine, Alzheimer's Disease, Anorexia Nervosa, Arthritis, and Asthma. And that's just some of the *A*'s.

  Clicking the <u>Lesbian Health</u> link in the FAQ takes you to an overview of health concerns as they affect lesbians, such as sexually transmitted diseases, screening for breast and cervical cancer, and insurance issues. The site also has a fact sheet on lesbian health at `www.4woman.gov/owh/pub/Lesbian.htm` that discusses the health status and health risks of lesbians.

- **Violence Against Women:** This area of the site tells you about the different forms of violence toward women and where you can go to get help. The areas covered include domestic and intimate partner violence, sexual assault and abuse, dating violence, and elder abuse. Each topic covered includes an overview, with links to online publications and organizations. Click the <u>State Resources</u> link near the top of the page for a list of state agencies dealing with domestic violence, along with contact information.

- **Healthy Pregnancy:** This area of the site contains information and further resources on each trimester of pregnancy, family planning, how to prepare for childbirth , and what to do after the baby is born.

- **Women with Disabilities:** Here, you find information and links to additional resources on various aspects of being a disabled woman in America. Topics covered include abuse, access to healthcare, financial assistance, minorities, reproductive health, sexuality, services and support, and substance abuse. This area of the site also contains information on various disabilities including learning, developmental, psychiatric, neurological, and hearing and vision impairment.

- **Body Image:** This area of the site tells you how to improve your health, start an exercise program and eat better, as well as provides information on eating disorders and total mind/body wellness. Each section of the Body Image area contains a brief overview of the topic and links to Web sites, publications, and organizations where you can find additional information. You can also find information on nutrition for teens.

- **Minority Health Information:** This sections focuses on health risks that are of special concern to women of color and what women of color can do to improve their health by working out, eating better, and reducing stress.

GayHealth

To get the lesbian-friendly look at health, go to GayHealth at www.gayhealth.com. This site covers gay, lesbian, transgender, and bisexual health. On the site's main page, click the General Health link in the menu on the left-hand side of the page. Then click the Women link in the expanded menu that appears on the General Health page. You can find out about female cancers, osteoporosis, and more.

List o' links

Here are a few sites that provide links to a whole host of online health resources for women:

- **The Office of Research on Women's Health** — part of the National Institutes of Health — has an index of sites that provide healthcare information for women. This index, which is located at www4.od.nih.gov/orwh/consumer.htm, is divided into these topics: Issues of Aging, Alcohol and Drug Abuse, Cancer in Women, Health of Children and Families, General Health Issues, Issues of Menopause, Pain and Disability, and Prevention, Treatments, Alternative Interventions, and so on.

- **The U.S. Food and Drug Administration's Office of Women's Health** has a long list of links on women's health at www.fda.gov/womens/informat.html. Clicking a topic name takes you to FDA information in other areas of the site. For example, clicking the Cosmetics category link takes you to the FDA's collection of articles on the safety of specific beauty products, such as hair dyes, tanning lotions, and nail care products.

  Women often keep track of medicines for the entire family, in addition to themselves. The FDA has an online brochure called *My Medicines* (www.fda.gov/womens/taketimetocare/mymeds.html) that you can print out in English and 13 other languages to help make your job easier.

- **Ask NOAH About: Women's Health** (www.noah.cuny.edu/healthyliving/womenshealth.html) has a page of links to specific issues, such as birth control, bladder and continence, hemorrhoids, hysterectomy, polycystic ovary syndrome, toxic shock syndrome, and varicose veins.

- **The Links on Women and Health Care Issues from the Boston Women's Health Book Collective** (www.ourbodiesourselves.org/links.htm) are organized alphabetically by subject. You can use the alphabetical index at the top of the page to find links for topics, such as alternative health, childbearing, female genital mutilation, fitness and exercise, miscarriage, parenting, smoking, women of color in the United States, and young women.

Prevention and Self-Care: The Keys to Staying Healthy

Women are extremely health-conscious. Here are some tools to help women take care of themselves.

Finding a doctor

On the American College of Obstetricians and Gynecologists' (ACOG) Find A Physician page (www.acog.org/member-lookup), you can click a map to find an ACOG physician in your state or in Canada, Mexico, Guam, Puerto Rico, and other countries. You can also search for an ACOG physician by name or by zip code.

Check out Chapter 3 for information of finding family physicians and internal medicine specialists.

 If you've never had a gynecological exam, and you're wondering what to expect when you have one, check out the GYN 101 Web site (www.gyn101.com/homefr.htm) for a step-by-step rundown of the procedure. First, the site helps you decide if you need to see a gynecologist, and from there, you find out how to choose a doctor, how to prepare for the appointment, what to expect from a pelvic and breast exam, and what the results mean. The site, which is sponsored by the drug company Pfizer Inc., also has sections on your rights as a patient, a glossary, and a list of related links.

Medical tests

Two great places to look for information on medical tests — what they're for, what they're like, and what the results mean — are the *ADAM Medical Encyclopedia* Test Reference section at MEDLINE*plus* at medlineplus.adam.com/ency/index/testidxa.htm and the *Harvard Medical School Family Health Guide to Diagnostic Tests* at www.health.harvard.edu/fhg/diagnostics.shtml.

In addition to those sites, you may also want to check out the sites in the next few sections for information on medical tests that are specifically for women.

Breast exams: Mammograms and self-exams

To help detect breast cancer in its early stages (when it is most treatable) you need to perform monthly breast self-exams and undergo regularly scheduled mammograms.

The American Cancer Society has instructions on how to perform a breast self-examination (BSE) at `www.cancer.org/NBCAM_breast_self_exam.html`.

The National Cancer Institute's What Women Should Know page (`rex.nci.nih.gov/MAMMOG_WEB/WOMEN.html`) has links to several NCI online brochures about mammograms. Click the <u>Learn at Your Desktop: Mammograms Up Close</u> link to find out the basics, such as when the test is recommended based on your age. You can also find information about the benefits and limitations of mammograms, as well as a list of questions you should ask your doctor.

To find the FDA Certified Mammography Centers near you, go to `www.fda.gov/cdrh/mammography/certified.html`. Here you find a brief explanation of mammography center certification that's worth checking out. Click the <u>Search for FDA Certified Mammography Facilities in Your Area</u> link to search for a center by entering the first three numbers of your zip code or your state.

If you want to find out more about breast cancer, see Chapter 10.

You can sign up with iVillage.com at `www.ivillage.com/auto/ford/windstar/race/self-exam.html` to receive e-mail reminders to do monthly breast self-exams and to get a yearly mammogram.

Pap test

To detect cancer of the cervix early, you must have regular Pap tests, or Pap smears, based on your doctor's recommendations.

Pap smears detect early, precancerous changes in cells in the cervix. The Pap test is the most effective test in medical history for early detection of cancer. Since the Pap examination was introduced after World War II, death rates from uterine and cervical cancer have decreased 70 percent in the United States. Of the women who do die from cervical cancer, 80 percent haven't had a Pap examination in five years or more.

To find out the basics on the Pap test, check out the National Cancer Institute's "Questions and Answers About the Pap Test" brochure at `cancernet.nci.nih.gov/clinpdq/detection/Questions_and_Answers_About_the_Pap_Test.html`.

You can sign up at the College of American Pathologists' Web site at `www.papsmear.org/english/index.html` to receive annual e-mail reminders to schedule yourself for a Pap. You register with your e-mail address and the date you'd like to receive the reminder.

MUM's the word: The Museum of Menstruation and Women's Health

No list of Internet sites on "that time of the month" would be complete without a nod to the Museum of Menstruation and Women's Health, MUM for short (www.mum.org).

The museum's mission, as outlined in its purpose statement, is "to be the world's repository for information about, and showcase for, menstruation, including as many cultures as possible." The statement goes on to say, "this would include collecting and displaying, when possible, stories, customs, and artifacts, and conducting education about menstruation."

And that's just what you see when you wander through the exhibits at the virtual MUM. You see tampons throughout the ages, belts, bidets, an underpants directory, and advertising campaigns for feminine products featuring famous faces.

Before leaving the museum, you may want to pause a moment and go — no, not to the museum's gift shop (there currently isn't one) — to the museum's frequently asked questions (FAQ) file. Click the FAQ link to read the details of how the museum came to be. Be sure to check out the second page of the FAQ in which Harry Finley, founder and former director of MUM and creator of this Web site, shares his bio. In explaining how MUM came about, Finley says of himself, "Besides having a B.A. in philosophy from Johns Hopkins — what can someone in this circumstance do but start a museum of menstruation?"

What indeed.

Birth control

Birth control is a responsibility for both women and men. Here are some sites where you can find information on this topic:

- **The National Women's Health Information Center's "Birth Control Methods" brochure** (www.4woman.gov/faq/Easyread/birthcont-etr.htm)**:** This brochure contains information about cervical caps, condoms for men and women, diaphragms, vaginal spermicides, the pill, the morning-after pill for emergency contraception, RU486, IUDs, natural planning, and more.

- **Ann Rose's Ultimate Birth Control Links** (gynpages.com/ultimate)**:** This site approaches the topic of contraception with an attitude and some wry humor. Ann Rose has been a women's health and family planning educator for over 20 years, and she has compiled this comprehensive list of links to sites that cover more than 20 different methods of contraception, including the pill, natural family planning, sterilization, abstinence, male and female condoms, spermicides, and methods that don't work.

When contraception fails, women may opt to keep the baby, put the baby up for adoption, or have an abortion:

- ✔ You can get the pro-life viewpoint from the National Right to Life Committee at www.nrlc.org, including information on RU486 and late-term abortions.

- ✔ You can find out more about adoption at the National Adoption Information Clearinghouse at www.calib.com/naic. This site has a database of private adoption agencies and support groups for adoptive parents and for people searching for birth relatives.

- ✔ If you want to know about abortion, go to the National Abortion Federation Web site at www.prochoice.org, where you can find fact sheets and a locator map to find clinics.

Pregnancy and childbirth

Are you expecting? Or do you expect to be expecting? Either way, you can find a lot great information about pregnancy and childbirth at the following Web sites.

MayoClinic.com

The MayoClinic.com has a Healthy Living Center devoted to pregnancy and reproduction. The easiest way to get there is to go to the MayoClinic.com's homepage at www.mayoclinic.com and select Pregnancy & Reproduction from the Health Living Centers drop-down list box.

If you scroll down the Pregnancy & Reproduction Living Center opening page, you come to these six areas that make up this center:

- ✔ **Conception and Fertility:** Articles on the factors that can influence conception and fertility, including how to prepare to conceive and fertility challenges and therapies

- ✔ **Prenatal Health for Mom and Baby:** Articles on each trimester; how pregnancy affects your lifestyle, career, and relationships; and prenatal care and tests

- ✔ **Labor, Delivery, and Newborn Care:** Articles on labor and delivery and baby basics

- ✔ **Pregnancy Complications:** Articles on problems with Mom's health, premature birth and problem deliveries, and miscarriage, birth defects, and medical problems in newborns

✔ **Reproductive Health:** Articles on contraception and family planning, how things work in both old and young women, and preventive health, screening, and tests

✔ **Reproductive Diseases and Disorders:** Articles on sexually transmitted diseases, women's reproductive diseases and disorders, and men's reproductive diseases and disorders

Other sites

Here are some sites that cover topics related to pregnancy and childbirth:

✔ **Breastfeeding:** Check out these sites for more on breastfeeding:

- **La Leche League International** provides breastfeeding information at `www.lalecheleague.org/bf.html`, including answers to commonly asked questions and information on how you can participate in chats.

- **Breastfeeding.com** (`breastfeeding.com`), shown in Figure 15-3, provides information, support, and fun, including an art gallery and cartoons, in a community atmosphere. The site has a national and international directory of lactation counselors at `breastfeeding.com/directory/lcdirectory.html`.

✔ **Childbirth education:** Lamaze International (`www.lamaze.org`) has a section for expectant parents that includes a locator service to help you find a Lamaze class in your area.

✔ **Cool tools and support:** BabyCenter has a page of interactive tools, quizzes, and calculators (`www.babycenter.com/tools.html`) for you to use before and during your pregnancy and after your baby is born. Scroll down the page to find a collection of interview sheets that you can print out and take with you when you meet with your obstetrician, pediatrician, or preschool director.

The BabyCenter also has an extensive list of bulletin boards you can join at `www.babycenter.com/bbs`. The bulletin boards cover topics, such as preconception, pregnancy, family, grief and loss, dads, sleep, birth, baby, toddlers, mothercare, multiples, and child development.

✔ **Postpartum depression:** Postpartum Support International (`www.postpartum.net`) offers articles on the causes, symptoms, prevention, and treatment of postpartum mood disorders and depression. The site suggests ways for new moms to find support and provides a list of Web sites with additional support and resources for new moms and dads.

The site also offers support through chats and bulletin boards and provides a directory with contact information for local support groups.

Figure 15-3:
Breast-
feeding.com
has all the
facts on
feeding your
baby.

Menopause

Any change can be upsetting. Here are some sites to help you understand
and cope with "the change" — menopause, that is.

The North American Menopause Society

The North American Menopause Society has a section that helps you understand menopause and answers your questions. Start at `www.menopause.
org/aboutm/facts.html`, which gives you the basic facts, and then use the
buttons at the top of the page to access these areas:

- ✔ **Menopause Guidebook:** This extensive online book covers the basics:
  perimenopausal changes, postmenopausal health, treatment options,
  and suggestions for achieving optimal health.
- ✔ **FAQ's for Consumers:** This area lists answers to questions that women
  commonly ask.

Other menopause sites

Here are a few other Web sites with menopause resources:

✔ **The National Institute on Aging's "Menopause" brochure (**`www.nih.gov/nia/health/pubs/menopause`**):** This brochure discusses, in easy-to-understand language, what menopause is, what kind of physical and emotional changes to expect, the risks and benefits of hormone replacement therapy, and tips for staying healthy. The brochure also contains a glossary with words that may be unfamiliar to you and a list of resources.

✔ **Menopause Online (**`www.menopause-online.com`**):** This Web site includes information on menopausal symptoms, hormonal and alternative treatments, osteoporosis, and heart disease. You can also find bulletin boards on a variety of topics on women's health issues.

✔ **Power Surge, the Community for Women at Midlife and Menopause (**`www.dearest.com`**):** Alice Lotto Stamm, the creator of this site, once described her first hot flash to an online bulletin board as a power surge, a term that is now commonly used to describe a hot flash.

Stamm developed a warm and sharing virtual community named *Power Surge* to help you through all aspects of the change of life. From the opening page (`power-surge.com/intro.htm`), shown in Figure 15-4, click the Menu link in the upper-right-hand corner to access over 50 message boards, Web chats, and live events; the Ask the Expert feature, and newsletters. The message boards cover topics, such as skin problems, memory loss, naturally compounded hormones, soy, and menopause humor.

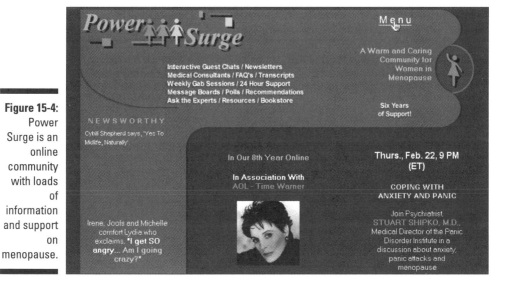

Figure 15-4:
Power Surge is an online community with loads of information and support on menopause.

Top killers of women

The National Women's Health Information Center put together an easy-to-read chart at www.4woman.gov/media/chart.htm that lists the following as the top ten leading causes of death for all American women:

1. Heart disease

2. Cancer

3. Cerebrovascular diseases (includes stroke)

4. Chronic obstructive pulmonary diseases

5. Pneumonia and influenza

6. Diabetes

7. Unintentional injuries

8. Alzheimer's disease

9. Nephritis, nephrotic syndrome, and nephrosis

10. Septicemia

The chart also lists the top ten leading causes of death for American women based on racial and ethnic groups: African American, Asian/Pacific Islanders, Caucasian, Hispanic/Latina, and Native Americans/Alaskans.

Women's Health Concerns

If you want to know more about a specific condition that affects primarily or only women, you can find informative Web sites and support online.

We cover a few such concerns from a woman's perspective throughout the book, including heart disease in Chapter 9, breast cancer in Chapter 10, and osteoporosis in Chapter 17. And healthfinder (www.healthfinder.gov) can help you find resources on virtually any women's health topic.

In next few sections, we look at what online information is available on infertility, gynecological cancers, and other women's health concerns.

Infertility

Three professional women who met in an online support group for couples facing infertility and pregnancy loss started the InterNational Council on Infertility Information Dissemination, known as INCIID. In total, these three women suffered 12 pregnancy losses spanning 16 years of infertility. The information they found led them to doctors who helped them achieve success. Incidentally, within days of creating INCIID, all three women became pregnant and carried their babies to term. Two of the women gave birth on the same day, and the third, two-and-a-half weeks later.

INCIID's Web site (www.inciid.org) has fact sheets, essays, and articles as well over 100 bulletin boards and chats and chat events on infertility, pregnancy loss, parenting, and adoption. You can find a glossary of infertility terms and acronyms at www.inciid.org/glossary.html and a directory of fertility specialists at www.inciid.org/webdocs.html. The site also provides a list of recommended links at www.inciid.org/links.

Gynecological cancers

OncoLink (www.oncolink.upenn.edu), shown in Figure 15-5, is an excellent Web site that covers many types of cancer.

It has a section focusing on gynecological cancers (www.oncolink.upenn.edu/specialty/gyn_onc) that provides fact sheets, links to online support, articles on therapy, news, summaries of medical articles, cancer survivor stories, an art gallery, and more. This section looks at cervical cancer, endometrial and uterine cancer, ovarian cancer, vaginal cancer, and other gynecological cancers.

The Women's Cancer Network (www.wcn.org) has useful information and links to women's cancer organizations. If you want to locate a *gynecologic oncologist,* a surgeon specializing in gynecological cancers, click the <u>Find a Doc</u> link on the site's main page.

You can find more information on how to research cancer online, including how to find research studies and journal articles, in Chapters 6, 7, and 10.

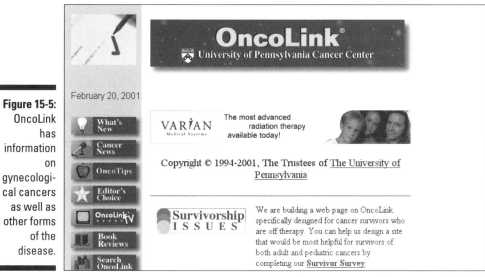

Figure 15-5: OncoLink has information on gynecological cancers as well as other forms of the disease.

Other health concerns

The following Web sites focus on other women's health issues:

✔ **Hyster Sisters** (www.hystersisters.com) offers pre- and post-operative online support for women undergoing hysterectomies. You can also find message boards, chats, and book recommendations at the site. Check out Princesses Tell Their Stories for first-hand accounts of women who have had hysterectomies.

✔ **The Endometriosis Association** (www.endometriosisassn.org) has information on the symptoms and treatment of endometriosis as well as contact information for local chapters, which offer support.

✔ **The Polycystic Ovarian Syndrome Association** (www.pcosupport.org) provides information on PCOS symptoms and treatment, e-mail lists, support groups, message boards, and a Do I Have PCOS? quiz.

The Centers for Disease Control and Prevention has a Web site at www.cdc.gov/nip/diseases/adult-vpd.htm that reminds adults that vaccines aren't just for kids. Here you find a table of vaccine-preventable adult diseases with the CDC's recommendations for when adults should be vaccinated for each disease.

Chapter 16

Men's Health

*N*ew York Yankee great Mickey Mantle said, "If I knew I'd live this long, I would have taken better care of myself."

You may only dream of hitting more than 500 homers, like The Mick did. But you need not have the same regret that the batting champ did about his health. Too many men do. They take care of their cars with oil changes every 3,000 miles, but they don't take care of themselves.

Not taking care of themselves takes its toll on men. They call it a man's world, but the life expectancy for American men is 74 years, while their female counterparts live to be nearly 80 years old. But men, you shouldn't give up. You may be able to improve your health, add years to your life and life to your years, by taking better care of yourself day in and day out.

We think the Internet can play a role in giving you the information you need to make informed decisions about your health. This chapter can help you seize the day by pointing you to Internet sites with the big picture on men's health and other sites that put the spotlight on special issues for men, including impotence, testicular cancer, prostatitis, and more.

Some health issues of concern to men, such as heart disease, stroke, and prostate cancer, are covered in Part IV. And others, such as enlarged prostate, are covered in Chapter 17.

Casey Stengel, a dentist who became baseball's greatest manager, said that Mickey Mantle had it in his body to be great. We're here to say that so do you. So go ahead and *carpe diem* and hit a few out of the park.

The Big Picture on Men's Health

You can get an overview on men's health and wellness at the medical megasites, such as CBSHealthWatch's Men's Health Channel at www.cbshealthwatch.com, InteliHealth's Men's Health at www.intelihealth.com, and WebMD Health's Men's Conditions at my.webmd.com/condition_center/mhp.

In next few sections, we show you a couple of sites that can give you the information you need about men's health.

National Women's Health Information Center

Women long have looked after their men's health. So maybe it's not surprising that a great place to get an overview on men's health is at a women's health site: the National Women's Health Information Center.

The center is run by a government agency, the Office of Women's Health. No comparable Office of Men's Health exists within the federal government, though there are efforts in Congress to change that.

So head over to the What About Men's Health page (www.4woman.gov/Mens), as shown in Figure 16-1. This section is a gateway to men's health information from the federal government and other sources and features fact sheets, online brochures, and links to health organizations.

Figure 16-1:
The National Women's Health Information Center has a comprehensive men's health section.

The National Women's Health Information Center
The Office on Women's Health - US Department of Health and Human Services

Search by Health Topic or Enter Keywords: [   ] Go

About Us - Contact Us - Site Index - Privacy Policy - Disclaimer

Text Only

What you need to know about Men's Health:

Alcohol and Drug Abuse

Cancer

Diabetes

Fitness & Nutrition

Heart Disease and Stroke

HIV & AIDS

What About **Men's Health?**

When we ask the question, "Why Men's Health?", we've discovered that a better question is "Why Not?" Statistically, men live 7 years less than women and face major health risks which are preventable and, more importantly, treatable if diagnosed early. Women are the major health caregivers/providers and consult a doctor 150% more frequently than men.

This section is specifically geared to help women learn more about the leading health concerns of the men in their lives. "What About Men's Health?" focuses on issues such as exercise, nutrition, and mental health. Working out, eating better, and paying attention to

On the left side of the men's health page, you find the following links to information:

✔ Alcohol and Drug Abuse

✔ Cancer

✔ Diabetes

✔ Fitness and Nutrition

✔ Heart Disease and Stroke

✔ HIV and AIDS

✔ Mental Health

✔ Men with Disabilities

✔ Prostate Health

✔ Reproductive Health

✔ Smoking

✔ Violence Prevention

The men's health section has information devoted to the following special groups: college-age men, minority men, and older men. You can find links to this information at the bottom of the left-hand side of the home page for men's health.

It's said that women hold up half the sky. On its pages, the National Women's Health Information Center is holding up more than its share. You go, girls!

Male Health Center

At his Web site, the Male Health Center, Dr. Kenneth A. Goldberg makes the point that women have special doctors available to them, obstetrician/gynecologists, who know everything about women's health.

But to whom can men turn? Goldberg says that men need ob/gyns of their own. He runs the Male Health Center in Dallas, but he's got a strong presence on the Net, too. His Male Health Center Web site (www.malehealthcenter.com) takes a treat-the-whole-man approach.

The site is well written and makes taking care of yourself seem like fun. If you scroll down the page, past the introductory material, you see a site map of what's available. You find links to such topics as symptoms, self-care, screening for major health problems, and sexual health.

Dr. G. has posted his syndicated "HIS HEALTH" column at the site, creating, in essence, an encyclopedia on male health issues. He organizes the columns under headings that include Aches and Pains, Medical Malfunctions, Medical Treatment, Prevention, Living Well, Exercise, Nutrition, Weight Loss, Cancer, Stressed Out, Growing Older, Father/Son Talk, Your Prostate, About Sex, About Sexual Dysfunction, and Birth Control and Infertility.

Some other sites for men's health

Here are some other places to go to get information on men's health:

- **MayoClinic.com at** `www.mayoclinic.com`**:** You can get to the Men's Health Center by choosing Men's Health from the Healthy Living Center drop-down text box on the right-hand side of Mayo's opening page. The Men's Health Center covers conditions and care on such topics as cancer, heart disease, hormonal conditions, and sexuality and reproduction.

- **mylifepath at** `www.mylifepath.com/topic/mens`**:** This site, from Blue Shield of California, has information on men's health topics, an Ask the Expert feature, and bulletin boards on male health issues.

- **GayHealth at** `www.gayhealth.com`**:** As shown in Figure 16-2, this is the site for gay, lesbian, transgender, and bisexual health. From the gay perspective, it goes beyond HIV/AIDS. For a gay-friendly look at health, click the General Health link in the menu on the left-hand side of the page. Then click the Men link in the expanded menu that appears on the General Health page.

- **NOAH at** `www.noah-health.org/english/wellness/healthyliving/menshealth.html`**:** NOAH's men's health page has links that cover the usual suspects, including impotence, hair loss, prostate problems, and testicular cancer.

Top killers of men

To help us live better and longer, researchers have to look at what kills us. The National Women's Health Information Center (`www.4woman.gov/Mens/twelve.htm`) lists the ten leading causes of death for men. Here they are in descending order:

- Diseases of the heart
- Cancers
- Unintentional injuries (accidents)
- Cerebrovascular diseases (stroke)
- Chronic obstructive pulmonary diseases
- Pneumonia and Influenza
- Diabetes
- Suicide
- Chronic liver disease and cirrhosis
- Homicide & legal intervention

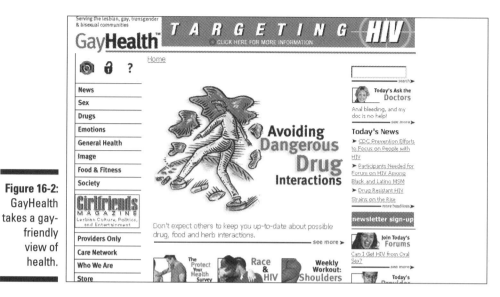

Figure 16-2:
GayHealth takes a gay-friendly view of health.

Immunizations aren't just for kids. You can find out whether and when you should have shots for the flu, tetanus, and so on from the National Coalition for Adult Immunizations at www.nfid.org/ncai/schedules. You can also print out (or cut and paste into a Word document) a record card to keep track of your immunizations.

Special Health Issues for Men Only

Just being who they are, men face some special health problems. That's just nature.

Some of these special health problems are covered elsewhere in Part IV and in Chapter 17. But in next few sections, you find out about Web resources for some special problems for men.

Testicular cancer

Testicular cancer was hardly a household phrase until national and world champion cyclist and two-time Olympian Lance Armstrong was diagnosed with — and then outraced — advanced testicular cancer. His comeback from testicular cancer by winning the Tour de France in 1999 was a tour de force. Armstrong has a Web site called Cycle of Hope (www.cycleofhope.org), which provides information for cancer survivors and their caregivers.

Armstrong isn't alone. Twenty-eight-year-old comedian Tom Green, best known as an MTV prankster and bad boy, showed that he was a better man when he took his fight against this cancer public. You can read all about it at Green's site at `www.tomgreen.com/about/articles/index.html`.

Testicular cancer is relatively rare, making up only one percent of all cancers in men. But it's a different story for young men, such as Armstrong and Green: Testicular cancer is the most common cancer in men 15 to 35.

Internet resources on testicular cancer can help you find the information you need on this cancer, including how it is diagnosed and treated, what's the prognosis, and its effects on sexuality and fertility.

Testicular Cancer Resource Center

If you want to know about testicular cancer, you should head over to the Testicular Cancer Resource Center (`www.acor.org/TCRC`), as shown in Figure 16-3. Some testicular cancer survivors have put together this terrific Web site to help those who are concerned about TC. TC is covered with TLC.

Here's some of what you find at the site:

- **The Self Exam:** How to do the monthly testicular self-exam
- **The TC Primer:** The basics on the condition
- **TC-NET:** The site's e-mail support group
- **The Testicle:** Everything you want to know about the male gland and were afraid to ask
- **TCRC Dictionary:** A glossary of testicular cancer terms
- **Questions to Ask:** A listing of what to ask your doctor
- **TC Links & Articles:** A library of TC info

The Testicular Cancer Resource Center also has information on interpreting pathology reports, information on *orchiectomy* (the operation to remove a cancerous testicle), information on radiation therapy and chemotherapy, and information on what happens after the therapy. The site also offers one-on-one buddy e-mail support.

Other topics you can find covered at this site include the effect of the condition on the survivor's sex life, fertility, alternative medical approaches, how much care costs, and faith and spirituality.

These guys have got all the bases covered: The site even has a humor page. Tom Green isn't the only one with a sense of humor.

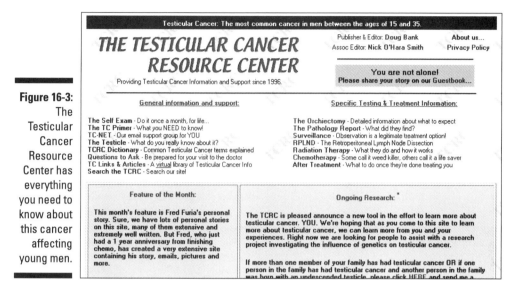

Figure 16-3:
The Testicular Cancer Resource Center has everything you need to know about this cancer affecting young men.

The National Cancer Institute and the American Cancer Society

The National Cancer Institute's CancerNet has the facts on testicular cancer at www.cancernet.gov/cancer_Types/Testicular_cancer.shtml. The American Cancer Society (www.cancer.org) also has a treatment center with information on this form of cancer. And both sites have information on the diagnosis and treatment of testicular cancer, which is considered highly curable if detected and treated early. (See Chapter 10 for more on researching cancer.)

If you're interested in joining a research study on testicular cancer, go to ClinicalTrials.gov at www.clinicaltrails.gov or CenterWatch at www.centerwatch.com.

Yahoo! Groups, at groups.yahoo.com, lists several online e-mail support groups for people with testicular cancer.

ED (also known as impotence)

Senator Bob Dole lost the presidency in 1996, but he gained the VIAGRA campaign.

In the early 1990s, Dole was diagnosed with and underwent surgery for prostate cancer. As a result of the surgery, as he famously announced in a commercial for early detection, he had ED (erectile dysfunction). That's the ten-dollar word for *impotence,* the inability to have an erection.

Warning signs for testicular cancer

The National Cancer Institute lists the following warning signs for testicular cancer in its "Questions and Answers About Testicular Cancer" fact sheet at `cis.nci.nih.gov/fact/6_34.htm`:

Men should see a doctor if they notice any of the following symptoms:

✔ A painless lump or swelling in either testicle

✔ Any enlargement of a testicle or change in the way it feels

✔ A feeling of heaviness in the scrotum

✔ A dull ache in the lower abdomen or the *groin* (the area where the thigh meets the abdomen)

✔ A sudden collection of fluid in the scrotum

✔ Pain or discomfort in a testicle or in the scrotum

If you experience any of these signs or symptoms, see your doctor.

The American Cancer Society (ACS), at `www.cancer.org`, says that experts are divided on whether testicular self-exam (TSE) helps detect the cancer early. The ACS doesn't feel that, for men with average testicular cancer risk, there is any medical evidence to suggest that monthly self-examination is any more effective than simple awareness and prompt medical evaluation. However, the ACS says that TSE may be in order for men with certain risk factors, such a personal or family history of testicular cancer and undescended testicles.

You can find directions on how to perform TSE at the Testicular Cancer Resource Center (`www.acor.org/TCRC`) and in the FDA Consumer Magazine (`www.fda.gov/fdac/features/196_test.html`).

Dole, it turns out, was in the early tests of VIAGRA and didn't mind telling the world about it, though he never actually mentioned the V-word in the ads for early detection. Pfizer, VIAGRA's manufacturer, paid for the ads.

Dole's efforts helped make the public aware of a serious health problem affecting as many as 30 million American men. ED affects men of all ages, although it's more common in older men. In virtually all cases, impotence has a treatable physical cause, such as disease, injury, or drug side effects, but it also can have psychological roots.

The Internet can help you find information on dealing with impotence. Here are some places to look:

✔ **Impotence World:** At `www.impotenceworld.org`, you can find information on the drug and nondrug treatments and a list of medical specialists.

✔ **impotence.org:** This site (`www.impotence.org`) has the background on diagnosis and treatment, information for partners, and chats.

✔ **National Kidney and Urological Diseases Information Clearinghouse:** This site has an online brochure on the topic at `www.niddk.nih.gov/health/urolog/pubs/impotnce/impotnce.htm`.

- ✔ `alt.support.impotence:` At `www.alt-support-impotence.org`, you can find the newsgroup's archives and information on joining the group.
- ✔ **The American Urological Association:** This group can help you find a *urologist,* a specialist in this kind of problem, at `www.auanet.org/patient_info/find_urologist/index.cfm`.

Birth control and safer sex

Birth control too often has been left to the ladies. Men, you should do your part, too.

Here are some sites with information to help you make informed choices:

- ✔ **Planned Parenthood at** `www.plannedparenthood.org/bc:` This site features all the birth control choices, including condoms and vasectomies. The site has an online brochure that demonstrates proper use of a condom at `www.plannedparenthood.org/bc/condom.htm.` You can find information on safer sex at `www.plannedparenthood.org/sti.`
- ✔ **AVSC International at** `www.avsc.org/contraception/cvas2.html:` This site tells you what you need to know about vasectomies, including the no-scalpel, no-stitch ones.

VIAGRA and the Net

If ever a drug was suited for the Internet, it's VIAGRA. The drug treats a common, but embarrassing, problem: *impotence,* which is the inability to have an erection. It's something that many of the millions of men would rather not talk to their doctor about.

Soon after the U.S. Food and Drug Administration gave VIAGRA the green light (in 1998) as the first oral drug for impotence, online hustlers, including medical doctors and pharmacists, started peddling the drug. Doctors were prescribing the medication online to men they had never examined in person. Some people in search of aphrodisiacs wanted in on the action, too.

Ethical issues about physicians prescribing medications for people they've never had in their care abound. Also, like any other drug, VIAGRA poses potential health problems:

VIAGRA isn't for everyone, and it is particularly risky for men with heart conditions who are taking nitrates, such as nitroglycerin.

To find out more about VIAGRA, go to the FDA's VIAGRA information page at `www.fda.gov/cder/consumerinfo/viagra/viagra_consumer.htm.` Pfizer Inc., the manufacturer of VIAGRA, has information at `www.viagra.com` on how the drug works, its potential side effects, and proper use of the medication.

Although the FDA, state attorneys general, and medical and pharmacy groups have cracked down on Internet sales of the medication, the online hucksters still haven't given up. E-mail and Web site pitches for VIAGRA are legion.

You can find more on avoiding the problems of Internet drug sales in Chapter 7.

You can find more information on avoiding HIV/AIDS and other sexually transmitted diseases in Chapter 13.

Prostatitis

The prostate is a small male gland that seems to cause more than its share of problems.

In Chapter 10, we look at prostate cancer, a major cancer in men. In Chapter 17, we look at *benign prostate hyperplasia,* the gland enlargement that sends older men scurrying to the bathroom throughout the night. But here we talk about another prostate woe: prostatitis.

The Prostatitis Foundation (`www.prostatitis.org`), shown in Figure 16-4, looks at the various symptoms and potential causes and treatment of this inflammation of the prostate gland.

Prostatitis, which can mimic urinary infections or other prostate diseases, can cause intense pain, urinary problems, sexual dysfunction, and infertility. Prostatitis can also be difficult to treat. This condition affects men of all ages in contrast with the other prostate diseases (such as prostate cancer and benign prostate hyperplasia), which primarily affect older men.

In the right-hand column of the site's home page, you can find links to information within the site. Look for the It Works for Me link, where men with prostatitis share their first-person stories on how they have dealt with the condition. A Studies Needing Patients link can help you find research studies that you can participate in.

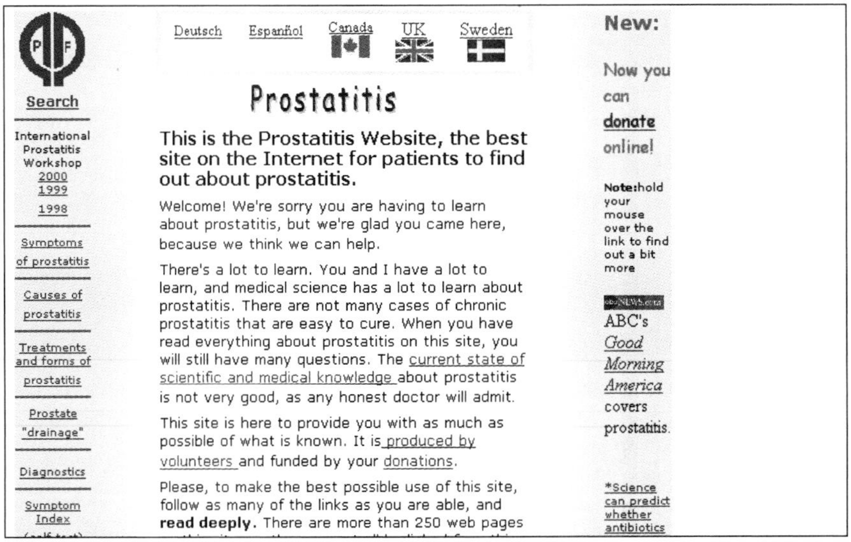

Figure 16-4: The Prostatitis Foundation shares first-person stories about coping with this sometimes hard-to-treat condition.

Deutsch Espanñol Canada UK Sweden

New:

Now you can **donate** online!

Search

International Prostatitis Workshop
2000
1999
1998

Symptoms of prostatitis

Causes of prostatitis

Treatments and forms of prostatitis

Prostate "drainage"

Diagnostics

Symptom Index

Prostatitis

This is the Prostatitis Website, the best site on the Internet for patients to find out about prostatitis.

Welcome! We're sorry you are having to learn about prostatitis, but we're glad you came here, because we think we can help.

There's a lot to learn. You and I have a lot to learn, and medical science has a lot to learn about prostatitis. There are not many cases of chronic prostatitis that are easy to cure. When you have read everything about prostatitis on this site, you will still have many questions. The current state of scientific and medical knowledge about prostatitis is not very good, as any honest doctor will admit.

This site is here to provide you with as much as possible of what is known. It is produced by volunteers and funded by your donations.

Please, to make the best possible use of this site, follow as many of the links as you are able, and **read deeply.** There are more than 250 web pages

Note: hold your mouse over the link to find out a bit more

ABC's *Good Morning America* covers prostatitis.

*Science can predict whether antibiotics

If you scroll down to the bottom of the Prostatitis Foundation's opening page, you can find a link to the foundation's <u>Moderated E-Mail Discussion List</u> and a link to the foundation's newsgroup, <u>sci.med.prostate.prostatitis</u>. (For more on online support, see Chapter 2.)

The American Foundation for Urological Disease takes a look at prostatitis symptoms and treatment (and has a glossary of relevant terms) at `www.afud.org/conditions/ps.html`.

Not for women only

Certain health problems have been viewed as "women's things." This category would include breast cancer, osteoporosis, and eating disorders, such as anorexia and bulimia.

Men can have these problems, too. Here's where you can find out more:

- ✔ **Osteoporosis:** About 2 million American men have this bone-thinning problem, which can cause serious fractures. The National Institutes of Health Osteoporosis and Related Bone Disorders Information Center has a fact sheet, "Osteoporosis in Men," on causes, symptoms, treatment, and prevention at `www.osteo.org/r603men.html`.

- ✔ **Breast cancer:** More than 1,000 American men a year are diagnosed with breast cancer, and 400 a year die from it. The Susan G. Komen Breast Cancer Foundation has information on the signs and symptoms, risk factors, and treatment for men at `www.breastcancerinfo.com/bhealth/html/male_breast_cancer.asp`.

- ✔ **Eating disorders:** An estimated one in six Americans with eating disorders is male. Anorexia Nervosa and Related Eating Disorders, Inc., has a fact sheet on anorexia, bulimia, and other eating problems for men at `www.anred.com/males.html`.

Chapter 17

Seniors' Health

. . . .

In This Chapter

▶ Staying well in the senior years

▶ Dealing with age-related conditions and diseases

▶ Finding out about nursing homes and assisted living

▶ Finding resources for caregiving, hospices, and grief support

. . . .

Legendary baseball pitcher Satchel Paige knew a thing or two about aging with style.

In his 40s, he became the oldest rookie in major league history, using his trouble-ball and jump-ball pitches to help the Cleveland Indians win the pennant and World Series in 1948. He's said to have relaxed in the bullpen in a rocking chair while waiting to be called to the mound.

At the tender age of 59, Satch pitched three innings for the Kansas City Athletics to become the oldest person to pitch in The Bigs. So believe it when the Hall of Famer said, "Age is a case of mind over matter. If you don't mind, it don't matter."

You can put to use the abundant information available on the Internet to minimize the curve balls that aging throws you and lead a healthy, active, and fulfilling life. In this chapter, you find online resources to help you stay well and help you cope with, and hopefully conquer, some of the health problems and concerns you encounter as you age.

Before we start, here's a Satchism to ponder: "How old would you be if you didn't know how old you were?" And by the way, the next time you're pitching, keep this sage Satch advice in mind: "You gotta keep the ball off the fat part of the bat."

Life, like baseball, is a game, so get out there and play ball!

Staying Well

Americans are living longer and better than ever before. According to the U.S. Census Bureau, a century ago, at age 65, people could expect to live only another 12 years. Today, on average, you have nearly 20 more years of life ahead if you reach age 65.

America's elderly population will increase dramatically as the baby boomer generation heads en masse into their senior years. By the year 2030, the United States government expects the number of older people to have doubled since the early 1990s.

It's gonna give a whole new definition to the 60s, man. It used to be said that life begins at 40. Now, they'd probably say that it begins at 60 or 65. Maybe older.

If you take good care of yourself, you can have a fulfilling life as a senior. AARP and MayoClinic.com are two sites that share this positive-aging approach.

AARP

There's something that people start noticing just before they turn 50. It isn't creaky joints, and it isn't those frustrating momentary lapses in memory, popularly called _senior moments_.

Nope, it's all that snail mail trying to entice them to join AARP (formerly the American Association of Retired Persons) with promises of travel discounts and mutual fund riches. Like death and taxes, that junk mail from AARP is one of the inevitabilities of life.

But AARP also happens to have a great Web page for finding health-related information. And you don't have to be a member to tap into the resources.

Go to the AARP health and wellness page (`www.aarp.org/healthguide`). Along the left-hand margin is a list of links to topics, where you can find articles on the following:

- ✔ **Wellness:** Here you can find tips on eating for your health, managing stress, preventing illness and disease, and staying fit. Online tools for health and fitness and information on grandchildren's health and safety also appear here.

- ✔ **Caregiving:** This area has pointers on balancing work and caregiving, caring for your parents at home, long-distance caregiving, managing stress when giving care, power of attorney, end-of-life issues, coping with grief and loss, widowed persons, and bereavement programs.

- ✔ **Health Insurance Options:** Here's what you need to know about managed care versus traditional insurance and about private long-term care insurance.

- ✔ **Medicare:** This area has information on Medicare basics, your Medicare rights, selecting Medigap insurance, and what to do if your managed care plan leaves Medicare.

- ✔ **Nursing Homes:** Here you can find out about choosing a good nursing home, Medicare hospice benefits, and your rights as a nursing home resident.

- ✔ **Community Help:** Here are tips on finding help for independent living, participating in AARP grief and loss programs, and avoiding elder abuse, plus an overview of AARP community programs.

The right-hand column of the AARP Web site's health and wellness page has a Discussions section, where you can find electronic bulletin boards so you can share your thoughts and feelings. Click the <u>Wellness Discussion</u> link to join a discussion on improving your health. Click the <u>Caregivers Circle</u> link for discussions on caring for a sick or frail family member. Click the <u>More Discussions</u> link to see other groups AARP offers on a wide variety of topics.

Live long and prosper

You know how they say it isn't how many years that you have in life, but how much life you have in those years?

In these United States, you get more of both. In the last century, huge gains were made in longevity in the United States, thanks to improved public health standards, such as the availability of a clean, safe water supply and healthier food, along with medical advances. According to the National Institute on Aging (NIA), the average American in 1900 had a life span of 47 years. Today, the average American's life span has surpassed 72.

Still, researchers believe that there's still room to grow . . . old. The NIA, in its online brochure, "In Search of the Secrets of Aging," at `www.nih.gov/nia/health/pubs/secrets-of-aging/p1.htm#p11`, tells the story of Shirechiyo Izumi. This Japanese man lived to a ripe — and well-documented — 120 years, 237 days. He died in 1986 from pneumonia.

In the United States, the fastest growing population group is *centenarians*. These people aren't Roman legionnaires; they're people aged 100 years and more. The U.S. Census Bureau reported that the number of centenarians had doubled to nearly 70,000 from the beginning to the end of the 1990s. The Census folks estimate that, by 2050, more than 800,000 Americans could be more than 100 years old.

Some researchers today believe that someone already alive now will live to be 150. We guess that person would be called a sesquicentenarian. That's far short of the 900 or so years of Methuselah's Biblical record, but still worthy of a George "I-made-it-to-100" Burns "see-gar".

MayoClinic.com

Many medical megasites have centers devoted to senior health. MayoClinic.com's Healthy Aging Center aims to encourage the physical, mental, emotional, and spiritual health of seniors.

To get to the Healthy Aging Center, go to www.mayoclinic.com and scroll halfway down the page. On the right-hand side, you'll see the Healthy Living Centers drop-down text box. In the list that appears after you click the downward-pointing arrow, choose Healthy Aging.

On the Healthy Aging Center page, you find the News and Feature Picks section with articles on topics of interest to seniors. Then, near the bottom of the page, you can find links to the following areas:

- **Living Longer:** How to make those later years longer and happier
- **Minding the Maturing Mind:** Ways to help keep that noggin nimble
- **Happily Aging:** Staying connected to family, friends, and community
- **Money Matters:** From home-care services to retirement planning, fast-forward on finances
- **Caregivers Corner:** Where looking after others and yourself intersect

Even further down the Health Aging Center page, you can find Mayo's exercise, weight loss, and smoking cessation planners and other tools.

Medical megasites usually have senior centers or information of interest to seniors. A few worth mentioning are the Senior Health channel at CBSHealthWatch at healthwatch.medscape.com, Aging Healthy at drkoop.com at www.drkoop.com/family/ seniors, and Seniors' Health at InteliHealth at www.intelihealth.com. (Use the link on the toolbar at the top of the page.)

Smoking is the nation's largest underlying cause of death. But according to the National Institute on Aging, the combination of lack of exercise and poor nutrition is number two. The Institute has a cool exercise guide aimed at seniors at www.nih.gov/nia/health/pubs/nasa-exercise. So get movin'. (You can find more on exercise, nutrition, and smoking cessation in Chapter 18.)

Dealing with Illnesses

Many of the major health concerns of older people are covered in Part IV of this book. Here, you find out about some other health problems of special interest to seniors.

Seniors often take a lot of medications to care for what ails them. At agenet.agenet.com, SeniorNet has reviews of more than 200 medications commonly used by seniors. Chapter 7 has more on finding out about medicines and purchasing them online.

Alzheimer's disease

People naturally become more forgetful as they get older, which results in those so-called senior moments that people joke about. A senior moment is forgetting where your keys are. Alzheimer's disease is forgetting what keys are used for.

Alzheimer's is a progressive degenerative disease that results in loss of memory, deterioration in language skills, impaired judgment, and other problems. Over 4 million American are living with Alzheimer's disease.

Typically, Alzheimer's disease begins after age 65, but it can begin as early as age 40. There is no cure for this devastating condition. Alzheimer's robs the person of his or her identity and can take a huge toll on his or her family. But information and support are available, as described in the following few sections.

ADEAR

The National Institute on Aging's Alzheimer's Disease Education and Referral (ADEAR) Center's Web site (www.alzheimers.org) offers information about Alzheimer's disease, its impact on families and health professionals, and research into possible causes and cures.

Here are some direct links to useful ADEAR services:

- ✔ **Publications:** Go to www.alzheimers.org/pubs/pubs.html for fact sheets on a variety of Alzheimer's-related topics. You can choose topics, such as depression, estrogen, forgetfulness, gingko biloba, and planning for long-term care from the drop-down text box on the page.

- ✔ **Alzheimer's Disease Centers:** The National Institute on Aging funds 30 research centers at major medical institutions, where top scientists are researching treatment for and prevention of Alzheimer's. The research centers also are good places to get care for people with the disease. To find the closest center, go to www.alzheimers.org/pubs/adcdir.html.

- ✔ **Alzheimer's Disease Clinical Trials Database:** If you're interested in research studies on Alzheimer's or other conditions in the category known as dementia, go to www.alzheimers.org/trials/index.html, shown in Figure 17-1. If you sign up on the site, ADEAR will e-mail you notification of new trials.

Figure 17-1:
The
National
Institute on
Aging's
Alzheimer's
Disease
Education
and Referral
Center has
information
on finding
research
studies on
the
memory-
robbing
disorder.

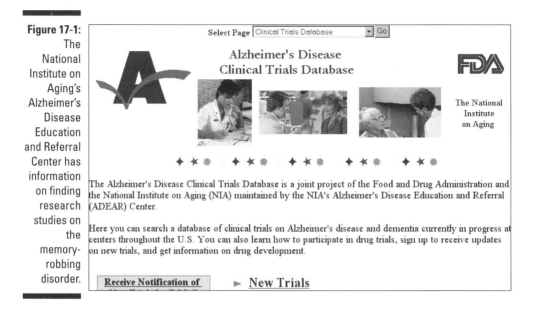

Alzheimer's Association

The Alzheimer's Association (www.alz.org) offers a variety of services online. To find support locally, go to www.alz.org/chapter, type in your zip code, and click the Find Local Chapter button. Local chapters offer helplines, support groups, and education.

The association also has a glossary of terms used in connection with the disease at www.alz.org/glossary.htm.

Osteoporosis

Osteoporosis, the bone-thinning disorder, is a major public health threat. People with osteoporosis are at risk for fractures of the hip, spine, wrist, and other areas.

Ten million Americans have the disease. Eighty percent are women. Another 18 million Americans are at risk for the condition that primarily affects the elderly, but it also can strike younger people.

Here are some places to get information and support.

Osteoporosis Resource Center

The National Institutes of Health's Osteoporosis and Related Bone Diseases National Resource Center (www.osteo.org), shown in Figure 17-2, has the basics you need to know about this condition, how it's diagnosed and treated, and what can be done to prevent it through nutrition and exercise.

Figure 17-2:
The
National
Institutes of
Health
Osteoporosis
and Related
Bone
Diseases
National
Resource
Center
provides
info on
osteo-
porosis.

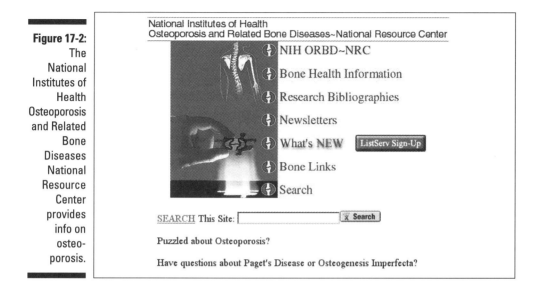

National Institutes of Health
Osteoporosis and Related Bone Diseases~National Resource Center

- NIH ORBD~NRC
- Bone Health Information
- Research Bibliographies
- Newsletters
- What's NEW   ListServ Sign-Up
- Bone Links
- Search

SEARCH This Site: [   ] Search

Puzzled about Osteoporosis?

Have questions about Paget's Disease or Osteogenesis Imperfecta?

Risk factors for osteoporosis

The National Institutes of Health Osteoporosis and Related Bone Diseases National Resource Center has an online brochure, "Fast Facts on Osteoporosis," at www.osteo.org/osteofastfact.html, which lists the major risk factors for osteoporosis as:

- Being female
- Thin and/or small frame
- Advanced age
- A family history of osteoporosis
- Postmenopause, including early or surgically induced menopause
- Abnormal absence of menstrual periods (amenorrhea)
- Anorexia nervosa or bulimia

- A diet low in calcium
- Use of certain medications, such as corticosteroids and anticonvulsants
- Low testosterone levels in men
- An inactive lifestyle
- Cigarette smoking
- Excessive use of alcohol
- Being Caucasian or Asian, although African-Americans and Hispanic Americans are at significant risk as well

Go to www.osteo.org/osteolinks.html for fact sheets on osteoporosis and how it affects Asian American women, African American women, Latino women, and men.

National Osteoporosis Foundation

The National Osteoporosis Foundation (www.nof.org) offers information on preventing, diagnosing, and treating osteoporosis and advice on finding a doctor. It has information on support groups at www.nof.org/patientinfo/support_groups.htm.

To find a newsgroup on osteoporosis, go to Google Groups at groups.google.com, enter **osteoporosis** in the Search Groups box, and click the Google Search button. Under the heading Relevant Groups, click the sci.med.diseases.osteoporosis link to read the latest postings to the newsgroup. (You can find more on newsgroups and e-mail support in Chapter 2.)

Eye diseases

As you age, you have an increased risk for certain diseases that affect your eyes.

The American Academy of Ophthalmology, the Eye MDs, presents its information on eye diseases at Medem at www.medem.com. From the Medem home page, go to the Medical Library. Scroll down the page to the Diseases and Conditions section and click the Eye Health link. On the Eye Health page, you can see a variety of links to articles from the Eye MDs, including those of special interest to seniors on macular degeneration, cataracts, and glaucoma.

You can take the screening test for *macular degeneration,* the loss of peripheral vision, at the Prevent Blindness America site at www.preventblindness.org/eye_tests/amd_test.html.

The National Eye Institute (one of the National Institutes of Health), at www.nei.nih.gov, also covers these topics. It has online brochures at www.nei.nih.gov/pubpat.htm and a long resource list with groups that can help with low vision at www.nei.nih.gov/publications/lowvis.htm.

To find support, you should go to the Association of Vision Science Librarians' Eye Resources on the Internet Web site at webeye.ophth.uiowa.edu/dept/websites/eyeres.htm. The librarians have created a comprehensive list of eye-related Web sites, e-mail lists, and newsgroups.

Prostate disease

The prostate is a small walnut-shaped gland that produces fluid for the semen to carry sperm. But this one-ounce bad boy can pack more than its weight in health troubles.

Prostate cancer, a major health concern for older men, is covered in Chapter 10. And prostatitis, affecting men of all ages, is covered in Chapter 16.

Symptoms of BPH

In "Treating Your Enlarged Prostate," which is available through a link at `www.ahrq.gov/consumer/consguidix.htm,` the Agency for Healthcare Research and Quality lists the following symptoms for benign prostatic hyperplasia:

✔ I feel that I have not completely emptied my bladder after I stop urinating.

✔ I urinate often.

✔ I stop and start when I urinate.

✔ I have a strong and sudden desire to urinate that is hard to delay.

✔ My urine stream is weak.

✔ I need to push or strain to start the urine stream. I often wake up at night to urinate.

If you have these symptoms, you should see a doctor for tests and a treatment strategy.

A common problem among older men is *benign prostatic hyperplasia* (BPH), an enlargement of the gland that occurs with age. BPH is responsible for many of those wake-up calls in the middle of the night for senior men. BPH is common in men after 50, and more than half of men have it by age 60. It can play a role in urinary tract infections and also can result in an interruption in urination.

For more on this condition, go to the Agency for Healthcare Research and Quality's <u>Treating Your Enlarged Prostate</u> link at `www.ahrq.gov/ consumer/ consguidix.htm`. The National Kidney and Urologic Diseases Information Clearinghouse has a fact sheet on BPH at `www.niddk.nih.gov/ health/ urolog/pubs/prostate/index.htm`.

For newsgroups on BPH, go to Google Groups at `groups.google.com,` enter **benign prostatic hyperplasia** in the Search Groups box, and click the Google Search button. Under the heading Relevant Groups, click either the <u>sci.med.prostate.prostatitis</u> or <u>sci.med.prostate.bph</u> link to read the latest postings to these newsgroups. (Chapter 2 has more on finding support online.)

Eldercare

When a loved one has been diagnosed with a chronic, disabling, or life-threatening condition, or has suffered a short-term health problem, you may need special help in caring for him or her. A wide variety of eldercare possibilities are available, and the Internet can help you make the decisions, locate the best services, and find support.

This section looks at some of the resources available in nursing homes, assisted living, and other choices.

Nursing homes

The Agency for Healthcare Research and Quality estimates that four in ten older people will stay in a nursing home at least once. One in ten will stay for five years or more.

If the time comes for you, your spouse, or parent to go into a nursing home, you can find help online. Various resources from AARP and Medicare can help you through this difficult time.

AARP

AARP's health and wellness Web site (`www.aarp.org/healthguide`) is one of the best places to look for information on nursing homes.

For information on nursing homes, go to `www.aarp.org/indexes/health.html#nursinghome`. The page has links to articles on the following topics:

- Choosing a Good Nursing Home
- Continuing Care Retirement Communities
- Nursing Home Admission Contract
- Medicaid and Paying for Nursing Home Care
- Medicare Hospice Benefits
- Resolving Nursing Home Problems
- Rights of Nursing Home Residents

Medicare

Medicare, the federal government's medical insurance program for seniors, has excellent advice and tools for finding out about nursing homes on its site at `www.medicare.gov`.

In the left-hand column, click the <u>Nursing Homes</u> link. You come to the Nursing Homes page with an overview on nursing homes at the top. Scroll down the page and you find links to other sections of the Medicare site that help you make informed choices about nursing homes.

Here are some of the links you may find helpful:

- **Nursing Home Checklist:** Here you find a form, shown in Figure 17-3, that you can print out to help you evaluate the nursing homes you may be considering.

  You can reach this checklist directly at `www.medicare.gov/Nursing/Checklist.asp`.

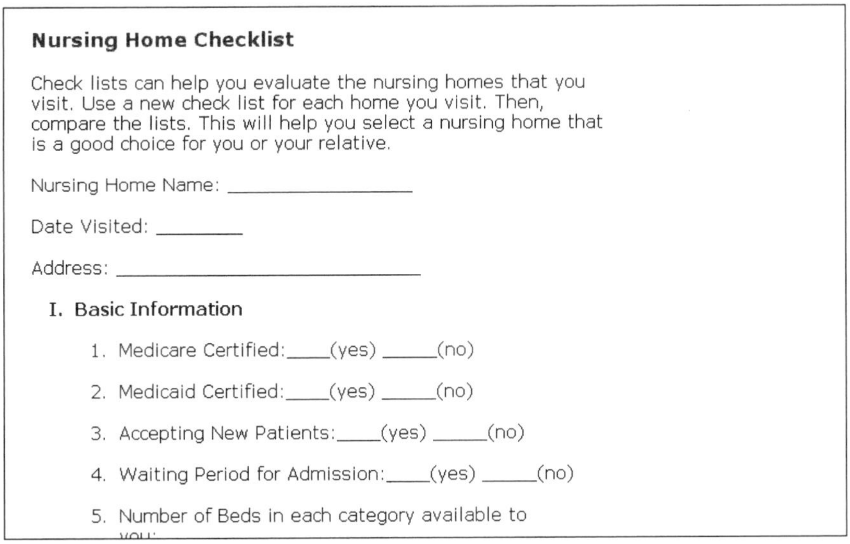

Figure 17-3:
Medicare's
Web site
has a
nursing
home
checklist
that you can
print out to
help
evaluate
nursing
homes.

Nursing Home Checklist

Check lists can help you evaluate the nursing homes that you
visit. Use a new check list for each home you visit. Then,
compare the lists. This will help you select a nursing home that
is a good choice for you or your relative.

Nursing Home Name: _____

Date Visited: _____

Address: _____

I. Basic Information

1. Medicare Certified:____(yes) _____(no)

2. Medicaid Certified:____(yes) _____(no)

3. Accepting New Patients:____(yes) _____(no)

4. Waiting Period for Admission:____(yes) _____(no)

5. Number of Beds in each category available to
you:

You'll get directions on how to grade the homes on factors, such as
whether the home and its administrator are licensed by the state,
whether it screens employees for history of abuse, whether it has waiting lists for special units for rehabilitation, Alzheimer's disease, and hospice, and whether it trains employees to recognize resident abuse and
neglect.

✔ **Paying for Care:** Here, you find out how nursing home care is financed
through the state-federal Medicaid plan, Medigap insurance, and (in
some cases) Medicare.

You can reach this information directly at www.medicare.gov/
Nursing/Payment.asp.

✔ **Nursing Home Compare:** Nursing Home Compare is an interactive tool
that enables you to compare information on nursing homes. It contains
information on more than 17,000 Medicare- and Medicaid-certified nursing homes, looking at factors, such as state inspection results and nursing staff information.

You can get directly to Nursing Home Compare at www.medicare.gov/
NHCompare/Home.asp.

Home care and assisted living

Some people who are unable to take full care of themselves can maintain
some of their independence with the help of home-care services, such as visiting nurses or live-in aides. Assisted-living and other residential-living
arrangements are another possibility.

Here are some resources to help you decide about such services and locate them:

- ✔ ElderSearch, at `www.eldersearch.com/welcome.html`, has information on senior housing, day care, and legal and financial information. The site features regularly scheduled chats.

- ✔ Administration on Aging, at `www.aoa.gov/elderpage/locator.html`, has an Eldercare Locator, a nationwide directory assistance service designed to help older persons and caregivers locate local support resources.

- ✔ HOMECARE Online from the National Association for Home Care, at `www.nahc.org/Consumer/coninfo.html`, has information on selecting home-care services and hospices, knowing your rights as a patient, and financing services, plus a listing of state agency resources and contacts for agencies that accredit home-care services. The site also has a link to the HomeCare & Hospice Agency Locator to help you find services in your area.

To check out the quality of long-term care and home health care services, the Joint Commission on Accreditation of Healthcare Organization's QualityCheck program, at `www.jcaho.org/qualitycheck/directry/directry.asp`, has reports online evaluating individual services. See Chapter 4 for help with using QualityCheck.

- ✔ The National Center for Assisted Living, at `www.ncal.org/consumer/consumer.htm`, has online brochures covering what you should think about in considering assisted living, what questions you need to ask, and what information you need about financing and long-term care insurance. Checklists for preparing to move into an assisted living facility are available here.

End-of-Life Issues

You're born, you mature, you grow old, and you die. That's the natural order.

We all know that it doesn't always happen that way. Sometimes, life is cut short as children die from cancer, teens die in auto accidents, young mothers die from breast cancer, and young fathers die from heart attacks.

This chapter on seniors seems to be the right place — in the natural order — to cover end-of-life issues. But the material you find here on caregiving, grieving, and hospice applies in all the seasons of life and death.

Caregiving

It's a tough and isolating experience to care for a person with a long-term or terminal disease. It can take its toll on the caregiver emotionally, physically, and spiritually.

Caregivers can get advice and support online relating to a dying or chronically ill spouse, child, or friend. Here are some places to go:

- ✔ **Growth House, Inc. (**www.growthhouse.org**):** This site has information on pain management, hospice and home care, death with dignity, eldercare, and chat for those facing life-threatening illnesses, their caregivers, and the bereaved.
- ✔ **Family Caregiver Alliance at (**www.caregiver.org**):** This site offers an e-mail support group for caregivers and fact sheets on end-of-life issues and on individual conditions, such as Alzheimer's disease, multiple sclerosis, brain tumors, and Parkinson's disease.

Hospice

At the end of life, caring, not curing, counts. And hospices are considered the model for compassionate caring for people who are dying.

Hospices provide supportive care so that patients can die pain-free with dignity and support to their family members. Hospices, which involve a team of health professionals, can be places, such as in hospitals or nursing homes; or hospice programs can come to an individual's home.

The National Hospice and Palliative Care Organization, an association of hospice groups, at www.nhpco.org, has some very useful information. In the left-hand column, click the Hospice Care Information link to go to the What Is Hospice? page, where you can get tips on choosing a hospice and learn about the Medicare hospice benefit.

Especially worth reading is "Communicating Your End of Life Wishes," which you can reach by clicking the link in the left margin of the What Is Hospice? page. The article notes that you plan for weddings, marriages, and other important events, so why not plan for your final days?

Here are some additional sites that provide hospice-related information:

- ✔ The American College of Physicians' *Home Care Guide for Advanced Cancer* offers advice that applies not only to cancer, but also to other conditions, at www.acponline.org/public/h_care/index.html. Click the Dying Person's Guide link for some sound advice from a physician who is dying from cancer.

- ✔ You can click the <u>Find a Hospice Program</u> link at `www.nhpco.org` to find a hospice in your area.

- ✔ The Partnership for Caring, Inc., at `www.partnershipforcaring.org`, has information about living wills and durable powers of attorney for health care, which are documents that instruct your family how to carry out your wishes if you become incapacitated. You can download these documents, which are available on a state-by-state basis. Because these are important legal documents, you may want to consult with your attorney.

- ✔ The Hospice Patients Alliance, at `www.hospicepatients.org`, is a consumer group that aims to make hospice patients and their families aware of their rights, including where to file complaints.

Grief support

If you're grieving the loss of a spouse, parent, child, or friend, you can get support online. Here are a couple places to go:

- ✔ **Death-Dying (`www.death-dying.com`):** This site has a variety of message boards and chats on loss and grief.

- ✔ **WidowNet (`www.fortnet.org/WidowNet`):** This site covers grief, bereavement, recovery, and other issues for people who have lost their spouses or life partners. The site features message boards and chats. Also, there's also a link to "Dumb Remarks and Stupid Questions (along with a few responses that come to mind)" to help you cope with those thoughtless remarks from people whom the site refers to as "terminally tactless."

Bill Moyers takes a comprehensive look at death and dying issues at the On Our Own Terms: Moyers on Dying Web site at `www.pbs.org/wnet/onourownterms/index.html`. You find end-of-life tools and information on all aspects of caregiving, grieving, and support at this site.

Part VI
Using the Web for Wellness

The 5th Wave   By Rich Tennant

@RICHTENNANT

"You know, anyone who wishes he had a remote control for his exercise equipment is missing the idea of exercise equipment."

In this part . . .

This part points you to online resources that help you stay healthy — both physically and mentally.

The online tools in Chapter 18 inspire you to eat right and exercise, support and advise you if you want to shed some pounds, and help you quit smoking. And in Chapter 19, you find out about tools that help you reduce stress and increase your mental well-being, as well as sites where you can get information and support for depression, anxiety, seasonal affective disorder, and eating disorders.

Chapter 18

Eating Right, Staying Fit

In This Chapter

▶ Finding out how to eat healthy

▶ Getting in shape

▶ Quitting smoking

*T*hree of the best things you can do to improve your health are to eat right, exercise, and quit smoking.

If you need to be convinced, keep these two facts in mind:

✔ **Cigarette smoking is the leading preventable cause of death in the United States.** It's responsible for one in five deaths, killing more people than AIDS, alcohol abuse, automobile accidents, illegal drugs, fires, homicide, and suicide, combined. One in four American adults smokes, and the numbers are even higher among high school students.

✔ **Poor nutrition, obesity, and lack of physical activity, combined, are the second leading preventable cause of death in the United States today.** Nutrition plays a critical role in the prevention and management of diseases including heart disease, cancer, and diabetes. As many as half of adult Americans are considered overweight or obese, and the obesity rate among children has doubled in the past 20 years.

In this chapter, you discover Web sites that provide information to help you lose that spare tire, improve your heart rate, and quit smoking. So, put down that Danish and be a couch potato no more.

Eating Right

When it comes to information about eating right, the Internet is a banquet. In the following sections, we introduce you to Web sites containing information on what constitutes a healthy diet, according to the federal government; how to lose weight; how to find a healthy substitute for a fatty ingredient; how to prevent or treat food-related illnesses, such as heart disease, cancer, and diabetes; and how to find online dieting support.

So let the info feast begin.

Nutrition.gov

Nutrition.gov (`www.nutrition.gov`), shown in Figure 18-1, is a megasite that pulls together nutritional information from a variety of government sources, such as the U.S. Department of Agriculture, the Food and Drug Administration, and the Centers for Disease Control and Prevention.

Of special interest is the Food Facts section, where you can find the following links:

- **Dietary Supplements:** Information on dietary supplements

- **Food Labels:** How to make sense out of food labels

- **Food Pyramid:** A guide to the government's official nutritional recommendations

- **Healthy Eating:** Tips on eating for people with high blood pressure, high cholesterol, and cancer, and recipes to keep your heart healthy

- **Nutrients:** Food composition tables

Figure 18-1:
Nutrition.
gov
provides a
cornucopia
of
information
on nutrition.

Click and shrink

Looking to shed a few pounds? Here are the Web sites for some popular eating plans:

✔ **At Home with Richard (www. richardsimmons. com):** Web site for diet guru and bon vivant Richard Simmons.

✔ **Atkins Diet (www.atkinscenter.com):** Dr. Robert Atkins' low-carb plan.

✔ **BodyforLife.com (www.bodyforlife.com):** Take the popular six-meal-a-day low-fat, high-protein diet and exercise challenge and cross the abyss.

✔ **Carbohydrate Addicts' Official Home Page (www.carbohydrateaddicts.com):** Controlled carb eating.

✔ **Dr. Dean Ornish (my.webmd.com/medcast_ channel_toc/3068):** Low-fat diet.

✔ **WeightWatchers.com (www.weight-watchers. com):** Losing weight with the Duchess.

✔ **Dr. Andrew Weil (www.drweil.com):** Dr. Weil offers what he modestly calls the best diet in the world.

✔ **ZonePerfect.com (www.zoneperfect.com):** The Zone diet.

Other food/nutrition sites

Here are some other sites with nutrition information you can chew on:

✔ **Nutrition Navigator (navigator.tufts.edu):** Tufts University presents its top-rated links to nutrition sites for parents, women, kids, and people with special health needs, and to hot topics, such as weight management, sports nutrition, and vegetarianism.

✔ **Center for Science in the Public Interest (www.cspinet.org):** This site has featured Nutrition Action Healthletter articles, a listing of ten foods you should never eat, a listing of ten foods you should eat, and Chemical Cuisine, a list of chemical additives in foods.

✔ **The American Dietetic Association's Find a Dietitian feature (www.eatright.org):** To locate a dietitian, type your zip code in the search box in the upper-left-corner of the page.

✔ **Cyberdiet (www.cyberdiet.com):** This site helps you lose weight and keep it off with a variety of Web tools, including 12-week meal plans designed for specific calorie levels and dietary restrictions, recipe makeovers, exercise and motivational tips, online support groups, guided meditation, and more.

- ✔ **WholeHealthMD.com** (`www.wholehealthmd.com`): This site features the Healing Kitchen, with information on the healing benefits of food; Food Remedies for particular conditions; a Recipe Makeover section; and a Recipe Database section.

- ✔ **VegSource** (`www.vegsource.com`): This site provides information on plant-based diets, including news, recipes, leads on veggie restaurants, and support through message boards and chats.

Getting Fit

The Internet can be your health club, your home fitness center, and your personal trainer, all in one, serving up the information you need to get in shape and stay that way. Here are a few sites that fit that bill.

Asimba

Asimba (`www.asimba.com`), shown in Figure 18-2, is a fitness megasite, earning letters in all sports. It covers the bases whether you're just starting to exercise or a particular sport is your passion.

Figure 18-2:
Asimba coaches you in exercise and fitness.

Asimba has a Tools section to help you assess your fitness level. These tools include the Fuel Up calculator, which helps you determine what and how much to eat and drink before, during, and after your workout; the Burn Calculator, which measures calories burned during a particular exercise; and the Resting Metabolic Rate calculator, which tells you how many calories you're burning while at rest, such as when you're reading this tome.

The Asimba Community section has bulletin boards to help you find a training buddy or help you find support on such topics as nutrition, weight loss, a particular exercise, or a specific sport, including walking, running, swimming, triathlons, or biking.

The site has an Ask the Asimba Expert feature, where you can pose questions about fitness, nutrition, equipment, or training. Asimba also has links to instructional videos demonstrating stretches, yoga, golf, badminton, martial arts, polo — you name it.

Other features include advice on the best gear for sports, links to other sites on a particular topic, and locators to find sporting events and coaches. Asimba requires you to register to use some services, and some services require a fee.

Why exercise? According to Asimba's logo: "Because endorphins feel good."

Some other fitness sites

Here are some sites that offer additional information on fitness:

- ✔ **"Exercise: How to Get Started"** (`familydoctor.org/handouts/015.html`): This online brochure from the American Academy of Family Physicians explains why and how to start an exercise program.

- ✔ **The Physician and Sportsmedicine's Personal Health section** (`www.physsportsmed.com/personal.htm`): You can browse this physician publication for advice on a wide variety of topics, such as the right way to do sit-ups, whether you should exercise when you're sick, how to choose the best sports bras and briefs, how to avoid and treat blisters, and using ice to treat sports injuries.

- ✔ **Stretching: An Overview** (`www.row2k.com/physio/overvie1.html`): The stretching information at this site was created for rowers, but it'll help anyone who wants to s-t-r-e-t-c-h. Ah.

- ✔ **Avoiding the Muscle Hustle: Tips for Buying Exercise Equipment** (`www.ftc.gov/bcp/conline/edcams/exercise/index.html`): The Federal Trade Commission's site tells you what to look for in home exercise equipment and also provides a handy link to click if you want to file a complaint against a manufacturer.

Stretch your body, stretch your mind

You can go online to find out about some ancient practices that can help keep your body lithe and relaxed and maybe even expand your mind. Here are some practices that help you breathe easy and get the qi — or energy — flowing, along with Web sites where you can find more information:

✔ **Meditation.** You don't have to grow a beard and climb to the top of the mountain to contemplate your navel.

Go to Learning Meditation at www.learningmeditation.com to experience the techniques in the comfort of your home. Head into the Meditation Room, where you can click links to try out various meditations with the help of RealAudio software.

✔ **Yoga.** This ancient practice of using postures — known as asanas — and breathing techniques can help you gain strength and flexibility and maybe even some peace of mind in this fast-paced Internet age.

Yoga Site (www.yogasite.com) is a yoga megasite that uses playful stick figures to demonstrate how to do yoga postures — such as the salutation to the sun, the bridge, and the triangle. The site also has a teacher directory, information on meditation, yoga therapy news, and links to other yoga sites.

✔ **Qigong.** This practice from China aims to get the qi, or life force energy, moving. The technique combines movement, meditation, visualization, and breathing exercises. Can the 200 million Chinese who practice qigong be wrong?

ChiLel Qigong, a form of qigong developed at a famed medicine-free hospital in China, has a Web site at www.chilel-qigong.com, where you can find information on the technique, a directory of teachers, and a downloadable page of 100 fill-in-the-smile faces to keep track of your 100-day gong. Embrace the qi.

Kicking Butts

Mark Twain said it was easy to quit smoking, and he did it hundreds of times. Maybe you have, too.

But back in Twain's time, people only suspected that cigarettes were bad for you. Today, it's known that smoking is the leading cause of premature death in the country.

More than 400,000 Americans die each year from heart disease, cancer, lung disease, or other problems attributed to this addiction, according to the Centers for Disease Control and Prevention (CDC) (www.cdc.gov/tobacco/research_data/health_consequences/mortali.htm). The CDC also notes that one in five deaths can be attributed to smoking.

Despite Twain's comments, it's difficult, though not impossible, to break the nicotine addiction. The U.S. Surgeon General says in his "You Can Quit Smoking: Consumer Guide" (www.surgeongeneral.gov/tobacco/consquits.htm) that it usually takes two or three attempts before you succeed.

To be successful, experts say you need to prepare to quit, find support, learn new skills and behaviors, get medication and use it properly, and be prepared for relapses. The following sections introduce some sites that offer the information and tools you'll need to quit.

QuitNet

QuitNet, an online smoking cessation community (www.quitnet.org), shown in Figure 18-3, can be the headquarters for your personal campaign to quit smoking for good.

QuitNet takes you through the whole smoking-cessation process: finding out why you should quit, setting a quit date, and then following through. The site even offers around-the-clock support by hooking you up with online buddies. You need to register to take full advantage of the site.

Here are some of the tools that the site provides (which you can link to from the site's main page):

- **Quitting Guide:** This is a comprehensive guide to smoking cessation.

- **Quitting Calendar:** This calendar can be personalized and is aimed at giving you day-by-day support to help you stop smoking.

- **Pharmaceutical Guide:** This section provides an overview of the pharmaceutical products that help you quit smoking, including the nicotine patch, nicotine gum, nicotine inhaler, and medications. This section helps you find the best method for *you*.

- **Q-Gadget:** This motivational tool helps you track the amount of money and years of life you've saved since you quit.

- **Talk:** You can get support from others who are trying to quit smoking through the site's message boards. The boards include QuitStop, where you can discuss the quitting process and get support in quitting, and Quitting Milestones, where you can celebrate quit anniversaries and stay motivated. Other message boards deal with weight control, depression, and addiction to other drugs. Registration is required.

QuitNet also has a host of other tools, including the QuitDate Wizard to help you set a quit date; the National Directory to help you find local smoking cessation programs; and the Quit Tips and Anniversary E-mails program to provide long-term support.

For links to information on all forms of substance abuse, including, alcohol, cocaine, and other drugs, go to MEDLINE*plus* at www.nlm.nih.gov/medlineplus/substanceabuse.html. Also, check out the Web of Addictions at www.well.com/user/woa.

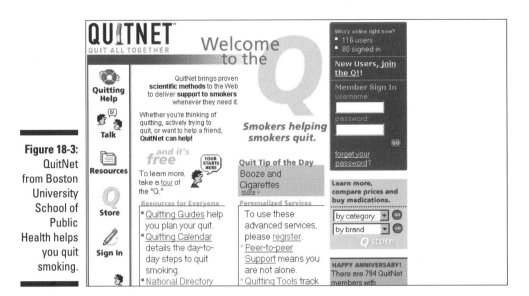

Figure 18-3: QuitNet from Boston University School of Public Health helps you quit smoking.

Other sites with quitting tips

Here are some other sites that help you kick the habit:

- ✔ The National Cancer Institute's "Smoking: Facts and Tips for Quitting" brochure at `rex.nci.nih.gov/NCI_Pub_Interface/Smoking_Facts/tips.html`

- ✔ The American Cancer Society at `www.cancer.org`

- ✔ The American Lung Association at `www.lungusa.org`

- ✔ The American Academy of Otolaryngology – Head and Neck Surgery at `www.entnet.org/spit-tobacco.html` (has information on quitting smokeless tobacco)

The Campaign for Tobacco-Free Kids at `tobaccofreekids.org` has excellent material aimed at encouraging kids not to start smoking or to quit. You can find additional information on teen smoking in Chapter 14.

Chapter 19

Mental Fitness

*N*ellie Bly made her name in the 1880s and 1890s as a *stunt reporter* for newspapers, which meant she took on the lives of her subjects to get her story. In one of her more famous stunts, she beat the fictional record of Phileas Fogg's journey in Jules Verne's *Around the World in Eighty Days;* Bly traveled around the world in just over 72 days. Another of Bly's stunts was getting herself admitted into an insane asylum to chronicle the conditions there. Her reports shocked the public and led to reforms at the time.

Much has happened since Nellie Bly's time. The causes of many mental disorders have been discovered, leading to new treatments. And there's a new appreciation of the importance of emotional wellness and stress reduction.

Heck, Bly led the way in that arena, too. After she left journalism, she ended up managing some industrial plants, where she provided her employees with pioneering mental and physical wellness programs along with gyms and bowling alleys.

In this chapter, which we dedicate to Bly, we point you to Web sites where you can get information to enhance your mental wellness, find information on mental disorders, and get support.

We wonder what Nellie Bly would make of the Internet. These days, she could get her word heard 'round the world in 72 nanoseconds, give or take.

Mental Wellness

The stresses of everyday life — the bills, the traffic, the job, the kids — can get the better of you. Fortunately, you can turn to theWeb for information and advice on managing anger, stress, the blues, and the like.

Here are a couple places that may help you get over the bumps in the road:

- ✔ **The American Psychological Association's HelpCenter** (`helping.apa.org`) has articles and advice on a variety of topics, including dealing with stress at work and at home, coping with being downsized, controlling anger, preparing for retirement, improving your well-being by exercising, and preparing your child for his first sleepover and for summer camp.

- ✔ **The National Mental Health Association** (`www.nmha.org`), shown in Figure 19-1, offers a series of fact sheets on reducing stress, controlling your anger, and coping with loss. To access these fact sheets, go to `www.nmha.org/infoctr/factsheets/index.cfm`.

- ✔ **KidsHealth for Parents** (`kidshealth.org/parent/emotions/feelings/stress.html`) has information on how stress affects kids and how parents can help them cope. Stress is a problem for kids of all ages. KidsHealth helps you recognize signs of stress in a child, such as disturbed sleep patterns, bedwetting, thumb sucking, and hair twirling.

Figure 19-1:
The National Mental Health Association has information on emotional wellness as well as mental illnesses.

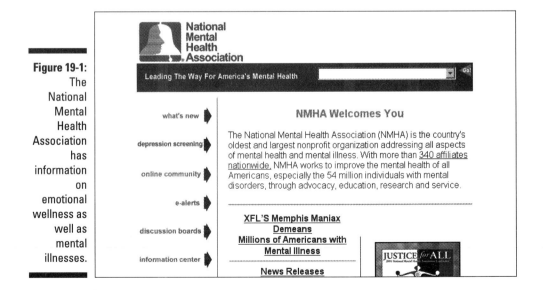

National Mental Health Association

Leading The Way For America's Mental Health   Go!

what's new ▶

depression screening ▶

online community ▶

e-alerts ▶

discussion boards ▶

information center ▶

NMHA Welcomes You

The National Mental Health Association (NMHA) is the country's oldest and largest nonprofit organization addressing all aspects of mental health and mental illness. With more than 340 affiliates nationwide, NMHA works to improve the mental health of all Americans, especially the 54 million individuals with mental disorders, through advocacy, education, research and service.

XFL'S Memphis Maniax
Demeans
Millions of Americans with
Mental Illness

JUSTICE *for* ALL

News Releases

The Big Picture on Mental Illness

According to the National Institute of Mental Health, about one in five adults — some 44.3 million Americans — have a diagnosable mental disorder in a given year. Mental disorders, including major depression, bipolar disorder, schizophrenia, and obsessive-compulsive disorder, make up four of the ten leading causes of disability. Also, mental illness plays a major role in suicide, a leading cause of death in this country.

In the next few sections, you find out about some mental health megasites where you can get information on many of these conditions, find out how they're treated, and get support.

National Alliance for the Mentally Ill

The National Alliance for the Mentally Ill (NAMI), a patient advocacy organization, has information on mental disorders on its Education Information and Programs page at `www.nami.org/education.html`. Here are a few areas you may want to check out (just click the appropriate links on the aforementioned page):

✔ **Information on Illnesses & Treatments:** Click this link to get fact sheets — including information about conditions, how they're treated, and where to get support — on the following topics:

- Anorexia nervosa

- Anxiety disorders

- Attention deficit/hyperactivity disorder

- Autism/Asperger's

- Bipolar disorder

- Borderline personality disorder

- Bulimia nervosa

- Depression

- Dissociative disorders

- Eating disorders

- Mental illness and substance abuse

- Obsessive-compulsive disorder

- Panic disorder

- Personality disorders

- Post-traumatic stress disorder

- Seasonal affective disorder

- Schizophrenia

- Sleep disorders

- Suicide

- Tourette syndrome

The site also has fact sheets on the medicines used to treat depression, obsessive-compulsive disorder, bipolar disorder, and schizophrenia.

✔ **Research:** Click this link in the left column for information on how you can participate in research studies.

You can search for local NAMI support groups by using your zip code or area code at `www.nami.org/cfapps/Affiliate_Finder/affiliate_finder.cfm`.

U.S. News names its picks for the best psychiatric programs at teaching hospitals at `www.usnews.com/usnews/nycu/health/hosptl/specpsyc.htm`. Chapter 4 also contains information on choosing and evaluating hospitals.

National Institute of Mental Health

The National Institute of Mental Health, known as NIMH, is the nation's leading research center on mental illness. The Institute's Web site (`www.nimh.nih.gov`) is a good place to start your search for information on mental problems.

Click the <u>For the Public</u> link to find online brochures on a variety of mental disorders, how they are diagnosed and treated, and what their prognosis is. Here are some of the topics covered on the For the Public page:

✔ Anxiety disorders

✔ Attention deficit/hyperactivity disorder

✔ Autism

✔ Bipolar disorder

✔ Child and adolescent mental health

✔ Children and violence

✔ Depression

✔ Generalized anxiety disorder

✔ Learning disabilities

✔ Medications and mental disorders

✔ Obsessive-compulsive disorder

✔ Panic disorder

✔ Post-traumatic stress disorder

✔ Psychotherapy research

✔ Schizophrenia

✔ Social phobias

✔ Suicide

The For the Public page also has a <u>Clinical Trials</u> link to information on research studies on mental health disorders. Chapter 7 also provides information on finding studies.

NIMH's Medications booklet (www.nimh.nih.gov/publicat/medicate.cfm) is a guide to the many medications used to treat mental disorders. This booklet suggests questions to ask your doctor about medications and covers the benefits and potential side effects of antipsychotic medications, antimanic medications, antidepressant medications, and antianxiety medications.

Some other mental health sites

Here are some other places where you can find information:

✔ **Internet Mental Health** (www.mentalhealth.com) has information on mental disorders, medications, and links to discussion groups and chats.

✔ **Dr. Ivan's Depression Central** (www.psycom.net/depression.central.html) covers all types of depressive disorders and also has links to information on other mental problems.

Artificial therapy

Wanna get some free psychotherapy? Then head over to see Eliza at www.mentalhelp.net/oracle. In the interest of fun and entertainment, Mental Help Net, a gateway for information and news on mental health, offers the Eliza Oracle, a computer program that acts like a shrink. If you enjoy asking a question and getting a question as an answer, you're all set.

Some Special Mental Health Concerns

In the next few sections, you find information focused on particular mental health topics, including depression, suicide, seasonal affective disorder, anxiety disorders, and eating disorders.

Depression

The National Mental Health Association's depression-screening.org is a good place to find out about depression, a common health problem and the nation's leading cause of disability. This site, which details the symptoms of depression, is located at www.depression-screening.org, as shown in Figure 19-2.

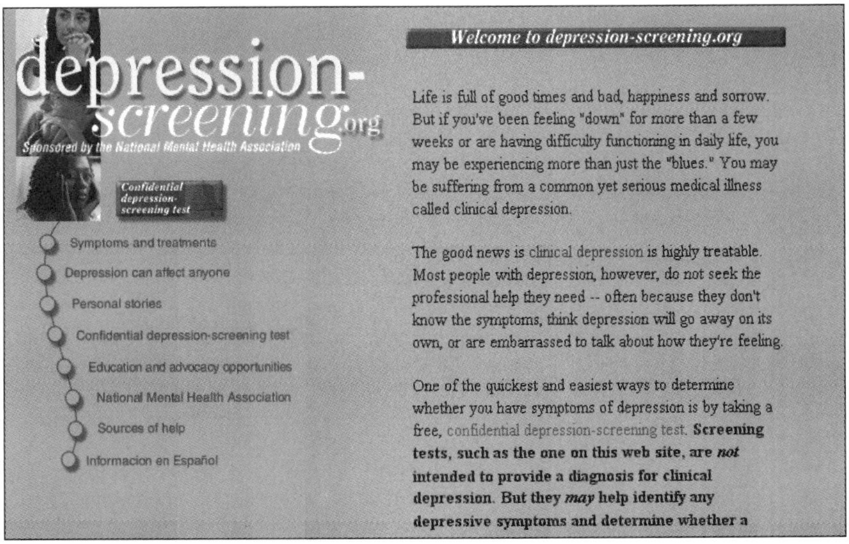

Figure 19-2: depression-screening.org has information on depression and offers confidential screening for the condition.

If you want to view video clips of people who have overcome clinical depression, click the Personal Stories link. You need RealPlayer G2 software (which is free) to hear the video clips, or you can opt to read transcripts of the interviews.

The site also offers confidential screening for depression. You can access the screening test by clicking the Confidential Depression-Screening Test button on the site's main page.

Symptoms of depression

The National Institute of Mental Health in its online brochure "The Invisible Disease: Depression" (www.nimh.nih.gov/publicat/invisible.cfm) lists the following symptoms of depression:

- ✔ Sad mood

- ✔ Loss of interest or pleasure in activities that were once enjoyed

- ✔ Change in appetite or weight

- ✔ Difficulty sleeping or oversleeping

- ✔ Physical slowing or agitation

- ✔ Energy loss

- ✔ Feelings of worthlessness or inappropriate guilt

- ✔ Difficulty thinking or concentrating

- ✔ Recurrent thoughts of death or suicide

The National Mental Health Association stresses that its depression-screening.org Web site is NOT designed to respond to a suicide crisis. If you believe you're at risk for suicide or know someone who is, dial 9-1-1 or go immediately to the nearest hospital emergency room for an evaluation. If you need to call a suicide hotline or want support, the American Society of Suicidology lists local crisis centers and support groups at www.suicidology.org/index.html.

Here are some additional sites that offer information on depression:

- ✔ **Personal accounts of depression:** The Depression and Related Affective Disorders Association offers first-person accounts of living with depression from TV personality Dick Cavett and writer Art Buchwald at www.med.jhu.edu/drada/firstperson.html.

  Cavett describes how he lost interest in everything, except books and articles on depression, and how he "couldn't pass a couch without falling in love with it." The site also features former U.S. Senator and presidential contender George McGovern describing his daughter Terry's unsuccessful battle with alcoholism and depression.

- ✔ **Information on various depressive disorders:** Dr. Ivan Goldberg, a New York psychiatrist, runs Dr. Ivan's Depression Central, an Internet clearinghouse for information on all types of depressive disorders. The site (www.psycom.net/depression.central.html) provides you with information on mood disorders and how they affect special groups, such as people with HIV/AIDS, people with cancer, the elderly, and African Americans.

> Dr. Ivan also lists support newsgroups for depression, such as `alt.support.depression`, `soc.support.depression.crisis`, and `soc.support.depression.family`. Yahoo! Groups at `groups.yahoo.com` lists some depression e-mail support groups. You can find out more about newsgroups in Chapter 2.
>
> ✔ **Local support groups:** The National Depressive and Manic-Depressive Association lists local support groups at `www.ndmda.org/chapters.htm`.

Suicide

Suicide is a major public health problem. The National Institute on Mental Health on its Suicide Facts page (`www.nimh.nih.gov/research/suifact.htm`) lists these grim statistics:

✔ Suicide is the eighth leading cause of death in the United States. More people die from suicide in a year than from HIV/AIDS and homicide combined.

✔ Suicide is most common among white men, with firearms being the most common method used. Four times more men than women commit suicide.

✔ Suicide is the third most common cause of death among young people ages 15 to 24.

✔ The highest suicide rate is among men over 85.

There are no definitive methods to predict suicide. However, medical professionals believe that early recognition and treatment of depression and other psychiatric illnesses can help prevent suicides.

If a person is displaying suicidal behavior, call 9-1-1 to get help. The American Association of Suicidology (`www.suicidology.org/index.html`) lists numbers for local crisis centers and support groups.

Seasonal affective disorder

The acronym for seasonal affective disorder — SAD — says it all. This depressive disease affects millions of people, typically starting in the fall and lasting through the winter months as the amount of daylight decreases. Some people are totally disabled by SAD, whereas others experience milder winter blues. The condition, which is four times more common in women, can cause weight gain, fatigue, cravings for sweet or starchy foods, and irritability.

Suicide risk factors

The National Institute of Mental Health in its "Suicide Facts" brochure at www.nimh.nih.gov/publicat/suicidefacts.cfm lists the following risk factors for suicide:

- One or more diagnosable mental or substance abuse disorder

- Impulsivity

- Adverse life events

- Family history of mental or substance abuse disorder

- Family history of suicide

- Family violence, including physical or sexual abuse

- Prior suicide attempt

- Firearm in the home

- Incarceration

- Exposure to the suicidal behavior of others, including family, peers, or in the news or fiction stories

NIMH says it's important to note that many people experience one or more risk factors and are not suicidal.

The American Academy of Family Physicians' familydoctor.org Web site has a handout on SAD at familydoctor.org/handouts/267.html. The handout notes that as many as 4 to 6 percent of the population has full-blown SAD and 10 to 20 percent has the milder form of SAD.

Special fluorescent lights can help combat the affects of SAD. You can find information on light therapy and SAD at the National Organization for Seasonal Affective Disorder (www.nosad.org) and the National Alliance for the Mentally Ill (www.nami.org/helpline/sad.htm).

Online support is available from the soc.support.depression.seasonal newsgroup. Refer to Chapter 2 for more on newsgroups.

Anxiety disorders

Anxiety disorders are the most common mental health disorders, affecting more than 19 million Americans.

The National Institute of Mental Health at its Anxiety Disorders Web site (www.nimh.nih.gov/anxiety/anxiety/index.htm) provides information on the symptoms and treatment for anxiety disorders. The disorders covered include panic disorder, obsessive-compulsive disorder, post-traumatic stress disorder, phobias, and generalized anxiety disorder. Because of widespread lack of understanding and the stigma associated with these disorders, many people with anxiety disorders are not diagnosed and thus are not receiving treatment that has been proven effective through research.

NIMH has a Does This Sound Like You? screening quiz (`www.nimh.nih.gov/soundlikeyou.htm`), shown in Figure 19-3, aimed at helping people decide whether they need to seek professional help.

Figure 19-3:
The Does This Sound Like You? screening quiz asks questions to screen for anxiety disorders.

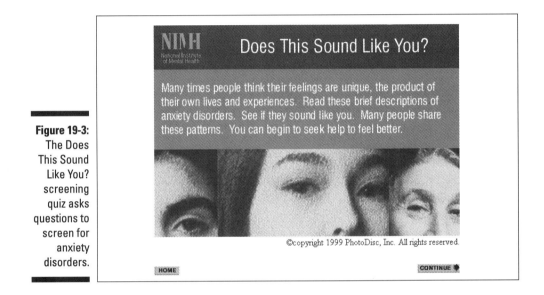

Here are a few additional sites to check out for information on anxiety disorders:

- ✔ **The Anxiety Disorders Association of America** on the opening page of its Web site (`www.adaa.org`) has links to consumer information, message boards, and chats. It also offers some self-tests for phobias.

- ✔ **The Obsessive-Compulsive Foundation** (`www.ocfoundation.org`) has information on symptoms and treatment of obsessive-compulsive disorder (OCD), an Ask the Experts bulletin board, and an online OCD screening test.

Yahoo! Groups at `groups.yahoo.com` lists e-mail groups for people with anxiety disorders, such as OCD-Teen for teenagers with obsessive-compulsive disorder and Avoidant for people with social phobia.

Eating disorders

Some big names in sports and entertainment, such as Karen Carpenter of the Carpenters, have made the news because of the tragic consequences of eating disorders. We live in a society that seems to prize thinness above all. One sign of this trend is that the *New York Times* bestseller list often includes diet books.

Here are some Web sites that offer information on eating disorders:

✔ **The National Association of Anorexia Nervosa and Associated Disorders (ANAD)** (www.anad.org) estimates that 8 million Americans — 7 million women and 1 million men — have anorexia, the starvation disease; or have bulimia, the binge-and-purge disease; or are compulsive overeaters. ANAD has information on the warning signs for anorexia and bulimia.

✔ **Caring Online** (www.caringonline.com) is an eating disorders mega-site. The site's opening page has links to information on eating disorders and athletes, binge eating, and body image. You can also find a link to poetry written by people with eating disorders and links to screening questionnaires.

On the site's main page, click the <u>Support</u> link to see a listing of support groups or click the <u>Treatment Centers</u> link for a list of centers where you can get help. The site also has message boards, which you can access by clicking the <u>Message Board</u> link.

✔ **The Something Fishy Website on Eating Disorders** (www.somethingfishy.org) also has lots of information on symptoms and treatments of eating disorders and links to online support.

Phobias

Phobias are fears. At Phobia List at www.phobialist.com, you can find a list of more than 500 different phobias. Fredd Culbertson — a word buff, not a mental health professional — compiled this list of phobias mentioned in medical papers. He can't explain why. He just did it. Here are a few of the fears on his list:

✔ Helminthophobia, fear of being infested with worms

✔ Motorphobias, fear of automobiles

✔ Orthinophobia, fear of birds

✔ Phobophobia, fear of phobias

✔ Rhytiphobia, fear of getting wrinkles

Culbertson's site includes information on how phobias are named, how they are treated, and some famous quotes about fear. Fear not — most phobias are treatable.

Part VII
The Part of Tens

The 5th Wave   By Rich Tennant

Ever since she got that thing, I'm afraid to fall asleep in my chair.

Home Defibrillator

In this part . . .

*E*very For Dummies book has a Part of Tens, and here's ours. In this part, we impart our parting shots on Internet health resources.

In Chapter 20, you find an online health fair with ten online quizzes and tests that help you assess your risks for a variety of health concerns, including heart disease, stroke, cancer, diabetes, osteoporosis, and stress. For those of you who can't get enough of this stuff, we even include a bonus round with more sites.

In Chapter 21, check out our top ten list of health Web sites, which we compiled after visiting thousands and thousands of sites.

Chapter 20

Ten Virtual Health Fair Booths

In This Chapter

▶ Assessing your risks for heart disease, stroke, cancer, and other major diseases

▶ Rating your stress, diet, and mental well-being

*H*ave you ever been to a health fair? You go to the high school gym and saunter from table to table, finding out about health and wellness. You may be able to have your blood pressure checked, have your vision screened, take a quiz on heart-healthy foods, get a free neck massage, or find out how straight your spine is. You may be able to take a cholesterol-screening test or undergo screening for osteoporosis. Such experiences are meant to be fun and educational.

Well, we've organized the first-ever *Healthcare Online For Dummies* Virtual Health Fair. Thanks for stopping by. We've set up ten virtual tables — and more — where you can review your risks for some common health problems.

Like real-world health fairs, we're not aiming to have you diagnose diseases online — that's best left between you and your doctor. These online tests and quizzes were created to alert you to potential problems and to motivate you to see your doctor.

Feel free to wander from booth to booth. Good luck. And good health.

How Stressed Out Are You?

Head on over to the YMCA Wellness Resource Center's table (www. ymca-portland.org/wrc/Stress/quiz.htm) to find out how well you're handling stress.

Are You at Risk for Heart Disease or Stroke?

The American Heart Association (www.americanheart.org/risk/quiz.html) sets you straight on what you can do to lower your risk for heart disease and stroke, two major killers.

Are You at Risk for Cancer?

Take the tests at the Harvard Center for Cancer Prevention's Web site, Your Cancer Risk Prevention, to find out about your risks for different cancers, including breast, prostate, lung, colon, bladder, skin/melanoma, uterine, kidney, pancreatic, ovarian, stomach, and cervical. Twelve all told. Go to www.yourcancerrisk.harvard.edu for the info.

Are You at Risk for Diabetes?

Sixteen million Americans have diabetes, but one in three doesn't know it. Find out about your risk for diabetes from the American Diabetes Association's booth at www.diabetes.org/ada/risktest.asp.

Are You at Risk for Osteoporosis?

Osteoporosis, the bone-thinning disorder, is a major cause of bone fractures in older women. But did you know it also affects men? Take the MSNBC healthy bones test at www.msnbc.com/Modules/quizzes/Osteoquiz.asp to find out your risks.

Are You at Risk for HIV?

The AIDS Action Committee has a series of quizzes for straight men, gay men, intravenous drug users, and straight women to see if they're at risk for human immunodeficiency virus (HIV), which causes AIDS. You can take the quizzes at www.aac.org/areyouatrisk_hivquiz.htm.

How Well Balanced Is Your Diet?

Are you sitting on top of the food pyramid? Or sliding down? At the American Dietetic Association booth at `my.webmd.com/nutr_quizstart`, you can find out how well balanced your diet is.

Are You Depressed or Anxious?

If you think that you may need psychological help, go to New York University School of Medicine's Department of Psychiatry Web site to be screened for anxiety and depression (at `www.med.nyu.edu/Psych/public.html`). The site also has tests on attention deficit disorders, sexual disorders, and personality disorders.

Are You Addicted to . . . ?

Head over to the AddictionSolutions.com virtual table (`www.addictionsolutions.com/self_assess`) for a series of tests to assess whether you might have an addiction problem. You can test yourself for addictions to drugs, alcohol, sex, gambling, food, nicotine, and Internet use. The site also has a test for co-dependency.

Are You at Risk for Hepatitis C?

Hepatitis C, the bloodborne liver disease, is a huge public health problem. You can find out if you're at risk for it over at the Hepatitis C: An Epidemic for Everyone Web site at `www.epidemic.org/theTest/personalRisk.html`. The C. Everett Koop Institute at Dartmouth College sponsors this table.

Bonus Round

You can find dozens of other online screening tests and quizzes at the following sites:

- **allHealth.com:** This site has a collection of tests, quizzes, and surveys at its Test Yourself Quiz Center at `www.allhealth.com/onlinepsych`.

- **drkoop.com:** Here you can find more than two dozen quizzes in the Tools section at `www.drkoop.com/tools/calculator/index.asp`.

- **HealthAtoZ.com:** This site has more than 30 health quizzes and risk assessment tools at its Healthy IQ's And Risk Assessments page at `www.healthatoz.com/atoz/RiskAssesment/quizbody.asp`.

- **ThriveOnline:** The ThriveOnline Assess Yourself page has more than 60 quizzes at `thriveonline.oxygen.com/quizzes.html`.

Chapter 21

Ten Must-See Health Sites

In This Chapter

▶ Describing what makes a health Web site a "must-see"

▶ Listing our ten must-see health sites

*A*fter looking at thousands and thousands of health and wellness Web sites to write this book, we realized we should've stocked up on computer eye drops.

We saw lots of useful and fun sites, but because this is one of those famous Part of Tens chapters that all *For Dummies* books have, we've narrowed them down to our top ten, must-see health Web sites.

But first, in case you're wondering, here's what we look for in a site:

✔ **Reliable and authoritative information.** If the site doesn't have useful and credible stuff in plain English, who needs it?

✔ **Easy-to-navigate and user-friendly design.** Sites need to be well designed and easy to get around in. Who wants to get lost in cyberspace?

✔ **Timeliness.** Yesterday's news just doesn't cut it when it comes to your health.

✔ **Clean, attractive design.** The contestants ought to be pleasing to the eye and make a good first impression.

✔ **Broad scope.** Even if the subject is narrow, we like to see that there's depth. Sometimes when it comes to health information, you want a snack, and sometimes, you want a meal. We like sites that can accommodate everyone's appetite for information.

✔ **Clear sponsorship.** We want to know who's backing the site. It's fine to have a point-of-view, but we want to know who's talking to the mouse.

✔ **Personality.** Every site has a personality of its own. If it's appropriate, a site should be friendly and welcoming. And a humorous touch can be a bonus when dealing with heavy subjects. As Mary Poppins, MD, said, "A spoonful of sugar helps the medicine go down."

Drumroll. Spotlight. Cue the music. Here are our favorites.

MEDLINEplus

www.medlineplus.gov

MEDLINE*plus,* a comprehensive site from the National Library of Medicine (NLM), is breathtaking in its scope and depth. It has links to tons of information on virtually any imaginable health topic or medication. MEDLINE*plus* also features the easy-to-read and lushly illustrated ADAM Medical Encyclopedia. After you look up a disease in the Health Topics section of MEDLINE*plus,* you're provided with links to news, relevant organizations, and convenient, automated searches on NLM's ClinicalTrials.gov (for info on research studies) and on Internet Grateful Med (for articles from medical journals). This is a great one-stop shop.

healthfinder

www.healthfinder.gov

healthfinder, a U.S. Department of Health and Human Services site, can be the shortest distance between a health question and the Web site that can answer it. It has links to online tools, such as medical dictionaries and databases; hot topics, such as AIDS, tobacco, and medical errors; and smart choices, such as prevention and self-care. It also has a special section for kids and parents.

MayoClinic.com

www.mayoclinic.com

MayoClinic.com maintains the high standards of the famed Mayo brick-and-mortar clinics. It's our favorite medical megasite, offering information we trust and an attractive design. Some Mayo on that Web sandwich, please.

familydoctor.org

www.familydoctor.org

Family doctors take care of people of all ages. And familydoctor.org from the American Academy of Family Physicians reflects that. It has patient handouts on a wide variety of topics for children, women, men, and seniors. The site also features Self-Care Flowcharts to help you decide when to go to the doctor and information on medications and herbal and alternative therapies.

The National Women's Health Information Center

www.4woman.gov

The National Women's Health Information Center provides health information for all women: young, old, minority, disabled, lesbian, and so on. It covers all the aspects of health and wellness of interest to women. And don't be fooled by the name; this is also a great site for information on men's health.

KidsHealth

www.kidshealth.org

KidsHealth isn't just for kids. This site has areas for parents and teens, too. It presents health facts authoritatively, in plain language, and, when appropriate, with a sense of humor. Where else can you find out what's a booger as well as how to help a kid cope with stress? KidsHealth rules.

Go Ask Alice!

www.goaskalice.columbia.edu

If you've got questions — no matter how offbeat — on health in general, fitness and nutrition, sexual health, emotional health, or on alcohol, nicotine, or other drugs, Go Ask Alice! The straight-shooting answers come from the experts at Columbia University's Health Education Program. Remember what Jefferson Airplane and the dormouse said, Go Ask Alice! and feed your head — and quench your curiosity.

OncoLink

www.oncolink.upenn.edu

OncoLink provides comprehensive information on all types of cancer, including daily cancer news updates and links to online support. You can also read reviews of books on cancer and visit an online gallery featuring art by people whose lives have been touched by cancer. OncoLink serves as a great information source for people with cancer and their families. Other disease sites should follow its lead.

Breastfeeding.com

```
www.breastfeeding.com
```

Breastfeeding.com looks, with style, at all aspects of breastfeeding, from technical information from doctors to fun stuff such as first-person accounts and art galleries. Breastfeeding.com may not be of interest to everyone, but it does capture the spirit of what's great on the Web.

QuitNet

```
www.quitnet.org
```

If you want to quit smoking, QuitNet is the place to go. The site has extensive information on smoking cessation and effectively uses interactive tools to aid ex-smoker wannabes with e-mail, bulletin boards, online buddies, and more.

Index

YOUR ONLINE RESOURCE

WWW.DUMMIES.COM

Discover Dummies Online!

The Dummies Web Site is your fun and friendly online resource for the latest information about *For Dummies* books and your favorite topics. The Web site is the place to communicate with us, exchange ideas with other *For Dummies* readers, chat with authors, and have fun!

Ten Fun and Useful Things You Can Do at www.dummies.com

1. Win free *For Dummies* books and more!
2. Register your book and be entered in a prize drawing.
3. Meet your favorite authors through the Hungry Minds Author Chat Series.
4. Exchange helpful information with other *For Dummies* readers.
5. Discover other great *For Dummies* books you must have!
6. Purchase Dummieswear exclusively from our Web site.
7. Buy *For Dummies* books online.
8. Talk to us. Make comments, ask questions, get answers!
9. Download free software.
10. Find additional useful resources from authors.

Link directly to these ten fun and useful things at **www.dummies.com/10useful**

For other titles from Hungry Minds, go to **www.hungryminds.com**

Not on the Web yet? It's easy to get started with *Dummies 101: The Internet For Windows 98* or *The Internet For Dummies* at local retailers everywhere.

Hungry Minds™

Find other *For Dummies* books on these topics:
Business • Career • Databases • Food & Beverage • Games • Gardening
Graphics • Hardware • Health & Fitness • Internet and the World Wide Web
Networking • Office Suites • Operating Systems • Personal Finance • Pets
Programming • Recreation • Sports • Spreadsheets • Teacher Resources
Test Prep • Word Processing

FOR DUMMIES
BOOK REGISTRATION

Register This Book and Win!

We want to hear from you!

Visit **dummies.com** to register this book and tell us how you liked it!

✔ Get entered in our monthly prize giveaway.

✔ Give us feedback about this book — tell us what you like best, what you like least, or maybe what you'd like to ask the author and us to change!

✔ Let us know any other *For Dummies* topics that interest you.

Your feedback helps us determine what books to publish, tells us what coverage to add as we revise our books, and lets us know whether we're meeting your needs as a *For Dummies* reader. You're our most valuable resource, and what you have to say is important to us!

Not on the Web yet? It's easy to get started with *Dummies 101: The Internet For Windows 98* or *The Internet For Dummies* at local retailers everywhere.

Or let us know what you think by sending us a letter at the following address:

For Dummies Book Registration
Dummies Press
10475 Crosspoint Blvd.
Indianapolis, IN 46256

...FOR DUMMIES™

BESTSELLING
BOOK SERIES